Gertrude Stein and the
Politics of Participation

Modern American Literature and the New Twentieth Century
Series Editors: Martin Halliwell and Mark Whalan

Published Titles
Writing Nature in Cold War American Literature
Sarah Daw
F. Scott Fitzgerald's Short Fiction and American Popular Culture: From Ragtime to Swing Time
Jade Broughton Adams
The Labour of Laziness in Twentieth-Century American Literature
Zuzanna Ladyga
The Literature of Suburban Change: Narrating Spatial Complexity in Metropolitan America
Martin Dines
The Literary Afterlife of Raymond Carver: Influence and Craftsmanship in the Neoliberal Era
Jonathan Pountney
Living Jim Crow: The Segregated Town in Mid-Century Southern Fiction
Gavan Lennon
The Little Art Colony and US Modernism: Carmel, Provincetown, Taos
Geneva M. Gano
Sensing Willa Cather: The Writer and the Body in Transition
Guy J. Reynolds
Gertrude Stein and the Politics of Participation: Democracy, Human Rights and Modernist Authorship, 1909–1933
Isabelle Parkinson

Forthcoming Titles
The Big Red Little Magazine: New Masses, 1926–1948
Susan Currell
The Reproductive Politics of American Literature and Film, 1959–1973
Sophie Jones
Ordinary Pursuits in American Writing after Modernism
Rachel Malkin
The Plastic Theatre of Tennessee Williams: Expressionist Drama and the Visual Arts
Henry I. Schvey
Exoteric Modernisms: Progressive Era Literature and the Aesthetics of Everyday Life
Michael J. Collins
Black Childhood in Modern African American Fiction
Nicole King
The Artifice of Affect: American Realist Literature and the Critique of Emotional Truth
Nicholas Manning

Visit our website at www.edinburghuniversitypress.com/series/
MALTNTC

Gertrude Stein and the Politics of Participation

Democracy, Rights and Modernist Authorship, 1909–1933

ISABELLE PARKINSON

EDINBURGH
University Press

Edinburgh University Press is one of the leading university presses in the UK. We publish academic books and journals in our selected subject areas across the humanities and social sciences, combining cutting-edge scholarship with high editorial and production values to produce academic works of lasting importance. For more information visit our website: edinburghuniversitypress.com

© Isabelle Parkinson 2023, 2024

Edinburgh University Press Ltd
13 Infirmary Street
Edinburgh EH1 1LT

First published in hardback by Edinburgh University Press 2023

Typeset in 10/13 ITC Giovanni Std Book by
Cheshire Typesetting Ltd, Cuddington, Cheshire

A CIP record for this book is available from the British Library

ISBN 978 1 4744 8432 9 (hardback)
ISBN 978 1 4744 8433 (paperback)
ISBN 978 1 4744 8434 3 (webready PDF)
ISBN 978 1 4744 8435 0 (epub)

The right of Isabelle Parkinson to be identified as the author of this work has been asserted in accordance with the Copyright, Designs and Patents Act 1988, and the Copyright and Related Rights Regulations 2003 (SI No. 2498).

CONTENTS

Acknowledgements	vi
Introduction: Gertrude Stein, Modernism, and Democracy	1
1. The Politics of Authorship in *Three Lives*	36
2. Authorship and Community in Stein's Pre-war Portraits and *Tender Buttons*	84
3. Modernism's Abject: *Geography and Plays* and Stein's Contested Authorship	140
4. *Useful Knowledge* and the Mind of Mass Democracy	189
Coda: Stein's Democratic Authorship in *The Autobiography of Alice B. Toklas*	227
Bibliography	238
Index	250

ACKNOWLEDGEMENTS

My first and most profound thanks are to Suzanne Hobson, whose generous support and guidance in the years during and after my PhD at Queen Mary, University of London have extended far beyond any possible obligation. I am also grateful to my adviser Morag Shiach for calling me to account until I learned to account for myself. Thanks are also due to Alex Goody and Robert Hampson, who examined my PhD thesis, a process that helped me determine the direction of this new project. The majority of this book was written whilst I was teaching in the Department of Comparative Literature and Culture at Queen Mary, and I have an enormous debt of gratitude to Kiera Vaclavik and Angus Nicholls for their mentorship and encouragement, and for the extraordinary opportunities they gave me to develop as an academic and teacher. Thanks also to all those modernist scholars I always look forward to meeting at conferences and whose lovely work and thrilling conversation has stimulated and developed my thinking, including Hannah Roche, Faye Hammill, Iain Bailey, Alix Beeston, Clara Jones, Sophie Oliver, Natasha Periyan and Jeff Wallace.

Particular thanks are due to Janet Lyon, inspirational modernist scholar and co-editor of the *Journal of Modern Literature*, whose forthright feedback proved to be a formative intervention at an important moment in the development of this study. I am very grateful for EUP's initial readers for continuing this work, and for the ongoing support of *Modern American Literature and the New Twentieth Century* series editors, Martin Halliwell and Mark Whalan.

Thanks also to Susannah Butler from EUP for her patient and gentle reminders.

I would like to acknowledge with deepest gratitude the bookish friends Claudia Jessop, Andrew Gray, Kate Bomford, Nick Dodd, Anneke Pettican, John Dunn and Emma Simpson who have listened and engaged with kindly attention to the long story of this text, and especially Asiya Bulatova, modernist, traveller and dearest padrooga. Finally, thanks to my best and most present reader, Marc Lancaster, for his thereness, and to Evie and Vic Lancaster for being Them.

Portions of *Gertrude Stein and the Politics of Participation* have been published elsewhere. A version of Chapter 4 appeared as 'Democrat or "imbecile"? Gertrude Stein's *Useful Knowledge* and Discourses of Intellectual Disability in the *To-day and To-morrow* Pamphlet Series' in *Journal of Modern Literature*, 43:3 (2020), and sections from Chapter 4 and from the Introduction appear in *Useful Knowledge* beyond the Beinecke: Gertrude Stein reading discourses of democracy and rights in *Life* magazine and the *Literary Digest*' in *Historicizing Modernists: Approaches to 'Archivalism'*, edited by Matthew Feldman (Bloomsbury Academic: 2021). Thanks to *JML* and Bloomsbury for permission to republish.

Introduction: Gertrude Stein, Modernism and Democracy

The pragmatic value of modernism lies in it's tremendous recognition of the compensation due to the spirit of democracy. [. . .] Modernism says Why not each one of us, scholar or bricklayer, pleasureably realise all that is impressing itself upon our unconscious, the thousand odds and ends that make up your sensery every day life. [. . .] Modernism has democratised the subject matter and la belle matière of art, through cubism the newspaper has assumed an aesthetic quality, through Cezanne, a plate has become more than something to put an apple on, Brancusi has given an evangelistic import to eggs, and Gertrude Stein has given us the Word, in and for itself.[1]

The most perfect example of this method is 'Italians', where not only are you pressed close to the insistence of their existence, but Gertrude Stein through her process of reiteration gradually, progressively rounds them out, decorates them with their biological insignia [. . .]. They solidify in her words, in ones, in crowds, compact with racial impulses. They are of one, infinitesimally varied in detail, racial consistency.[2]

Modernism and Democracy

Mina Loy's 1924 celebration of Gertrude Stein's work, written in the form of two letters to *The Transatlantic Review*, reveals a contemporary association of modernism with democracy that has Stein's authorship as the literary exemplar of its democratising force. In Loy's account, modernism is democratic both because of its subject matter and formal experimentation and because of its openness to broad participation. By 1924, definitions of modernism were being formed and contested after more than twenty years of radical practice by a profusion of international artists and writers in European centres and, to a lesser extent, in rapidly modernising American cities. Loy's expression of allegiance shows that Stein's authorship was both produced by and generative of the expansive possibilities of early-twentieth-century Anglo-American literary culture. Stein's significant position on the modernist scene reflected and encouraged an expansion in authorship, notably in her case the proliferation of women writers and of new modes of collective production. Her practice and her presence exemplify a necessary symbiosis in the ecology of modernism in a period characterised by the florescence of both mass and coterie publication, the rise of new audiences, the exploration of innovative aesthetic forms and subjects, and by the emergence of new forms of authorship and the recognition of a greater range of authorial subjects.[3] This expanding literary culture courted and created audiences for radical work through small presses and, increasingly after the late 1910s, through publication in a vast and steadily enlarging popular press. As Loy points out, Stein's writing, like much modernist work, also defined new aesthetic subjects in experimental forms, including her explorations of working-class experience, of complex sexualities and gender formations, and of the everyday life of the ordinary consumer. Loy's paean to Stein demonstrates her optimistic belief that these significant shifts in literary culture reflected and intersected a simultaneous expansion in the political sphere, following extensions in suffrage as liberal democracies in America and Europe consolidated their moves to mass democratisation in the first decades of the twentieth century.

One might therefore, along with Loy, think of this as a democratisation of culture that reflects a wider political democratisation, in which participation in the production of and engagement with the arts opens up, in which the right to write expands as other rights are extended. The story is, of course, much more complex and much knottier than this. Loy's apparently optimistic characterisation of this democratic modernism and of Stein's democratic writing simultaneously signals the underlying tensions and some of the darker implications of the growth of mass democracy in the inter-war period. Her reference to the 'pragmatic value' of modernism in its recognition of 'the compensation due to the spirit of democracy' offers an alternative to the narrative of break or rupture reflected in much avant-garde rhetoric, positing instead a more gradualist participatory shift.[4] It also, however, reflects the anxiety of a bourgeois cosmopolitan class about the potential engagement of others (for example, the 'bricklayer') in public life, and by the challenge to the class structure that this might presage. In Loy's formulation, modernism is pragmatic in that it makes the best of a bad job: the social and political disadvantages of democracy are compensated for by the cultural advantages of (and for) the arts. Loy's close reading of Stein's 'Italians' points to another problematic in the emergence of the inter-war international order: the entrenchment of nationalistic ideologies that accompanied mass democratisation. As many scholars have argued, the organicist nationalism of the nineteenth century deepened in the early twentieth century as biological theories of race proliferated and the state became increasingly interested in the bodies of citizens as a mass.[5] In his study of nationalism and the modernist novel, Pericles Lewis argues that the persistence of organicist nationalism complicated liberal democratic conceptions of citizenship because 'legal, formal equality of citizenship in the liberal state was insignificant next to what the organicists considered the real brotherhood arising from shared blood and a shared linguistic or cultural heritage'.[6] Loy's insistence on the 'biological insignia', 'racial impulses' and 'racial consistency', of the Italians that Stein depicts reflects an understanding of 'race' as the identification of nationality with biology, in which individuals are deeply bound by a shared genetic inheritance defined as coterminous with nationality. This is of a piece with Loy's earlier – though short-lived – association with Filippo Marinetti, the founder of Italian Futurism and supporter of Benito Mussolini, including her 1914 feminist manifesto in which she advocated for 'superior' women to reproduce in order to promote the genetic purification of the race.[7] Thus, Loy's optimistic exemplification of the reciprocity of modernism and democracy in the work of Gertrude Stein is shadowed by these hints at the inherent inequalities and the biopolitical horrors that accompanied the extensions of rights to citizens in the mass democracies of the twentieth century.

Looking back from the post-Second World War moment at the actualisation of conceptions of rights in Western democracies, Hannah Arendt notes that, rather than being '"inalienable," "given with birth"', or originating in '"self-evident truths"', equality, 'in contrast to all that is involved in mere existence, is not given us, but is the result of human organization insofar as it is guided by the principle of justice'. She goes on: 'We are not born equal; we become equal as members of a group on the strength of our decision to guarantee ourselves mutually equal rights'.[8] Thus, the membership of a national group, with all the potential for inequality and violence the organicist racial identification of nationality entails, was the ground upon which rights had been granted.[9] Arendt scholar Hauke Brunkhorst neatly delineates the inherent problem in the paradigm of national membership and expanding rights that Arendt addresses when he points out that

> If we tell the whole story then we have to accept that in many cases (and in some way in all cases) the expansion of social inclusion was with the price of new exclusion, or new forms of first latent, later manifest oppression.[10]

As I argue in this book, what we can see in Stein's authorial practices, in her formulations and reformulations of herself as author, and in arguments over the legitimacy of her authorship across the first decades of the twentieth century, is that, as is evident in Loy's contribution to Stein's authorial consecration, literary culture was a site of discursive contestation with complex ties to these parallel discourses of democratic rights and national belonging. Just as equality in the public sphere more generally is based on membership of a group, so the right to authorial equality is founded on the recognition and legitimisation of a writer as author in a specific literary and artistic unit. This study of Stein and her milieu is a study of the corresponding processes of cultural inclusion and exclusion that shape her work and define her authorship.

The relationship between the literary and the political is, of course, complex and difficult to map, and it would be inaccurate to say that the paradigms of inclusion and exclusion in early-twentieth-century democracies and in modernist literary circles have the same origins, causes or effects. Pascale Casanova offers a productive framework for the analysis of these interactions that enables an attention to the uneven yet connected historical shifts in the configurations of literary and political (economic, social) space. In her study *The World Republic of Letters* (2004), Casanova identifies 'world literary space' as a 'world made up by lands of literature; a world in which what is judged worthy of being considered literature is brought into existence'.[11] The space of literature is therefore a sphere with its own rules and norms in which the adjudication of value – indeed, of literariness as such – and the status of authorship are conferred by its 'consecrating authorities' (12). Despite the fact that it has its own rules, its own authorities, and an internal structure continually formed in contestation on an international literary scene, the idea of 'a literature emancipated from all historical and political attachments' is, for Casanova 'a fiction'. In the world of literature, alternative and contested or competing literary forms were first mapped to national boundaries as states emerged in the fifteenth century, and later claimed in the service of nineteenth-century nationalism, but 'its boundaries, its capitals, its highways, and its forms of communication do not completely coincide with those of the political and economic world' (11). The relationships between the literary and political spheres change over time, and they interact with each other differently at different moments. The literary world is thus a space that has a relative, fluctuating and unevenly distributed autonomy that means it is never fully divorced from the political sphere, but neither is it, by the same token, ever analogous or equivalent with the political. Casanova concisely sets out the relations between the literary 'world' and the political domain in an essay written to accompany the English translation and publication of her book. Here, the 'world of literature' is a space in which 'struggles of all sorts – political, social, national, gender, ethnic – come to be refracted, diluted, deformed or transformed according to a literary logic, and in literary forms.'[12] Casanova's conception of the relations between the literary and the political is key to the way my study interrogates the changing configurations of Stein's authorship in relation to the social, political and economic sphere of the early-to-mid-twentieth century that is continually refracted and transformed at the porous border of the literary world. Casanova argues that the 'world republic of letters has its own mode of operation: its own economy, which produces hierarchies and various forms of violence' (*World Republic of Letters*, 11). What I am arguing in my discussion of Stein's unstable author status is that the hierarches and forms of violence – including her own – involved in her fluctuating literary fortune refract, dilute, deform and transform political discourse and the realities it creates.

Several others of Casanova's conceptions and observations are important for this study. First, her understanding of the intricate webs of cause and effect, exemplified in her discussion of Paris in the late nineteenth and early twentieth centuries:

> The incessantly proclaimed universality that, by a sort of mutual contamination of causes and effects, made Paris the intellectual capital of the world produced two types of consequences: the one imaginary, which helped construct and consolidate a Parisian mythology; the other real, associated with the inflow of foreign artists, political refugees, and isolated artists. . .without its being possible to say which ones were the consequences of the others (*World Republic of Letters*, 30).

The reciprocity of the imaginary and the real offers a way of accounting for the power of language and of myth and the oscillation of cause and effect in Stein's literary fate. The language used in the construction and reconstruction of her author status often emerges out of political realities, creating an imaginary of her authorial subjectivity that in turn shapes responses to her work. The political reality of the American Progressive settlement houses with which she is associated early on, for example, is an imaginary (Stein was never involved in this kind of activism) that pins her to a certain category of 'worthy woman' and so diminishes the power and radicalism of her text. As we shall see in Chapter 1, the work of middle- and upper-class American women such as Jane Addams in educating and supporting working-class women from spaces established within the community was presented in the popular press as comfortable charitable work and associated with negatively feminised depictions of missionaries and do-gooders. This means, however, not just that Stein is less likely to be read seriously because of her fictional association with a category of women's work whose own radicalism had already been obscured, but that women's writing more broadly, even the most innovative and ground-breaking, can be easily categorised and so dismissed. To make an example of Stein is to have an effect on the real lives of other women.

Second, Casanova's observation that literature, however obliquely, is tied to the development of the nation, that authors carry with them an idea of nation that they must confront in order to write, is important as a framework for exploring the ways Stein's authorship is tied to her American nationality. Casanova argues that, by virtue solely of their 'membership in a linguistic area and a national grouping' the author 'embodies and reactivates a whole literary history' and is 'therefore heir to the entire national and international history that has "made"' them what they are (*World Republic of Letters*, 41). However mutable these relations, nationality remains a significant influence on literary value. For Casanova, 'literary capital is inherently national' and 'literary heritage is a matter of foremost national interest'. Because literature has as its material the national language that defined and unified emerging states, 'language and literature jointly provide political foundations for a nation and, in the process, ennoble each other' (34). More precisely, the emphasis on nationalism in the recent prehistory of this moment is still a significant factor in the designations of authorship and literary value in the first half of the twentieth century. In the mid-to-late-nineteenth century 'with the spread of nationalist ideas . . . the construction of world literary space proceeded once more through national rivalries that were inseparably literary and political' (35). Writers in the twentieth century, however, enabled by the protections afforded by those liberal 'legal, formal' forms of nationality, shake loose geographical constraints and travel abroad under the protective aura of citizenship, bringing with them an idea of national identity with which they can frame their literary work. Indeed, Casanova cites 'Stein's permanent concern to develop a modern American national literature (through the creation of an avant-garde)' to exemplify the significance of national identity for writers working in Paris outside their geographical nation. In terms of the assembly and reassembly of her author status, however, both the identification of Stein as an American author and her own expressions of allegiance are fluctuating and contingent. At some stages in her career, Stein's national identity is asserted: at one moment by her champions, at another by her detractors. At other points, her Americanness is downplayed in order to imagine her either positively as a central figure in an important international avant-garde, or negatively as a European decadent.

Finally, the question of how far and in which conditions literature can attain the status of autonomy is also relevant here. I will argue in my discussion of Stein scholarship below that, however esoteric or experimental a work seems, however divorced from political reality it appears to be, autonomy is always an illusion. The status of autonomy may be claimed or posited, but this in itself is the result of historical conditions and political reality.[13] As Casanova argues, the conception of the literary sphere as 'an enchanted world, a kingdom of pure creation, the best of all possible worlds where universality reigns through liberty and equality' (*World Republic of Letters*, 11) is a fable. In the key strand of Stein scholarship that I critique below, Stein the 'real' woman, living in a world defined by social, economic and political realities and with her own specific political views, is separated from Stein the experimental, apparently autonomous writer who exists in a world of literature, a 'kingdom of pure creation' governed by the 'liberty and equality' of an abstract and idealised imaginary democracy divorced from actual democracies and their often ugly and violent realities. At its core, this book situates Stein in the political reality that impinges upon and is refracted in the literary 'world' that is the context for her authorship.

Inclusion/Exclusion

The view that a dichotomy of inclusion and exclusion characterises this period in the history of Western democracy is shared by historians, philosophers and modernist scholars. Approaching rights more broadly in his recent study of the historiography of human rights, Samuel Moyn's contention, that 'the first crucial fact is that humanitarianism could underwrite violations of rights as well as their defense' offers a succinct rendering of this paradox.[14] Modernist scholars considering the relationship between modernism and democracy point out that the duality of rights becomes more acute in mass democracies as they emerge in the twentieth century. In her 2006 book on modernism and democracy, Rachel Potter underscores the significance of this view of democracy for a nuanced understanding of some modernists' increasing resistance to liberalism. For Potter, 'at the heart of many modernist texts is the idea that modern democracies become formally inclusive at the historical moment when the state extends its power over the individual citizen'. She argues that many modernists experienced 'the change from restricted to mass democracy', the moment 'when the state becomes inclusive' as also the point at which 'the terms of this inclusion become opaque'. In Potter's view, 'these anxieties feed into the modernist imagination in powerful ways'.[15] These anxieties shape modernist texts, but they also shape modernist literary culture in ways that move beyond imagination. As my study will show, narratives of inclusion and exclusion bled into the discourse of modernism itself during the inter-war period, eventually performing, in the influential configuration around T. S. Eliot, the discursive dismantling of modernism as such, accompanied by the resurgence and ratification of an ahistorical notion of individual authorial genius reimagined to both transcend the terms for inclusion that might be set by a particular group and, paradoxically, to fix a permanently exclusionary definition. However rhetorical and however temporary this dismantling, it reveals both the power of modernist literary culture to define authorship *per se* and the increasing urgency of definitions of authorship in the shifting and contested space of modernism as Western democracies – in their struggles to control and contain the mass of individual citizens in legal and bureaucratic frameworks with an increasingly biopolitical cast – edged their way towards extreme solutions. On this point, as Lyndsey Stonebridge argues, 'writers had been debating and challenging the rights of writing since it had become clear just how extreme the twentieth century was going to be'.[16]

Central to the inclusion/exclusion paradigm is a concept of rights emerging out of what Moyn describes as 'a justification for state sovereignty'. Taking a long view of rights, and echoing Hannah Arendt, Moyn argues that 'For most of modern history, rights have been part and parcel of battles over the meanings and entitlements of citizenship, and therefore have been dependent on national borders for their pursuit, achievement and protection' (79).[17] Rights, therefore, are from the outset firmly tied to citizenship, to nationhood, and to national sovereignty. Andrew John Miller attends to the significance of this paradigm for modernist literary culture in *Modernism and the Crisis of Sovereignty* (2008). Setting out some of the consequences of mass democratisation founded on the nation-state, Miller elaborates the dichotomy as it is expressed in the modernist period: 'confronted with the growing instability of the inside/outside binarisms on the basis of which nation-states are founded, government authorities, over the course of the first half of the twentieth century, developed increasingly effective means of policing and regulating identity'.[18] As the tension grew between a developing bourgeois cosmopolitanism, emerging models of internationalism, and intensifying waves of migration (both voluntary and forced) on the one hand, and the attempt to rigidly circumscribe the nation-state on the other, so the demarcation of the rights-bearing citizen became increasingly reliant on precise and complex bureaucratic mechanisms to define, measure and control an unstable mass of individual bodies.[19] Thus, Miller argues, 'the work of defining and documenting the division between insiders and outsiders became one of the chief functions' of a new 'administrative order' (viii). Miller pins this to modernist culture in that, while modernism is characterised by cultural flows that represent 'a worldwide emergence of transnational forms of cultural identity', this is accompanied and challenged by 'an intensification of the nationalistic tendency to insist on narrowly territorial and/ or ethnocentric models of group membership' (x–xi). For Miller, the 'realm of discursive exchange' is perceived as 'a contestatory scene' in which 'contradictory articulations of the conflict between the claims of nationalism and the claims of cosmopolitanism' are made. This is what Miller defines as 'the civil war of language that defines the modernist moment' (xxii). The analogous relationship between the discourse of citizenship and the concurrent discourse of modernist cultural belonging that Miller identifies is also borne out in my examination of both Gertrude Stein's changing delineations of authorial belonging and of contestations among modernists over the validity of her authorship. At some points claiming allegiance to an international avant-garde and at others asserting her status as American author, the shifting positions taken by Stein, her supporters and her detractors reflect their contemporary political currents. It is important to note that these formulations and struggles operate at the level of discourse and that these are discursive forces at play, and that, while their rhetoric may often coincide with that of the political and social sphere, their intersection with those spheres in general remains very much at the level of discourse. It is also important, however, to consider the role that discourse has in forming and directing political and cultural opinion and activity. I have no doubt, for example, that Stein's critiques of Woodrow Wilson, a range of pieces published in a variety of contexts, from *Life* magazine to an Oxford University student paper, had no effect on his fortunes, but they do intersect and interact, as we shall see in my discussion below, with a political discourse that did.[20] And while the brutal discourse of annihilation generated by Stein's detractors did not destroy her reputation in her lifetime, their legacy and its post-war ascension did effectively erase Stein from the modernist canon for thirty years.

As indicated in Loy's letter, the heightened discourse of nationalism and the attendant rise of administrative and disciplinary technologies that accompanied the emergence of mass democracies was also increasingly tied to a pseudo-scientific imaginary of genetic purification. This dark backdrop, I would argue, informs attitudes to cultural production and leaches into the discourse of modernist authorship in the early twentieth century. Perhaps the most extensive formulation of this view of Western democracies in relation to the first half of the twentieth century in particular occurs in the work of Italian theorist Giorgio Agamben. Working through the ideas of Hannah Arendt and Michel Foucault and taking as its point of departure the paradigm of the state of exception developed by Nazi jurist Karl Schmidt, Agamben's 2005 *State of Exception* explores the implications of theories of biopower to track the move from mass democracy to totalitarianism, on terms that he first developed more generally in *Homo Sacer: Sovereign Power and Bare Life* (1998). His argument in the earlier text that 'only because biological life and its needs had become the politically decisive fact is it possible to understand the otherwise incomprehensible rapidity with which twentieth-century parliamentary democracies were able to turn into totalitarian states' puts the state's interest in the body of the citizen at the heart of this metamorphosis.[21] In *State of Exception*, Agamben develops his theory that totalitarianism was inherent to early-twentieth-century democracies by arguing that 'the modern state of exception is a creation of the democratic-revolutionary tradition and not the absolutist one'.[22] For Agamben, a permanent state of exception in which the rights of citizens are suspended in order to preserve the constitutional order defines the totalitarian state. In the first half of the twentieth century, emergency powers, assumed ostensibly to protect and preserve democracy itself, gave the state absolute power over the 'bare life' of citizens whose citizenship is determined by their inclusion (and therefore by their threatened exclusion) in a system that legitimates them as worthy of the protection that enables life. This system, the democratic nation-state, is one that, to use Foucault's formulation, works on the logic that the role of the state is the decision 'to make live' or 'to let die'.[23] In Agamben's configuration, this is 'a "protected democracy"', which 'is not a democracy at all' but is, rather 'the paradigm of constitutional dictatorship' that 'functions instead as a transitional phase that leads inevitably to the establishment of a totalitarian regime' (15).

Tracing the history of the state of exception as it proliferated across western liberal democracies, including, as well as the more obvious examples represented by the emerging fascist states of Germany and Italy, examples in Britain and the United States, Agamben develops the inclusion/exclusion paradigm as the defining mechanism of democracies in the period.[24] This is a context ruled by a paradoxical logic in which the process of democratisation immediately engenders the imperative to define and protect the zones – at every level of territoriality – determining and therefore circumscribing the rights of citizens. The increasing emphasis on national purification in the early decades of the twentieth century is inextricably bound to the framework of protected democracy that enables the suspension of rights in order ostensibly to preserve the integrity of the nation. It is also intimately tied to the mechanisms of biopower that Agamben explores in *Homo Sacer*. For Agamben, this was a historical situation in which 'politics had already turned into biopolitics, and in which the only real question to be decided was which form of organisation would be best suited to the task of assuring the care, control, and use of bare life' (*Homo Sacer*, 122). The apparent liberalisation represented by mass democracy was therefore deeply troubled and contradictory: as democracy expanded, conceptions of nation and citizen became attached to ideas of biological purification, and the democratic subject as the subject of rights also became increasingly subject to new forms of regulation and control, in a rapid extension of biopower that coincided with developments in the science (and pseudo-science) of evolutionary genetics. Gertrude Stein's work, her activity on the cultural scene, and debates about the legitimacy of her authorship engaged and refracted those discourses in significant ways, as she became the focal point for a debate over the right to write in a scene involved in the reformation, construction and legitimation of authorship that accompanied the opening of new spaces for writing and for new kinds of writers. Both Stein's work and its reception are shadowed by discourses of biopower as apparent new freedoms generated further definition, identification and regulation of bodies in the demos. Both the discussions around Stein's authorship and the various forms of Stein's own cultural production engage with the expansion of democracy in ways that reveal discourse traces of the biopolitical trajectory of modern democracy.

Stein's 'Democratic' Writing

By setting Stein's authorship explicitly in the context of the historical consolidation of mass democracy and exploring in detail her response as an author to rapidly changing political and cultural conditions, this study engages critically with a significant strand of scholarship in which, echoing Loy's 1924 characterisation, Stein's work is claimed as inherently democratic. Many of these scholars argue that the democratic quality of Stein's work marks her off as an author from canonical Anglo-American modernism and its perceived institutionalisation. From the outset, the scholars involved in Stein's critical recuperation in the 1970s invariably posited arguments for her exceptionality on these terms. Since then, a diverse and influential body of scholarship has sustained this view of her authorship, constructing a Stein who stands outside the modernism that had begun to contract by the end of the 1930s, a reactionary turn that, in this narrative, paralleled the rise of fascist dictatorships in Europe. This conception of Stein's authorial position is an adjunct to the now well-worn account of the canonisation of a handful of modernists in the later 'post-war settlement' consecrated by the publication of the 1950 *Penguin Book of Contemporary Verse*.[25] In the arguments claiming her exceptional status, it is the democratic quality of Stein's work that enables her to be free from the dictatorship of a reactionary, anti-democratic modernist institution. The critics involved in Stein's recuperation read her outsider status as voluntary act of resistance, and her texts become resistant writing that struggles against the closure of modernism. This position has a long and persistent legacy that still colours Stein studies today.

In tackling this critical tradition and in examining the relationship between authorship and democracy in Stein's literary production and its contexts, my study commences from two premises. First, that Stein's outsider status was not a choice but an imposition against which she struggled in, at times, perturbing ways, resisting through various more or less complex and entangled methods those other designations that are invoked to exclude her from the designation of 'author': her gender, her Jewishness, her sexuality. Second, that Stein's engagement with democracy and the status of her authorship in relation to democracy are much more complex, more contradictory, and more interesting, than a characterisation of her writing as 'democratic' will allow. This study confronts the question of how far and in which senses Stein's work, as produced and distributed in the context of early-twentieth-century democracy, and her concomitant authorial position, as imagined, constructed and reconfigured in the context of the literary cultures of western democracies, can be called 'democratic'.

The scholarly exploration of Stein's 'democratic' potential thus far forms a loose yet highly significant critical strand that views Stein's writing, in itself, as enabling a form of participation characterised as anti-authoritarian and, thus, radically egalitarian. The primary iteration of this understanding of Stein emerged out of the avant-garde literary scene around the Language poets that saw itself as sustaining the political activism of 1968 into the late 1970s,

1980s and 1990s.²⁶ This was a creative-critical engagement with Stein that was arguably consolidated in more formally academic scholarship with Peter Quartermain's 1992 *Disjunctive Poetics* and Marjorie Perloff's 1999 *The Poetics of Indeterminacy: Rimbaud to Cage*. Quartermain characterises Stein's writing as 'thoroughly democratic, resistant to institutionalised power and meaning', whereas Perloff develops the Language poets' Marxist readings of Stein's work as resistant to the authority of meaning and its easy consumption by suggesting the egalitarian effect of an 'indeterminacy' that encourages the reader to 'be able to fill in the gaps in whatever way suits us'.²⁷ This reading of Stein's authorship as radically democratic has been sustained through a tranche of criticism associated with the 'experimental' or 'innovative' poetics working out the legacy of Language poetry and other late iterations of the avant-garde, such as Juliana Spahr's *Everybody's Autonomy* (2001), in which Stein's work represents an 'egalitarian project' manifested in her 'particular turn to avant-garde modernism in order to write a literature for "everybody"'.²⁸ These arguments for the political force of the formal features of Stein's work are also sustained, for example, in Joan Retallack's 2008 edited collection *Gertrude Stein: Selections*. In her introduction, Retallack often contextualises Stein's work politically, and she does not shy away from critique. Her conclusion, however, that Stein's work can 'counter . . . much of the politics we deplore in her time and our own' because of a 'self-complicating poethics' in which 'ethos is enacted by . . . form', implies that the formal properties of Stein's writing can except it from political life as it is enacted and experienced.²⁹

Beyond the scholarship associated with experimental poetry, arguments for the democratic quality of Stein's writing have also emerged in work across the field of modernism studies over the last two decades. Exemplary of this strand is Barbara Will's highly influential study *Gertrude Stein, Modernism and the Problem of 'Genius'* (2000). The overarching contention in this examination, Will's first monograph on Stein, is that Stein's conception of genius is democratic because it is 'dialogic' and inclusive. Will argues that, by the late 1920s, Stein is engaged in an effort 'to rewrite the American national myth as an ideal relationship between the individual unit . . . and the collective "whole"' and to represent an 'enlightened American collectivity'.³⁰ For Will, as for the scholars around the experimental poetry scene, the form of Stein's work in itself encourages a mode of reading that enables readers to share in her new participatory model of 'genius'. Ulla Dydo, 'the preeminent Gertrude Stein scholar of our time', also shares this view that the formal qualities of Stein's writing are inherently democratic qualities, expressed in the unequivocal statement, 'all her work is a demonstration of the possibilities of grammar for democracy'.³¹ Developing this view, G. F. Mitrano (2005) argues that Stein's texts themselves are concerned with 'the right of individuals to full cultural access and participation'.³² In more recent critical essays, Aidan Thompson has argued that Stein's use of repetition opens a space which allows 'choice and agency', which 'provides a valuable practice – one that is democratic in its undoing of hierarchical mechanisms', and Julie Goodspeed-Chadwick describes her writing as an 'egalitarian diffusing and recombination of meanings'.³³

In these readings, democracy is treated conceptually rather than historically, as a broad and nebulous ideal that includes general notions of egalitarianism, openness, inclusion or participation, identified in a linguistic experimentation that seems to offer the reader agency. Almost invariably, however, and as is hinted at in Retallack's distinction, the 'democracy' in Stein's writing is set at an awkward angle to the politics of the historical Stein. Spahr expresses this problematic succinctly in the ambivalent statement 'if Stein is not the democrat that I am arguing her work suggests she could be, still there is much to be learned from the anarchic democracy of the works themselves' (49). This simultaneously reveals an uneasy disconnect between Stein and her work and a generalised representation of democracy that means it can be aligned with anarchism, a form of social organisation that a number of modernists supported in opposition to democracy as it was practised in both its pre-war and inter-war iterations.³⁴

Similarly, GF Mitrano sidesteps Stein's political views to attend to a set of generalised concepts when she notes 'While not negating her controversial politics. I am interested in arguing that she reaches us more effectively when she asks about desire, access, and full cultural participation' (5). Aidan Thompson is more specific about what she views as Stein's undemocratic interest in her own status in a hierarchical structure, in that 'Her concept of herself as an artistic leader and her aspiration to be recognized in bourgeois culture run in opposition to the notion of democracy', and yet even here there is little recognition of the nature of democratic politics in the period, not least the significance of 'bourgeois culture' for definitions and circumscriptions of democracy in the first half of the twentieth century (131). These interpretations often read – and puzzle over – Stein the author as a more troubling presence than the work she produced; as radically democratic in her language experiments, yet conservative and reactionary in her nationalism and anti-democratic in her support for authoritarian regimes, hinted at, for example, in Spahr's reference to Stein's friendship with the Nazi collaborator Bernard Fäy. Indeed, Barbara Will's more recent critical examination of Stein's politics, *Unlikely Collaboration* (2011), which I discuss below, continues to assert the view that there is a tension between writing that seems 'democratic' and 'the reactionary political views that Stein overtly expresses in her later writings of the 1930s and 1940s'.[35] These readings of Stein's practice as democratic rest largely on the inherent qualities of the text, bringing those purely ideal notions of democracy to bear on them, and, thus, a nebulous and generalised concept meets a series of highly abstract texts.

The divide between Stein the historically situated woman with political views, and Stein the private experimental writer also exists in feminist scholarship. Among feminist scholars who pay close attention to Stein's work, there is a tendency to read it as a discrete entity and as, however experimental, an esoteric engagement primarily with the personal and the quotidian. Marianne DeKoven's *A Different Language*, Harriet Scott Chessman's *The Public is Invited to Dance*, Lisa Cole Ruddick's *Body, Text, Gnosis* and Ulla Dydo's *Gertrude Stein: The Language that Rises* all do important work in reading Stein's writing in terms of its emphasis on the significance of the domestic world and the world of sexuality and intimate relationships.[36] Seeing Stein's private experimental language as an alternative to the patriarchal discourse of public culture, these readings have put the argument for Stein's importance for feminism, and, indeed the related interest in the 'everyday' of modernism has been and remains a productive strand of research.[37] Yet I would maintain that reading the work as a personal project also isolates it from the political and cultural scene with which it intersects and, once again, sees only half the story.

In *Unlikely Collaboration*, the reassessment of her own earlier characterisation, Barbara Will explores in detail Stein's relationship with the collaborator Bernard Fäy, beginning with an outline of the problem I have identified: 'the very work for which Stein is best known...is significant precisely because it appears so profoundly dissociated from time and place, from an author and her "views". Will goes on, 'To this extent, Stein's experimental writing also seems open to the reader in the radically democratic way that Roland Barthes discusses in his famous essay "The Death of the Author"' (12–13). As we have seen, the scholars in the loose tradition I am outlining here tend to distinguish Stein's texts and their esoteric, private democracy from the public Stein who might express political 'views'. Will's more historicised way out of this is to identify Stein's troubling politics as a later phase, an expression of ideas that do not emerge until Stein's explicit approval of the authoritarian European nationalism of the latter part of the inter-war period. Will outlines Stein's 1930s nationalism as at some moments 'extreme' and at others, 'a basic nationalist credo' (9), identifying it as a dangerous, 'reactionary' (15) nationalist feeling that is formulated 'as the more optimistic decade of the 1920s turned into the hollow years of the 1930s' (24). Will therefore also marks off Stein's 'democratic' writing from her 'nationalist' ideology by separating her earlier work from her 1930s expressions of nationalism. This is made explicit in Will's methodology: to look for answers to the question of how Stein seems to become a radical nationalist, 'not by searching for political ideas in Stein's experimental writing – writing, again, that abstains from "ideas" and "views" – but rather by looking at the principles that guided her through her aesthetic development' (15). Thus, the work of the early Stein does not yet seem to have a 'politics', allowing the texts written before the 1930s to be read as exemplary of a pure linguistic experimentation that is 'democratic' in the most abstract sense of the term. They are therefore untainted by the problematic nationalism that appears in the 1930s and the result of a personal, esoteric engagement with an abstract ideal of democracy divorced from its ground-level realities.

This book begins from the premise that Stein's authorship has a more direct relation to the discourse of democracy in the first three decades of the twentieth century than these arguments for the democratic nature of her work might indicate. Focusing on the changing iterations of her work and authorial identity before the mid-1930s, I will explore the ways Stein, her modernist milieu, and the 'world of literature' refract, dilute, deform and transform the politics of early-twentieth-century democracy.

Cultural Constructions of Authorship in the Context of Mass Democracy

In the last few years, in keeping with the historicist approach to modernist cultural production that has emerged since the turn of the century, modernist scholars have turned their attention to the cultural construction of authorship, notably in relation to constructions of celebrity and the mainstreaming of apparently esoteric works and unconventional, even aberrant, authorial identities in the mass-market publications whose proliferation and growth accompany mass democratisation. These examinations of authorship in the context of an interaction of cultural, social and economic fields owe much to Pierre Bourdieu, generating an understanding of authorship succinctly summarised in the introduction to Franssen and Honings's collection of recent essays on the subject: 'An author's stature is created within a variable tension field of power relations where different parties claim authority'.[38] Aaron Jaffe's influential study *Modernism and the Culture of Celebrity* argues that, within the broad field that includes popular culture, modernist authorship depends on the construction and maintenance of the specificity of the author's imprimatur, a 'textual mark of authorship' that distinguishes 'a high literary product from the inflating signs of consumption'.[39] Subsequent scholars, however, have argued that Stein, in particular, was much more attuned to the mass culture that the writers around Eliot appeared to disdain. While Jaffe argues that the imprimatur as a construct covertly co-opts the mechanisms of celebrity status and the logic of the market, Stein scholars point to her more explicit attentiveness to popular culture and, in doing so, have revealed the greater engagement with mass-market publications and audiences among modernists more generally. That Stein consistently attempted – with some success – to have her work published in American magazines with large popular readerships is commented on and documented by a range of scholars. Deborah Mix points out that 'Stein and her work were not only known but also discussed in substantive ways throughout the United States in the 1920s and 1930s', and that 'She doggedly sought publication for her work . . . via major presses and mainstream magazines', with success in a range of publication contexts including the *Saturday Evening Post, Vanity Fair*, the *Atlantic Monthly* and *New York Times Magazine*.[40] Karen Leick's painstaking archival work consolidates, moreover, the prevalence of mainstream discussion and – to a lesser extent – publication of Stein's work from the 1909 appearance of *Three Lives* onwards.[41] As Ann Ardis points out, print media was 'center-stage in the period's conversations about the possibility of radical democracy in a mass society, the function of the arts in a republic, and the intellectual "health" of modern culture'.[42] This was a context where, in fact, 'any number of turn-of-the-century writers multiplied their authorial identities in ways that defy a Foucauldian conception of the author-function or a modernist notion of an authorial imprimatur' (42). Constructions and reconstructions of Stein's authorship, along with those of other modernists, therefore, are circulating from the outset in a broad and diverse field of American print culture engaged with the production and distribution of cultural, social, economic and political knowledge to a massive and increasingly engaged demos.

One striking example of Stein's work in the mainstream media is the appearance of her text 'A League' in the 18 September 1919 edition of *Life* magazine. The publication of this short piece, a critique of Woodrow Wilson and the League of Nations, situates Stein's authorship firmly in the context of a broad print culture dealing explicitly with a complex contemporary scene of democracy in flux. *Life* magazine engages a broadcast audience with 'light' or 'humorous' treatments of issues around rights and gender, rights and labour, and rights and class, touching on the question of designations of humanity and on developments in biological science. The subject matter and publication context of this work trouble the readings that ascribe to Stein's work inherently 'democratic' properties reflecting an abstract and very personal engagement with democracy, the separation of her work from her political views, and the accompanying notion that, before 1930, her authoritarian nationalist leanings were not apparent, and enables an understanding of the ways she engages with the realities of democracy in 1919. In particular, democracy and nationalism have a far more complex relationship than is suggested by Will's 2011 attempts to mark off Stein's 'democratic' experimental work from her nationalism, and something of this can be identified in this early inter-war text and its publication context.

'A League' reappears later in the 1928 collection *Useful Knowledge*, a publication often read as Stein's late-1920s reconciliation with her American identity and a significant expression of her commitment to democracy. The most influential example is perhaps Will's 2000 account of it as 'Stein's idealized resolution of the earlier concerns that had plagued *The Making of Americans*' where she argues that 'in *Useful Knowledge* "America" serves as a utopian "landscape" which neither subsumes individual "value" nor abandons the larger frame that is integral to the collective' (*Gertrude Stein*, 121). This reading has *Useful Knowledge* as evidence to support the view that Stein's work is democratic, developed, in Will's interpretation, to argue that at this point Stein's artistic modes are aligned with a new formulation of her American identity where America is reimagined as an idealised egalitarian landscape. 'A League', however, published in 1919, represents not a facet of an abstract, oblique, conciliatory ode to American democracy written towards the end of the 1920s, but a quite precise response to a particular political moment just after the First World War. Responding to the expansion of mass democracy in the context of debates around the role of internationalism for the democratic nation-state, 'A League' engages directly with questions about the status and role of American democracy in the post-First World War geopolitical landscape.

Stein's Nationalism

Internationalism was understood in large swathes of opinion in the popular weeklies as a threat to American democracy. Stein's 'A League' is a complex but clearly identifiable criticism of the internationalism represented by Wilson and the League of Nations, countering the idea either that her works simply perform an abstract ideal of democracy, or that she did not directly express political positions in her writing before the 1930s. Indeed, 'A League' indicates that Stein's 1930s 'reactionary' nationalism cannot be marked off from her earlier political positions (or from their imagined lack). Well before the 1930s, Stein's nationalism is apparent, and it is influenced by the popular press. Stein's submission of 'A League' to *Life* magazine in 1919 reflects her interest in the popular weekly and her belief that the American mass-market publication was the appropriate context for her experimentation. It is also the expression of an American nationalism that is in keeping with the many articulations of anti-League nationalism represented in *Life*. 'A League' mediates the popular discourses of democracy in the American weekly. Indeed, this publication suggests that, as an ex-pat in Paris since 1903, Stein, at least in part, gets her America, her politics, and her sense of national identity through this reading.

Predating the photojournalism associated with its later iteration, *Life* was an American humour magazine, a weekly publication aimed at a broad audience founded in 1883, in emulation of the successful British magazine *Punch*, and sustained in that form until 1936. *Life* reached its highest distribution in the period after the First World War, with 'a circulation of nearly one-half million in 1920'.[43] With an adult American population in the period of around 70 million, and considering this paper would have likely been bought for the whole household and circulated informally beyond that, this would have meant that a significant proportion of the American public was reading it. This publication positions itself as an important vehicle in the promulgation and maintenance of American democracy. The 18 September 1919 edition of *Life*, in which Stein's 'A League' appears, references a broad audience and the democratisation of print distribution by bordering its subscription advertisement with cameo heads of men, women and children from across the social strata, with an elaborately coiffured woman, a bowler-hatted businessman, a straw-chewing farmer, and a maid in uniform in continuous succession.[44] More explicitly, the cover illustration of this edition has a depiction, in sentimental painterly style, of George Washington and Ulysses S. Grant in uniform on horseback saluting General Pershing (in military vehicle with Allied Powers flags) from heaven, accompanied by the caption 'When Johnnie Comes Marching Home'.[45] The implication is that American victory in the First World War is a third iteration of the American tradition of key battles for freedom and democracy, initiated by the Revolutionary War and reasserted in the Civil War. This construction of a mythos of America as the torchbearer for democracy in the Western world is sustained in the connection with the French tradition in the poem, 'The Spirit of the Maid', on the first page. In a series of (again) sentimental octaves in simple, reassuring rhyme, the poet invokes the image of Joan of Arc as 'the spirit of Democracy' and 'the incarnation of unconquered France' in order to elevate America's role in the war as the continuation of a mythic battle for democracy that France and America, as the first republics, jointly originate (*Life*, 74, 485).

The inclusion of Stein's work in this magazine embodies a complex network of cause and effect in conceptions of her authorship. Appearing in the mid-section of the edition, juxtaposed with the usual mix of light-hearted responses to current affairs and homely humour about American life, Stein's text could be received by the unwitting reader of *Life* as a slightly opaque ditty in the same vein. In many ways, this is what it is: Stein knows this audience and she wants to appeal to them, but she also wants to move them in the direction of her literary experimentation. Stein's submission to *Life* promotes her American authorship and represents an intervention into American political discourse. This engagement with a broadcast American magazine overtly committed to democracy is an attempt to present her authorship as a valid aspect of democratisation, both in terms of acceptance of her authorial identity as an American writer and of her unusual work as a legitimate contribution to mainstream American debate. The integration of her piece in the textual fabric of the magazine is, however, disrupted by a note from the 'Editor of *Life*' which reads, 'Miss Gertrude Stein is one of the pioneers of Free Verse. We gladly publish her poem as a fit accompaniment to President Wilson's elucidation of the League of Nations' (*Life*, 74, 496). Setting 'A League' apart from the other unattributed contributions in the section, this rather arch framing of her text identifies its difference and heightens its incongruity. The emphasis on the decision to publish indicates that it is outside their usual range, and the light mockery in the comparison with Wilson's difficulty in communicating his vision of the League to Americans prepares the reader to encounter Stein's piece as unintelligible. Thus, Stein's efforts to normalise her authorship are undermined by the assertion of normative standards of publication and poetic expression in the editor's note.

The designation of Stein as 'one of the pioneers of Free Verse', however, while it contributes to the impression that her appearance is an anomaly, also situates Stein within a group and a movement, indicates her pre-eminence, even her prestige, and, significantly, reveals that a familiarity with poetic innovation is expected of the readers of *Life*. Despite its relatively recent coinage and distribution in the Anglophone literary world, and its even more recent recognition in the American context, this reference suggests that 'Free Verse' already has currency in the mainstream media.[46] Stein's status as innovative author and the literary culture that legitimises that status are therefore asserted even as they are mocked. Stein's appeal to democracy and her expectation that cultural and political space will be open to her authorship because of democratisation is in keeping with Loy's later conviction that this is one of its compensations. What is true of Loy's engagement with inter-war democracy is, however, also true of Stein's: while it insists on the rights of the author, it also offers a conception of rights that is shadowed by a racialised theory of nationality in conflict with the legalism of liberal democracy.

'A League' explores through linguistic experimentation, as does much of Stein's work in this period, a contemporary cultural practice in a specific medium. It is an experiment in writing the verbal-visual medium of the political cartoon genre, a discourse mode that Stein quite rightly associated with the production of knowledge about this political moment, and one which is the mainstay of political expression in *Life* magazine. Although *Life* is editorially in favour of Wilson and the League, it includes much anti-League and anti-Wilson content. These views are invariably expressed in the political cartoons that make up most of the content, and that, in the 18 September edition, contrast sharply with the rather defensive pro-League editorial in the middle section of the paper, which argues that its opponents are 'stupid' and 'brutish' (500). The cartoons in this edition also tend to be vehemently anti-internationalist in general, offering caricatures of the League of Nations and the Russian Revolution as internationalist movements that present twin threats to American democracy and national sovereignty.

Stein's choice of genre, therefore, indicates an alignment with the anti-internationalist stance so often reflected in the political cartoons in *Life*. Among the raft of such cartoons in the 18 September edition, two target Wilson and the League in particular. In the first example, a depiction of an encounter between Uncle Sam and Woodrow Wilson, Uncle Sam angrily presents his large stovepipe hat, inscribed 'Monroe Doctrine', to Wilson with the exclamation 'Say! Do you know you sat on my hat!' (506). Wilson stands mute, brandishing a smaller hat with 'League of Nations' feather. The implication is clear: the League of Nations is a threat to American sovereignty and heralds the return of the meddling colonial powers that were seen off by the Monroe Doctrine, the 1823 policy designed to protect the Americas from European imperialism. The second, anti-League, example depicts Uncle Sam once again, this time engaged in defending American democracy and national sovereignty by pushing a 'League of Nations' Humpty Dumpty off the wall protecting a distant White House from its incursion (498). Further signifiers in these cartoons contribute to the national feeling their scenarios evoke. In the 'Monroe Doctrine' cartoon, Wilson is portrayed with hand on hip and carelessly flourishing his feathered hat. This, in conjunction with the small wire-rimmed glasses obscuring his eyes and rather distracted, weak smile, suggest intellectualism coupled with effete and simpering politesse distinct from Uncle Sam's simple bluntness and direct gaze, and Wilson's refined, understated attire registers a European style that again contrasts with Uncle Sam's stars-and-stripes brashness. Indeed, the hat that Wilson holds denotes at once the properties of an English bowler and a 'Tyrolean'. Uncle Sam is the plainspoken direct American, and Wilson's urbane carelessness bespeaks a foreign indifference to or disdain of the American national story. The Humpty Dumpty example has Uncle Sam once again as the indomitable, straight-talking spirit of America who has no truck with the

League. More significantly, the wall in the nursery rhyme becomes a border-wall separating American democracy, represented by the image of the White House in the background, from the rest of the world. Both of these cartoons have the representatives of the League – a foppish scholar and an egg – as weak, flimsy, even degenerate in the face of the strength of American national identity.

As we can see, the political cartoon is a complex genre that has traditionally 'drawn meaning from a broad range of public knowledge and experience', using allegory, metaphor and symbolism and prompting 'readings of the human body' to translate political abstractions into tangible visual representations, often deploying juxtaposition, literary allusion or references to familiar stories and characters, the distortion of recognisable traits in stereotype or caricature, and visual and verbal punning.[47] 'A League' replicates these features in a writing experiment with this mode of political discourse. With its facile rhymes and prominent, awkward rhythm – formal features suggestive of the inevitable pratfalls of slapstick humour – it satirises President Wilson's campaign for the League of Nations, part of which took the form of a national tour throughout September 1919. The title 'A League' uses a pun that evokes the familiar folktale trope of seven-league boots, mocking both the League of Nations and Wilson's gruelling tour of America to promote it – 8,000 miles in 22 days – as fanciful or absurd quests. In the first line 'Why don't you visit your brother with a girl he doesn't know?', the reference to a 'visit' begins to elaborate the caricature of Wilson's tour, with 'brother' suggesting an American 'brotherhood' to satirise the purpose of the trip in enabling Wilson to get closer to ordinary Americans (*Life*, 74, 496). It also hints at an idea of national belonging in which the basis of the social contract is not a bond of mutual recognition but what is common to a group by birth. In this context, the 'girl he doesn't know' is not a brother, and, I would argue, is representative of the League, or at least its overseas outsiders. As a replication of the visual form of the cartoon, this line invokes an image of a man being advised to marry a girl off to his brother in a pragmatic transactional arrangement, an analogy that concretises Wilson's political aims as an attempt to sell America into a loveless foreign marriage.

Introduction / 27

The following line 'And in the midst of emigration we have wishes to bestow' compounds this imputation of betrayal by implying that Wilson has revoked his American nationality (*Life*, 74, 496). The tour comes shortly after Wilson's protracted stay in Europe for the Paris Peace Conference. He was the first American president to travel to Europe while in office, and he remained at the Peace Conference for more or less the entirety of its six-month duration, bar a two-week return visit to the US. The text, representing this as 'emigration' in an exaggerated form typical of the cartoon genre, caricatures the situation by implying Wilson is a president who has given up his citizenship. He is, therefore, no longer a brother, no longer native. It is notable that, here, Stein imputes to Wilson a conceptualisation of nationality in terms of purely legal status: emigration is only possible if citizenship is not predicated on birth. Stein's satirical representation of Wilson's attitude to his own nationality foregrounds the tension between opposing conceptions of nationality as either the organicist notion of brotherhood and belonging or as a status ascribed as the result of liberal democracy's official processes. The image this line evokes – of Wilson returning temporarily from Europe to 'bestow' wishes on Americans in order to gather support – implies an arrogance that is also a caricature of internationalist paternalism. The conception of nationality as citizenship conferred purely through a legal process is thus associated with liberal internationalism. Wilson, rather than being part of an American brotherhood, is a member of a global elite who can live anywhere. In the end what this adds up to is a reinforcing of the paradigm of nation and birth as the authentic form of nationality in contrast to a sterile legality for which nationality is simply a matter of expediency.

The central section of the text appears to move to Wilson's perspective, characterised as the de-individuated plural of institutional authority: 'We gather that the West is wet and fully ready to flow/ We gather that the East is wet and very ready to say so' (*Life*, 74, 496). These lines indicate the superficiality of Wilson's endeavour, with 'the West' and 'the East' representing a view of the nation as a map of voter preferences that Wilson can 'gather' (in all the senses of 'infer', 'assemble' and 'garner') and that are 'ready' to support him. The map image reiterates the imputation that Wilson is both disdainful of and separate from ordinary Americans because it evokes an impression of America seen from above or from a distance. The intimation of the superficiality of Wilson's engagement is sustained in the empty phrases that make up the last in this series of four increasingly lengthening sentences, 'We gather that we wonder and we gather that it is in respect to all of us that we think', where the first person plural and the stative verbs recall the hollow gestural forms of a politician's rhetoric. The final line of the text 'Do you want a baby. A round one or pink one' evokes an image of the politician's half-hearted engagement in ordinary lives (kissing babies, talking to people about their hopes and dreams), and so suggests the cynicism of Wilson's attempt to win Americans to his cause by encountering them directly on his tour (496). This grotesque semblance of a baby, reminiscent of the distortions of political caricature, perhaps also embodies the result of that dubious alliance suggested in the first line, shadowing the conception of a nationality of birth and brotherhood with intimations of blood heritage and a horror of miscegenation.

For Stein, Wilson represents the liberal, internationalist, paternalistic democracy she rejects. Stein's text is critical of the League for its internationalism and of Wilson for his betrayal of the principle of nation, presented as a racial allegiance that seems to include both identity and biology. In 'A League', Stein's democracy is not a universal ideal but an exclusionary, embodied reality asserted in the name of a nationalism that veers into racism. *Life* magazine in part echoes this view and in part contradicts it, revealing a complex landscape of opinion, from expressions of white supremacy, scepticism about the ability of women to make decisions and parodies of internationalism, to strongly argued support for the League of Nations and for the recent progress in ratifications of the Nineteenth Amendment that would, a few months later, give American women the right to vote.

The Right to Write

While it may be true that, as Stonebridge argues, 'literature speaks to the possibilities of freedom that political systems are often blind to' because 'writing anchors human rights law by providing images of the persons whose rights must be defended', Stein's work, her authorial identity, and her milieu show us that literature and the literary culture that enables and shapes its production can also be the site of discourses of exclusion and can enact forms of discursive violence.[48] And just as a sober view of Western democracies will admit that 'after their founding it swiftly became apparent that such rights followed the Athenian pattern of granting privilege only to those assumed to be part of the polis: property-owing men (largely) in; women, slaves and children (largely) out', so the legitimacy of literature and the right to write in itself can be conferred or withheld by normative discursive procedures (3). On these terms, Gertrude Stein's work, her authorial identity and the literary culture that wrangled over her authorship represent much that is difficult and troubling, but by engaging with such difficulties we can work through the politics – and the ethics – of literary participation, of writing and rights, and of what it means to write as a citizen of early-twentieth-century democracy.

The first chapter of this book, 'The Politics of Authorship in *Three Lives*', opens with a discussion of Stein's first publication in 1909. The chapter explores how this text represents Stein's struggle with American progressivism as a struggle with realist forms. It argues that *Three Lives*, in extending representation to new subjects as a mode of progressive political activism, simultaneously produces and problematises a quasi-clinical taxonomy aligned with the progressive discourse of social Darwinism. From there, it moves to the reception of *Three Lives*, considering the tendency of reviews to see the text as either promoting a progressive 'democratic' expansion of participation and representation or as an example of the aberrant practices of an avant-garde figured as a degenerate strand of literary production.

Chapter 2, 'Authorship and Community in Stein's Pre-war Portraits and *Tender Buttons*', turns to the early modernist scene of the 1910s and examines the place of Stein's work in a context of new conceptions of the artist and author expressed in modernist magazines and exhibitions that posit collective forms of authorship legitimised through the manifesto and the group. It explores the relationship of these ideas to discourses of liberalism, moving from debates within the emergent modernist literary culture to their reception in the broader public discourse of newspapers and magazines. It shows how, in broader print culture, Stein becomes a signifier of the new artist and author as aberrant, onto which scepticism about and dismissal of the new practices are loaded. It is here, I argue, that the figuring of Stein as an inappropriate biological subject for author status is constructed and begins to circulate.

The third chapter, 'Modernism's Abject: *Geography and Plays* and Stein's Contested Authorship', traces the seepage of the popular discourse of Stein as illegitimate or aberrant into modernist literary culture of the 1920s, exploring the ways modernist writers deploy these tropes to delimit aesthetic practice and legitimate particular forms of authorship. The chapter focuses on an extensive debate about the validity of Stein's work, prompted by the publication of *Geography and Plays*, the serialisation of *The Making of Americans* in *The Transatlantic Review* and the appearance of *Composition as Explanation* in Leonard and Virginia Woolf's Hogarth Essays series. In the context of extra-literary anxieties around democracy and rights, many of the louder voices in this literary culture insist on individual authorship as opposed to collective practice, and on the assertion of a normative model of authorship that enacts the identification and exclusion of those 'others' who had begun to participate in authorship during the pre-war period.

'*Useful Knowledge* and the Mind of Mass Democracy', extends into the fourth chapter the discussion of Stein's 1920s configuration by exploring her presentation, on the one hand, as the limit case for authorship and, on the other, as the ultimate democratic author. I argue that she becomes the focus for anxieties about literary and artistic participation that reflect discussions of the consequences of mass democracy, with an emphasis on the related issues of mental capacity, education and intellectual disability and often framed as ethical questions about the value of life, or as scientific or pseudo-scientific enquiries into genetic inheritance, reproduction and eugenics. On the other side of the debate, I look at the way Stein is framed as the mind of democracy and the exemplary democratic author, a representation that also echoes and engages with discussions of the positive potential of mass participation. Finally, the chapter considers Stein's 1928 text *Useful Knowledge* as a response to this discourse, arguing that the material Stein produces to frame

Useful Knowledge as American and democratic makes it an intervention that serves to reassert rather than resist the terms underlying her exclusion.

The book's Coda examines how Stein's authorial positioning as an authentically American writer is strongly reasserted in her bestseller *The Autobiography of Alice B. Toklas* in response to the sustained attacks on her authorial legitimacy discussed in Chapters 3 and 4. I argue that Stein offers an idealised vision of her authorship as representative of the liberation of identity in American mass democracy that is, however, subtended by an obfuscation of her own strategies of exclusion. Thus, while the *Autobiography* reconstituted Stein's American authorial identity after the attacks of the late 1920s in a highly successful recuperation, it also continued to reflect the problematic political views expressed in her earlier texts, revealing that her reactionary politics of the 1930s must be seen in terms of continuity rather than break.

Notes

1. Mina Loy, 'Gertrude Stein', *The Transatlantic Review*, Vol. 2, No. 4 (October 1924), 427–430 (429–430). Idiosyncrasies of spelling and grammar are in the original.
2. Mina Loy, 'Gertrude Stein', *The Transatlantic Review*, Vol. 2, No. 3 (September 1924), 305–309 (306).
3. This is the ecology of modernist culture in the sense of media ecology. For a recent overview of theories of media ecology, see Lance Strate, *Media Ecology: An Approach to Understanding the Human Condition* (New York: Peter Lang Publishing, 2017).
4. For a full and enlightening discussion of this strand of modernist thinking, see Lisi Schoenbach, *Pragmatic Modernism* (Oxford: Oxford University Press, 2012). Schoenbach discusses Stein and William James at length as exemplary of a 'gradualist, mediating approach to social change and artistic innovation'.
5. Foucault argues that, in the twentieth century, organicist conceptions of race and the associated discourse of race struggle are co-opted as 'state racism' in the emergence of biopolitics. See Michel Foucault, 'Society Must Be Defended', Lecture at the Collège de France, 17 March 1976, in *Biopolitics: A Reader*, ed. Timothy Campbell and Adam Sitze (Durham, NC and London: Duke University Press, 2013), 61–81 (79). See also Mark Mazower: 'the idea that . . . the nation needed racially sound progeny . . . ran right across the political spectrum of inter-war Europe, reflecting the tensions and stresses of an insecure world in which nation-states existed in rivalry with one another': Mark Mazower, *Dark Continent: Europe's Twentieth Century* (London: Penguin Books, 1999), 78.

6. Pericles Lewis, *Modernism, Nationalism, and the Novel* (Cambridge: Cambridge University Press, 2000), 6.
7. Mina Loy, 'Feminist Manifesto', in *The Lost Lunar Baedeker*, ed. Roger Conover (New York: Noonday, 1996), 153–156.
8. Hannah Arendt, *The Origins of Totalitarianism* (New York: Meridian, 1962), 301.
9. Pericles Lewis points out one of the most prominent examples: 'Organic nationalists found the existence of ethnic minorities within the borders of European states intolerable' (*Modernism, Nationalism and the Novel*, 7).
10. Hauke Brunkhorst, 'The Crisis of Legitimization in the World Society', in *The Twilight of Constitutionalism?*, ed. Petra Dobner and Martin Loughlin (Oxford: Oxford University Press, 2010), 179.
11. Pascale Casanova, *The World Republic of Letters* (Cambridge, MA: Harvard University Press, 2004), 3–4.
12. Pascale Casanova, 'Literature as a World', *New Left Review*, Vol. 31 (January/February 2005), 71–90 (72).
13. For example, the classic text on this, *Theory of the Avant-Garde*, defines autonomy as the result of the ascendancy of the bourgeoisie that creates the conditions in which the historical avant-gardes attempt to return art 'to the praxis of life': Peter Bürger, Michael Shaw and Jochen Schulte-Sasse, *Theory of the Avant-Garde* (Minneapolis: University of Minnesota Press, 1984), 58.
14. Samuel Moyn, *Human Rights and the Uses of History* (New York and London: Verso, [2014] 2017), 24.
15. Rachel Potter, *Modernism and Democracy: Literary Culture 1900–1930*, (Oxford: Oxford University Press, 2006), 9.
16. Rachel Potter and Lyndsey Stonebridge, 'Writing and Rights', *Critical Quarterly*, Vol. 56, No. 4 (December 2014), 1–16 (6). See also Lyndsey Stonebridge, *Writing and Righting: Literature in the Age of Human Rights* (Oxford: Oxford University Press, 2020).
17. See Arendt: 'The whole question of human rights, therefore, was quickly and inextricably blended with the question of national emancipation; only the emancipated sovereignty of the people, of one's own people, seemed to be able to insure them. As mankind, since the French Revolution, was conceived in the image of a family of nations, it gradually became self-evident that the people, and not the individual, was the image of man': Hannah Arendt, *The Origins of Totalitarianism* (New York: Meridian, 1962), 291.
18. Andrew John Miller, *Modernism and the Crisis of Sovereignty* (New York: Routledge, 2008), viii.
19. These shifting extranational currents were, of course, also very much in tension with each other, particularly in the inter-war period. Cosmopolitanism is a position made possible by citizenship, whereas the status of the refugee marks the opposite. See Lyndsey Stonebridge's discussion of modernist attitudes to statelessness: 'Where the cosmopolitan had been the figure for an earlier moment of modernism, by 1938 it was the refugee who had become, as Giorgio Agamben has put it, a "new paradigm of historical consciousness". Even as Virginia Woolf famously declared herself detached from her country on the grounds of her sex, a cosmopolitanism that since Kant had dreamt of a

universal humanity framed by a global understanding of rights, was confronted with the calamity of the radically stateless': Lyndsey Stonebridge, 'Refugee Style: Hannah Arendt and the Perplexities of Rights', *Textual Practice*, Vol. 25, No. 1 (2011), 71–85 (71).
20. See my discussion below and in Chapters 3 and 4.
21. Giorgio Agamben, *Homo Sacer: Sovereign Power and Bare Life* (Stanford, CA: Stanford University Press, 1998), 122.
22. Giorgio Agamben, *State of Exception* (Chicago: University of Chicago Press, 2005), 5.
23. Foucault, 'Society Must Be Defended', 62.
24. Agamben gives the examples of the Wilson administration, in which, 'from 1917 to 1918, Congress approved a series of acts . . . that granted the president complete control over the administration of the country'; and Franklin D. Roosevelt's assumption of 'extraordinary powers to deal with the Great Depression' (*State of Exception*, 21).
25. See Raymond Williams's influential 1989 discussion of modernism's canonisation: 'After modernism is canonized, however, by the post-war settlement and its complicit academic endorsements, the presumption arises that since modernism is here, in this specific phase or period, there is nothing beyond it. The marginal or rejected artists become classics of organized teaching and of travelling exhibitions in the great galleries of the metropolitan cities. "Modernism" is confined to this highly selective field and denied to everything else in an act of pure ideology, whose first, unconscious irony is that, absurdly, it stops history dead. Modernism being the terminus, everything afterwards is counted out of development. It is after; stuck in the past': Raymond Williams, 'When Was Modernism?' *New Left Review*, Vol. 1, No. 175 (May/June 1989), 48–52 (51). For Peter Quartermain, writing much later, in 2013, it is the publication of the 1950 collection that finally sealed a canonical modernism. See Peter Quartermain, *Stubborn Poetries: Poetic Facticity and the Avant-Garde* (Tuscaloosa: University of Alabama Press, 2013), 2.
26. This conception of Stein's writing has precedents in the responses of some modernists in the 1920s. See Chapter 4.
27. Peter Quartermain, *Disjunctive Poetics: From Gertrude Stein and Louis Zukofsky to Susan Howe* (Cambridge: Cambridge University Press, 1992), 43. Marjorie Perloff, *The Poetics of Indeterminacy: Rimbaud to Cage* (Evanston, IL: Northwestern University Press, 1999), 105–106.
28. Juliana Spahr, *Everybody's Autonomy: Connective Reading and Collective Identity* (Tuscaloosa: University of Alabama Press, 2001), 50.
29. Gertrude Stein, *Gertrude Stein: Selections*, ed. Joan Retallack (Berkeley: University of California Press, 2008), 75; 25.
30. Barbara Will, *Gertrude Stein, Modernism and the Problem of 'Genius'* (Edinburgh: Edinburgh University Press, 2000), 14.
31. Charles Bernstein, 'Ulla Dydo, 1925–2017', *Jacket 2*, 1 January 2018, https://jacket2.org/commentary/ulla-dydo; Ulla Dydo, *Gertrude Stein: The Language That Rises 1923–1934* (Evanston, IL: Northwestern University Press, 2003), 17.

32. GF Mitrano, *Gertrude Stein: Woman Without Qualities* (Aldershot: Ashgate, 2005), 5.
33. Aidan Thompson, 'Language and Democracy: Meaning Making as Existing in the Work of Gertrude Stein', *Arizona Quarterly: A Journal of American Literature, Culture, and Theory*, Vol. 69, No. 3 (Autumn 2013), 129-155 (130-131); Julie Goodspeed-Chadwick, 'Reconfiguring Identities in the Word and in the World: Naming Marginalized Subjects and Articulating Marginal Narratives in Early Canonical Works by Gertrude Stein', *South Central Review*, Vol. 31, No. 2 (2014), 9-27 (9).
34. Expressed, for example, in the very distinctive versions of anarchism imagined by Hutchins Hapgood (see my discussion in Chapter 2), Wyndham Lewis and Laura Riding (see my discussion in Chapter 4).
35. Barbara Will, *Unlikely Collaboration: Gertrude Stein, Bernard Faÿ, and the Vichy Dilemma* (New York: Columbia University Press, 2011), 13.
36. Marianne DeKoven, *A Different Language: Gertrude Stein's Experimental Writing* (Madison: University of Wisconsin Press, 1983); Harriet Scott Chessman, *The Public Is Invited to Dance: Representation, the Body, and Dialogue in Gertrude Stein* (Stanford, CA: Stanford University Press, 1989); Lisa Cole Ruddick, *Reading Gertrude Stein: Body, Text, Gnosis* (Ithaca, NY: Cornell University Press, 1990). These are all important feminist engagements with Stein which, along with the work of other scholars such as Jayne L. Walker, Shari Benstock, Sandra Gilbert and Susan Gubar, Catharine R. Stimpson and Bonnie Kime Scott were significantly involved in her initial recuperation and the development of Stein studies. See Jayne L. Walker, *The Making of a Modernist: Gertrude Stein from 'Three Lives' to 'Tender Buttons'* (Amherst: University of Massachusetts Press, 1984); Shari Benstock, *Women of the Left Bank: Paris, 1900-1940* (Austin: University of Texas Press, 1986); Sandra M. Gilbert and Susan Gubar, *No Man's Land: The Place of the Woman Writer in the Twentieth Century* (New Haven, CT: Yale University Press, 1989); and Bonnie Kime Scott, *The Gender of Modernism: A Critical Anthology* (Bloomington: Indiana University Press, 1990). Catharine Stimpson has published numerous articles on Stein, for example 'The Mind, the Body, and Gertrude Stein', *Critical Inquiry* Vol. 3, No. 3 (1977), 489-506; 'Gertrude Stein: Humanism and Its Freaks', *Boundary* Vol. 2, No. 12/13 (1984), 301-19; and 'The Somagrams of Gertrude Stein', *Poetics Today* Vol. 6, No. 1/2 (1985), 67-80. Chessman and Stimpson's shared interest in Stein culminated in their joint editorship of *Gertrude Stein: Writings 1903-1932* and *Gertrude Stein: Writings 1932-1946* (New York: Library of America, 1998).
37. For example, the 15th Modernist Studies Association conference, 'Everydayness and the Event', considered the significance of the everyday as a major theme.
38. Gaston Franssen and Rick Honing, eds., *Celebrity Authorship and Afterlives in English and American Literature* (London: Palgrave Macmillan, 2016), 2.
39. Aaron Jaffe, *Modernism and the Culture of Celebrity* (Cambridge: Cambridge University Press, 2005), 1.
40. Deborah Mix 'Gertrude Stein's Currency', in *Modernist Star Maps*, ed. Aaron Jaffe and Jonathan Goldman (Farnham: Ashgate, 2010), 93-104 (98).

41. See Karen Leick, *Gertrude Stein and the Making of an American Celebrity* (New York: Routledge, 2009).
42. Ann Ardis, 'Staging the Public Sphere: Magazine Dialogism and the Prosthetics of Authorship at the Turn of the Twentieth Century' in *Transatlantic Print Culture, 1880–1940: Emerging Media, Emerging Modernisms*, ed. Ann L. Ardis and Patrick Collier (London: Palgrave Macmillan, 2008), 30–47 (30).
43. David E. E. Sloane, ed., *American Humor Magazines and Comic Periodicals* (Westport, CT: Greenwood Press, 1987), 150.
44. *Life*, Vol. 74, No. 1925 (18 September 1919), 482.
45. Ibid., cover.
46. This terminology appears in American little magazines, such as the *Little Review* (1914–1929), *Others* (1915–1919) and *Rogue* (1915–1916), only after 1914.
47. Richard Scully and Marian Quartly, 'Using Cartoons as Historical Evidence', in *Drawing the Line: Using Cartoons as Historical Evidence*, ed. Richard Scully and Marian Quartly (Clayton, Victoria: Monash University Press, 2009), 01.3; 01.4.
48. Rachel Potter and Lyndsey Stonebridge, 'Writing and Rights', *Critical Quarterly*, Vol. 56, No. 4 (2014), 1–16 (2).

CHAPTER 1

The Politics of Authorship in *Three Lives*

The Struggle with Realism

This chapter considers the conception of authorship represented in Stein's earliest publication, *Three Lives*, which, despite its small circulation, attracted much commentary. Prevailing scholarly opinion regards *Three Lives*, written in Paris, as both a break from American realist literary forms and a reflection of Stein's dissatisfaction with the bourgeois progressivist culture of her university days.[1] For many, it marks the moment when she shakes off the Jamesian realism adopted in her first attempts at writing, the unfinished novels *Fernhurst* and *Q.E.D.*, and, influenced by the Parisian avant-garde in general and Matisse and Picasso in particular, moves into the first phase of the experimentation that would characterise her subsequent literary oeuvre.[2] I argue in this chapter that, although it is more overtly experimental than her other early works and, without doubt, reflective of her new cultural experiences, Stein's first publication retains significant aspects of the American realism of the early twentieth century, in particular the *progressivist* vision of the American author as pioneering chronicler of social reality engaged in the cataloguing of contemporary American life. I would contend that, rather than manifesting a rejection of American reformist politics, *Three Lives* sustains the progressive attitude to the demos, informed by the ideology of social Darwinism, in which the documenting and regulation of types accompanies the drive toward greater social inclusion and the extension of rights. Stein's funda-

The Politics of Authorship in *Three Lives* / 37

mentally progressivist desire to increase representation and participation in cultural life, here by extending literary representation to new subjects in new forms, ends up with a set of detailed classifications expressed in limiting biological terms that reproduce the pseudo-scientific taxonomies fundamental to American progressive thinking. What I also argue, however, is that, while identifying the same issues on similar terms, *Three Lives* simultaneously problematises progressive methods and approaches aimed at improving social conditions and moulding fitter democratic subjects, and, in doing so, begins to develop a new conception of authorship.

This chapter also considers the reception of *Three Lives*, exploring what I argue is a tension in the tendency of contemporary reviews to see the text as either deploying realist techniques to promote the expansion of participation and representation in which the author is actively involved in the promotion of such a vision of American democracy, or as an example of the aberrant practices of an avant-garde figured as a degenerate and un-American strand of literary production. My argument here is that these apparent contradictions in the way Stein's authorship was understood reflect the ambivalent position vis-à-vis American progressive ideas that is expressed in *Three Lives*. In this text, Stein grapples with progressivism and its representative literary genre, realism, and attempts to develop her own philosophy of human nature through a set of formal configurations influenced by her engagement with the continental avant-garde. Stein is, however, strongly indebted to progressive ideology and to the realist genre even as she wrestles with them, and this endeavour shapes the content and form of the text and, importantly, Stein's understanding of her own authorship at this stage.

The story of Stein's three-year attempt to get her first book into print has been told many times.[3] *Three Lives*, completed in 1906, was finally published, at Stein's expense, in September 1909 by Grafton of New York, a vanity press that typically produced family ancestry, memoir and local history rooted in the north-eastern region of the United States.[4] *Three Lives* cannot be said to exemplify any of these genres, but the text's engagements with modes of genealogy, biography and social history and its setting in the Maryland city of Baltimore in the Mid-Atlantic section of the Northeastern seaboard make this private publisher a particularly appropriate choice. In its engagement with early-twentieth-century American progressive discourses of heredity increasingly connected to theories of genetic inheritance and social evolution, *Three Lives* transmutes the genres of pedigree and lineage typically produced by this press. The text's associated attention to 'character', 'type', national and ethnic identities, and the role of social environment in the development and inheritance of traits, also refracts and extends Grafton's stock of memoir and local history. As I have pointed out, *Three Lives* has often been read as Stein's first attempt at writing influenced by the innovative European art with which she was becoming immersed. Traces of that other, still very potent influence of the American social, cultural and political sphere she had recently left, however, strongly inflect the modes of the text as well as the subject matter of ordinary lives lived out in a Northeastern American city. Stein, who grew up in California, took up residence in Baltimore in 1897 to study medicine at Johns Hopkins University following her preliminary studies at Radcliffe, the women's annex of Harvard. Thus, her experience of the Northeast was as a student immersed in the discussions, debates and activism of a middle-class intellectual milieu in which American progressivism was very much in the ascendant.[5]

Before settling for a private press, Stein and her friends, and, eventually, a literary agent, attempted to place the manuscript with a number of publishers.[6] One significant choice, third on Stein's list and her first choice of magazine publication, was the popular American monthly, *McClure's Magazine*.[7] Stein's interest in the magazine as a potential home for the text is clear from literary agent Flora M Holly's report that 'Miss Roseboro is still with *McClure's*, and I will send the manuscript over there as you suggest'.[8] Stein's desire to have the stories published in the magazine and her belief that this was the place for them indicates that she saw them as an appropriate contribution to its mix of 'muckraking' journalism, social commentary supporting calls for reform, character sketches detailing examples of American types, swashbuckling tales in the vein of Melville, and, throughout its history, but increasingly under the literary editorship of Willa Cather from 1906, realist fiction capturing the qualities of American contemporary life.[9] This was a programme that was very much attuned to progressive political, social and cultural ideals. Indeed, *McClure's* is where the new genre of journalism was born, pioneered by the journalist Ida Tarbell and exemplified by her exposé of Standard Oil in a series of articles from 1902 to 1904.[10] The influence and support of this form of journalism for the progressive drive for reform was significant, as evinced by President Theodore Roosevelt's response (in which he coined the term that came to define it): 'it is very necessary that we should not flinch from seeing what is vile and debasing. There is filth on the floor, and it must be scraped up with the muck rake'.[11] While Roosevelt is critical of the tendency to take it too far, arguing that it needs to be temperate, calling for 'honesty, sanity, and self-restraint' and arguing that there is 'little good in a mere spasm of reform', he is clear about the significance of this kind of reporting for the reformist cause (420). The progressive tendency in *McClure's* is expressed in much of its content, and there are parallels in *Three Lives* that reveal the significance and persistence of progressivism in Stein's vision of the purpose of innovation in literary fiction and the function of authorship at this early moment in her development as an author.

That Stein proposed *McClure's* as a suitable vehicle for *Three Lives* reflects her continued attachment to the sphere she inhabited while at university, and it also points to her concomitant association of literary fiction with the documentation of social reality and of authorship with political engagement. From its inception, *McClure's* published the work of originating American realists, Mark Twain, William Dean Howells, Hamlin Garland and Sarah Orne Jewett, and later, the work of Frank Norris, Stephen Crane and Jack London, short stories with naturalistic treatments of American working-class life that both created and served a popular demand.[12] Indeed, Jack London's story 'The Unexpected', published in August 1906, is footnoted with the claim that 'Mr London's story is a real human document, based upon actual incidents', an overdetermination of the story's authenticity – 'real', 'document', 'actual' – that reflects the editorial perception of readers' interest in stories of real life and foregrounds its value as such.[13]

These early-twentieth-century forms of American realism, their contexts and their origins are discussed in detail in a key textbook of the period written by Stein's English Professor at Radcliffe, William

Vaughn Moody, and his colleagues Robert Morss Lovett and Percy H. Boynton. *A First View of English and American Literature*, first published in 1902, would undoubtedly have reflected the teaching that Stein had received as an undergraduate, and it offers important insights into the way that American realism, its history, its function and its contemporary relevance were perceived at the time. *A First View* views realism as 'the characterizing impulse of the early twentieth century', a situation prompted by the 'democratic tendency in literature' that 'has been intensely stimulated by popular education' that has in turn generated 'the interest of the new vast reading public in realities, in the facts that govern our habitation of the earth'.[14] Arguing that 'contemporary realism is very different from the interest in the phenomena of the surface of society which goes under that name in the past' because of 'the influence of science', Moody et al. suggest that 'it looks deeper and values facts for their significance' and is, at the same time, 'acutely conscious of the meaning of fact for the immediate present'. Concluding that, 'it is, in other words, journalistic', and thus, that 'Journalistic realism may then be accepted as a definition of the leading tendency of contemporary literature', this contemporary understanding of the nature and role of realism is borne out in the magazines that Stein was evidently reading, and in the first such publication to which she submitted her own work of American realism (384).

Both William James (professor at Harvard at the time), who taught Stein psychology while she was at Radcliffe and with whom she maintained a connection until his death in 1910, and the publisher Pitts Duffield understood that *Three Lives* was most readily intelligible as a form of 'realism'.[15] In commenting on the potential reception of *Three Lives* as literary realism, however, Duffield notes two important distinctions. First, he points out that, in *Three Lives*, Stein has moved beyond realism in her 'application of French methods to American low life', but that the text would nevertheless be understood as 'only another piece of realism' to the majority of readers 'ignorant of any sense of literary values'. Second, he suggests that 'realism nowadays doesn't go'.[16] What he recognises is significant: that *Three Lives* reads like realism and retains many of the elements of realism, that realism as a genre is becoming outdated, and that Stein is struggling to move beyond a passé form but has not been able yet to make this intelligible to the 'average' reader. The fact that Stein places *Three Lives* with *McClure's* after Duffield's commentary marks her own understanding of the text as a form of realism that she believes, on the contrary, will indeed be accessible to readers still engaging with the popular realism published in the magazine, even if it won't 'go' for readers investing seriously in literary texts.[17] Understood on those terms, Stein's text makes sense in the context of the magazine's role as a vehicle for progressive ideals. The documentary aspects of these genres, their depictions of 'real' American lives, form the basis of social commentary and critique to support the calls for reform. These are potent ways of identifying inequalities and evoking affect.

Three Lives as Character Sketch

The mode Stein uses for her experiment with realism, however, is significant: Flora Holly described the stories as 'more character sketches than anything else'.[18] While the realist story could show the struggles of the working classes, the character sketch was not fiction but a form of reportage that often attended to the wealthy and powerful men who were the target for progressive critique or (less often) who represented progressive ideals. Stein's deployment of this form suggests the continued influence of this American idea of authorship because it reflects the anxiety that attended early-twentieth-century American realist fiction in particular: the apparent enthusiasm for journalistic rather than fictional accounts of American life. This is hinted at in the suggestion of Stein's other reader, F. H. Hitchcock at the Grafton Press, that she change the title of the text from her original 'Three Histories' because 'I do not want it to get confused with my real historical publication'.[19] While of course this reflects the prevalence of biography and history in Grafton's output, it also points to an important shift that is responding to the market for social documentary, and which is testament to the ways progressive ideas are forming taste.

The *Atlantic Monthly*, another publication that Stein, throughout her life, felt could or should be a vehicle for her work, had moved from the publication of the realism that had been its mainstay in the late nineteenth century to reportage documenting real lives such as that of Jacob Riis.[20] By the 1890s, the *Atlantic Monthly*, along with many other American monthlies, had become sympathetic to progressivism. For its new literary editorial team, 'literature' was increasingly understood as the space of the imaginary, the quasi-romantic and the conservative, holding on to the older 'genteel' audience, whereas reportage and other forms of first-person documentary became the place of innovation and progressive ideals.[21] This shift is also reflected in the proliferation of reportage and social commentary in *McClure's* throughout the first years of the twentieth century, exemplified by the contributions of Josiah Flynt, whose forays into the 'underworld' of American cities ran through the first years of the twentieth century and were often heavily promoted on front covers. On the other hand, Flynt's popular accounts of the criminal underclass also extended to fiction in collections of short stories, *The Powers That Prey* (1900), written in collaboration with Stein's close friend Alfred Hodder (writing pseudonymously as Francis Walton) and *The World of Graft* (1901), both published by McClure, Philips and Co. This reflects the appetite for realist fiction alongside documentary accounts and indicates the porous boundary between fiction and non-fiction, suggested in the introduction to *The Powers That Prey*, which asserts that 'The following tales are records of incidents' and represent the 'history of certain inconspicuous events' of which the reader 'will have read notices in the public prints'.[22] The editorship of Willa Cather from July 1906, during her 'realist Jamesian mode', also meant that *McClure's* heightened its attention to the strands of realist fiction that are working out, as we see with Flynt and Hodder, the relations between journalistic reportage, social commentary and literary art.[23] It is clear that, in a magazine market where the appetite is for 'reality', realist fiction was increasingly the only literary genre worth printing. Given both Stein's suggestion that *Three Lives* be placed with *McClure's* and her experimentation with a hybrid form of realist fiction drawing on multiple aspects of the character sketch (as we shall see), it is also apparent that Stein is responding as much to the literary milieu of the American progressivist magazine as she is to the Parisian avant-garde scene.[24]

Character sketches formed an important part of *McClure's*' offer in the first decade of the twentieth century. Subjects included American naval commander Admiral William T. Sampson, businessman and Republican Senator Mark Hanna, Tammany Hall leader Richard Croker, financier and banker J. Pierpont Morgan, and, perhaps the most influential sketch, that of John D. Rockefeller, founder of the Standard Oil Company.[25] The character sketch was often very subtle in its critique (or its praise), providing a sense of latitude in which the reader is encouraged to draw conclusions from the factual clues set before them, from Ray Stannard Baker's reference to reports of J. Pierpont Morgan's childhood 'sturdiness and independence' to his documenting of the position of the banker's desk.[26] Almost invariably, they also drew on a discourse of heredity set in relation to environmental factors in order to identify and explicate the formation of character often cast in terms of 'type'. The origin-story of migration and family lineage is a common element, as exemplified in Ida Tarbell's depiction of 'Rockefeller's origin': 'it is typically American. He sprang from one of the migrating families. . .coming to this country in the seventeenth century' out of which 'he and his brothers were the first great product of a restless family searching a firm footing in new soil'.[27] Indeed, William Allen White's sketch of Croker, whose family arrived much later, in the mid-nineteenth century, attributes the survival of the 'un-American' Tammany Hall to an 'atavism' that 'makes the European immigrant and his family stagger a bit under the first burdens of citizenship', and thus to the difficulties of adaptation.[28] The character sketch was often deployed in the service of critique, but it also served to mark and elevate exemplary men. Stannard Baker's 1899 depiction of Admiral William T. Sampson, for example, reflects the reformist emphasis on conditions by attributing Sampson's success to a mix of genetic inheritance and environment. Sampson is genetically 'north of Ireland stock', that, 'nurtured' in an environment of 'poverty and Presbyterianism', is one in which 'genius seems always smoldering just beneath its surface' and which is enabled to 'leap forth' under the influence of a mother who is 'ambitious for them with all the keen ambition of mother-love' and in the environment of the 'good, green country, with weather-colored houses and big red barns' of central New York State.[29]

The relations between heredity and environment suggested by Tarbell's reference to the subject of her sketch as the 'product' of a 'restless family' and 'new soil' and Baker's narrative of 'stock' and 'country' are more explicit in William Allen White's 1900 sketch of Mark Hanna, which opens with a reference to Herbert Spencer, the social Darwinist whose theories of evolution, underpinned by the neo-Lamarckian belief in the inheritance of acquired characteristics, were popular in the late nineteenth century and formed the basis of much progressive-era social policy thinking.[30] The neo-Lamarckian conception of the heritability of adaptations to environment reflected in Spencer's sociological and philosophical systems, although challenged by biologists since the late nineteenth century, was widely sustained by progressives in the development of social and economic theory and psychology well into the twentieth century.[31] The sketch of Hanna is framed, with explicit reference to Spencer, in terms of this perspective on environment: 'Mr. Herbert Spencer believes that life is a series of relations, and that man and the other creatures of the earth are the reflections of their environment', and the article develops this understanding of character throughout, attributing Hanna's success to his absorption of the mechanical power of industrial capitalism, the 'mines and ships and steel things that he loved' that are 'a part of him'.[32] For many progressives, social reform is necessary for the development of what pastor and leading progressive Washington Gladden described as 'a different kind of man and woman'.[33] If environment in all its aspects has a profound effect on the living being which is subsequently inherited by successive generations, then the improvement of material, social and cultural conditions is necessary for the improvement of Americans both in their lifetime and for their genetic legacy.

White's sketch of Hanna takes this paradigm as the starting point for an analysis of his political powerplay – he ran the election campaign of Republican President William McKinley – offering a vision of a man both shaped by and shaping his environment. After introducing Hanna's town of Cleveland, Ohio, entering his office and panning across the room documenting its contents – including photographs of 'the interior of a power-house with four huge engines . . . mechanically eloquent of power . . . waiting the touch of a master to release their energy' and of 'the men of the Republican National Committee', and with a 'litter of blue prints' on the desk – the article zooms in on Hanna and concludes:

Hanna's personality exudes from everything. The photographs of the great engines become vitally a part of him. The blue prints seem to crystallise themselves into him. The politician's faces, the chairs, the table with the shapeless legs, all in an instant become living, component parts of this man's existence. The room, the building, the town on the inland sea – they are all parts of him and products of him, and he is a part and product of them (57).

Prefaced by a quasi-evolutionary theory of the relations between environment and character, what might have been understood as a series of metaphors describing Hanna as invested with 'mechanical force' and 'the practical energy of a trip-hammer' become deeply defining characteristics that are the result of a profound reciprocity of organism and environment.

Describing Hanna as an 'American type', however, White broadens this conception to present him as expressing the essential characteristics of a group, and, toward the end of the piece, as a 'representative American' (64). The article nuances cartoon depictions of Hanna as 'a crusher of labor, an industrial octopus, a commercial Moloch' by grounding the reason for his success in the environment that *makes* Americans (62). This analysis forms the basis of White's proposal for a new 'remedy for Hannaism' which lies in the ability of reformist critics to 'give to the exemplification of high civic ideals the force of unqualified success and the charm of virile personality' that are the characteristics Hanna has developed in the environment of modern American life (64). White is arguing that the traits and concomitant energies that the conditions of industrial capitalism produce in Americans need to be channelled into the 'high civic ideals' of progressivism in order to shift the balance away from corporate gain and monopoly power. The article therefore presents the understanding of character through the lens of environment and adaptation as an accurate epistemological tool and an effective method for the promotion of the reformist cause to 'remedy . . . Hannaism' – that is, to regulate the power of business interests.

This is the milieu within which Stein first begins to consider authorship seriously, moving away from her experimentation in the emerging sciences of psychology and neurology and toward experiments in realist fiction. Stein's text engages with the problems of early-twentieth-century American realism, and these are, at the outset, progressivist problems in which authorship is conceived as activism and in which literary fiction is a vehicle for social reform. In employing the genre of the character sketch to present the lives of working-class immigrant and African American women, Stein merges realist fiction, the genre of ordinary life, with the sketch form usually reserved for prominent, powerful men in a way that calls for the inclusion of these lives in a typology of American character. What the character sketch and the realist fiction of this period have in common is their exploration of the relation between the individual and environment that is at the heart of progressive ideology. The epigraph with which Stein opens *Three Lives*, attributed to the French Symbolist poet Jules Laforgue, engages this very problem. The apparent riddle, 'donc je suis un malheureux et ce n'est ni ma faute ni celle de la vie' ['therefore, I am unhappy and this is neither my fault nor that of my life'] paraphrases rather than quotes Laforgue in a form of Stein's making that evidently serves her in the critical engagement with progressive ideas that motivates the text.[34] If a state of being is the result neither of the individual ('my fault') nor of environment or experience ('my life'), then the epigraph frames the stories with a question that is central to progressive thinking: the relationship between individual and environment.

As scholars have argued, the close observation of individual subjects in *Three Lives* correlates with and extends Stein's psychology experimentation and her experiences as a medical student at Johns Hopkins. Shadowing her apparent elevation of her working-class immigrant and black women characters is the mode of clinical observation, a residue of her experimental work on the motor functions of the brain and nervous system at Harvard and her medical training at Johns Hopkins, in particular her experience of obstetrics rounds in the working-class areas of Baltimore.[35] The role of character sketches in magazines associated with the progressive cause, and their deployment of Lamarckian narratives of acquisition and heredity, however, also needs to be taken into account in an understanding of how Stein viewed the text and her authorship as she conceived of and worked on *Three Lives* through 1905 and 1906.

This text documents the beginning of Stein's move, literally and artistically, but also *politically*, out of the direct influence of the progressivist milieu. Because these stories were conceptualised within the framework of a social reformist model of authorship, however, they remain very much tied to these roots even as they begin to problematise them. The genre of the character sketch enables a close scrutiny of individual traits and a theoretical account of their provenance, acquisition and development. Throughout the three stories, Stein presents the complex of genetic and environmental factors that shape and direct each character's temperament, behaviour and physique. The resultant sketch of an embodied nexus of effects echoes the exploration of the relations between genetic inheritance and environment in the character sketches in reformist magazines such as *McClure's*.

'The Good Anna', in keeping with the mode of the character sketch, opens *in medias res* with a set of indicative details that produce an outline of the subject through her immediate relations with her environment. Anna's economic relations with local tradesmen and her relation to the space of the 'funny little' Baltimore house are foregrounded, indicating the apparent determinism of her role as housekeeper, consistent with the progressive belief in the reciprocity of individual traits and environmental factors typified in the sketch of Hanna which has him as 'a part and product' of industrial capitalism.[36] The formative effects of environment are shown in their functional relationship with the foundational individual characteristics Stein also introduces here, and which she reiterates throughout 'The Good Anna'. Anna is 'a small, spare, german woman, at this time about forty years of age' to which Stein adds the details 'Her face was worn, her cheeks were thin, her mouth drawn and firm, and her light blue eyes were very bright. Sometimes they were full of lightning and sometimes full of humor, but they were always sharp and clear' (3). Set among an initial flurry of descriptions detailing a succession of unsatisfactory under-servants – the 'pretty, cheerful irish girl' (3) Lizzie, Molly, 'born in America, of german parents' (3), Old Katy, the 'heavy, ugly, short and rough old german woman' (5) and Sallie, 'a pretty blonde and smiling german girl' (7) – Anna's German ethnicity is made central in Stein's identification of her character, replicating the convention of the character sketch which tends to present such a delineation of 'stock' and ethnic heritage. The function of the dual influences of genetic inheritance and environment in producing and reproducing character is reiterated throughout 'The Good Anna' and accompanied and reinforced by the recursive reworking of the core description of Anna in which the mechanism of their reciprocal structuring is located. Introduced for the first time here, the details of Anna's worn face, thin cheeks, 'drawn and firm' mouth and light blue 'very bright' eyes return in the analepsis of Part II:

> At this time Anna, about twenty-seven years of age, was not yet all thin and worn. The sharp bony edges and corners of her head and face were still rounded out with flesh, but already the temper and the humor showed sharply in her clean blue eyes, and the thinning was begun about the lower jaw, that was so often strained with the upward pressure of resolve (13).

This narrative structure is consistent with the formula of the character sketch, in which the journalistic immediacy of the opening scenario, providing observational clues to the character's nature and its formation, is invariably followed by a return to the origins of the subject in question. Here, Stein's return to the past contains within it the promise of Anna's future state, determined by her inherited traits and their interaction with an environment that includes economic realities, social configurations and institutions, and interpersonal interactions.

The core characteristics of Stein's subjects are deepened by their engagement with their imperfect environments – as the text repeatedly points out and decries. These characteristics, the result of the interaction between heredity tied to ethnicity and environment as a powerfully conservative field of social and economic interaction, are punctuated in Part I by the reiteration of the refrain 'Anna led an arduous and troubled life' (1), 'You see that Anna led an arduous and troubled life' (3, 8). The chorus indicates the process through which her existence conforms to the determining interplay of biological and social life, a repetitive mechanism whose every reiteration asserts itself more insistently. These parallels – the attention to environment strongly suggestive of its formative role and the emphasis on family lineage tied to a narrative of ethnic bloodlines – reflect both the prevailing influence of literary and journalistic forms associated with early-twentieth-century progressive thought and strong traces of a progressive understanding of genetic inheritance, environmental influence and the heritability of acquired characteristics in Stein's thinking. While, as Sean McCann argues, the apparent determinism represented in *Three Lives* might indicate Stein's rejection of 'progress', it can just as convincingly be read as a critical account of the formative role of socio-economic environment hinted at in reformist-leaning character sketches and confronted more explicitly in the social documentary and short realist fiction prevalent in *McClure's* and other prominent American magazines of the period.[37]

In 'The Good Anna', Stein plays out the unfurling of Anna's nature to suggest the inevitable warping effects of the interaction of originary traits with a constraining or mismatched environment. This is an effect created in all three *Lives*. In 'Melanctha' the protagonist's 'subtle, intelligent, attractive' (55) elements are clouded from the start with a concomitant tendency to 'mystery', 'subtle movements', 'complicated denials' (57) and the 'complex, desiring', liminal qualities that Stein pins to her being 'half made with real white blood' (55). Melanctha's core characteristics are simplistically associated with her racialisation: in Stein's representation, mixed blood is complicated blood. Nonetheless, these traits suggest the potential for a full and complex form of life. Set in an environment defined by narrow stratifications of class and race, however, Stein indicates that Melanctha's complexity and subtlety mean that she cannot anchor herself in that territory, whose distinctions she encounters from a position of permanent transgression. From the opening, the dissonance created by Melanctha's liminality makes her wonder 'often, how she could go on living when she was so blue' (55) and 'how it was she did not kill herself when she was so blue' (57). Just as with Anna, the worn edge where Melanctha's nature interacts with her environment expresses itself finally in her death at the end of the story: she dies, according to the relation of her traits to her social context, not through the decisive act of suicide, but of the slow and 'subtle' dwindling caused by consumption, the result of her placeless 'wandering'.

Progressive Attitudes to Race in *Three Lives*

Stein's representations of race have all the features of the progressive discourse that formulates a taxonomy of racialisation underpinned by an ideology of racial hierarchy. The complications arising from Melanctha's racial liminality are emphasised by contrast and comparison throughout the text. The uncertainty of her racial identity is set against the insistently 'black' racialisation of Melanctha's friend Rose Johnson and her father James Herbert, which is foregrounded in crassly racist associations with, in Rose's case, 'simple, promiscuous immorality' and, in James's, with a 'virile' sexuality and 'brutal' physical power, stereotypes that carry with them a long history of concocted fear and fascination. Both Rose and James are associated with a crude and powerful simplicity that fixes their social position among the African-American working class, associated in Stein's taxonomy with the type of 'blackness'. The middle-class doctor, Jeff Campbell, on the other hand, the character for whom inheritance and environment appear to coincide most successfully, is the product of 'light brown' and 'pale brown' parents who 'had of course been regularly married'. His racialisation is coordinated with his social position in the most simplistic form: he is 'brown' and he is 'regular' and he therefore occupies the middle-class position of a 'young doctor'. Jeff also 'love[s] his own colored people', is 'always very interested in the life of the colored people' and, unlike the other characters, as Stein repeatedly points out, laughs with 'the free abandoned laughter that gives the warm broad glow to negro sunshine'. In other words, he is the figure of the acceptable African American who keeps his place among his 'people' and offers neither threat nor fascination. These representatives of racialised social ranks provide a contrast with Melanctha's troubling indeterminacy, whereas the other character identified as 'mulatto', Jane Harden, echoes Melanctha in her inability to locate herself securely in the shifting intersections of class and race and thus serves to reinforce Stein's identification of miscegenation with transgression and social instability. Jane is 'so white that hardly anyone would guess' and has 'had a good deal of education', a combination that Stein associates with the 'wandering' she attributes to both Jane and Melanctha. In Stein's account of their relationship, as scholars have argued, this wandering is a signifier for sexual experimentation, but it is also explicitly tied to a failure or refusal to find a place in the social order.[38] Thus, Stein constructs a relationship between racial and social stratification that reflects the relations between nature and environment, self ('ma faute') and life (la vie') she sets up in the epigraph.

Stein's taxonomy of race and status is a crass and undeniably racist attempt to give a critical account of relationships between genetic inheritance and social environment that is very much in keeping with progressive discourse. The topics of the 'negro question' or the 'color line' were regularly addressed in *McClure's* and other magazines in serious articles on the subject of race from a range of perspectives, in contributions as diverse as the Republican Senator Carl Schurz's wide-ranging critique of attitudes to African-American suffrage in the South, and the lawyer and novelist Thomas Nelson Page's series on the history and legacy of slavery.[39] Indeed, the advertisement for the March 1904 edition of *McClure's* refers to the magazine's attention to the 'negro question' as exemplifying its status as 'the first attempt at national journalism'.[40] The subject of race, and the issue of miscegenation in particular, are also treated, however, in the sensationalist fiction providing thin imitations of the Melville tradition, for example in the grotesquely racist figure of the 'giant Negro of the Keys' in 'Beneath the "Bulldog's" Bilge' by T. Jenkins Hains, or in Henry C. Rowland's 'Oil and Water', a lurid sea-faring tale of the dangerous products of miscegenation that provides much pseudo-scientific reference to 'plasma' and 'strains'.[41] Thus, the hyperbolic racism of these residually 'romantic' forms is published in parallel with serious journalistic discussions of African-American rights. In relation to this context, Stein's character sketch is more closely affiliated with the progressive journalism attempting to explore issues of race and twentieth-century American democracy with some seriousness than with the melodramatic and overtly racist pulp whose black characters are distorted caricatures narrated from the point of view of an alternately fascinated, horrified or disgusted white male authority. This is not to say that Stein's depictions are not racist, or that progressive journalism is not racist, but that, in Stein's attempt to publish in *McClure's*, given it has set no precedent for the printing of avant-garde work, she surely means to situate her representation of African Americans in alignment with the progressive strand of the magazine's offer.

The most prominent 'muckraker' treatment of the subject, exemplifying progressive journalism on the matter, is Ray Stannard Baker's book *Following the Color Line: An Account of Negro Citizenship in the American Democracy*. Although published in 1908, after Stein had finished *Three Lives*, chapters of Baker's book had previously been printed in *McClure's* and *The American Magazine*, a new incarnation of the failed *Leslie's Magazine*, founded by a number of 'muckraking' journalists in 1906.[42] Baker's account of African Americans in the North points out the change in attitude of the white world following the increase in internal migration from the South. While documenting and decrying the new expression of northern 'race prejudice' and the conditions that arise from it, for example at Harvard, where 'the Negro has always enjoyed exceptional opportunities' but where 'conditions are undergoing a marked change', and the 'line has already been drawn, indeed, in the medical department', Baker remains firmly attached to a narrative of racial hierarchy.[43] Despite his understanding of the 'forces and counter forces – economic, social, religious, political' that 'are at work', he nonetheless views the attempts of African Americans to gain a foothold in the North as 'the struggle of a backward race for survival within the swift-moving civilisation of an advanced race' (147). Similarly, although Baker defends African-American male suffrage, he contends that 'Negroes as a class are to-day far inferior in education, intelligence, and efficiency to the white people as a class' and that 'the mass of Negroes for years to come must find their activities mostly in physical and more or less menial labour'. His argument that, 'Like any race, they must first prove themselves in these simple lines of work before they can expect larger opportunities', offers an interpretation of the progressive theory of nature and environment in which the 'evolution' of a race is achieved through fixed stages of development, as if African Americans can be conceived of as a whole, and as if, as a whole, they must first, like Early Man, learn to use tools before they can use their minds (304). This well-meaning paternalistic garbling of evolutionary theory, even as it was understood in the early twentieth century, is characteristic of progressive thinking.

The association of whiteness with intelligence and cultivation and blackness with brutality and primitivity is clearly present in *Three Lives*, as it is in Baker's study. Melanctha is 'half made with real white blood' and 'intelligent', 'bright and learned', and 'went to school rather longer than do most of the colored children' (62), whereas the darker Rose is 'stupid' and 'childlike' despite, Stein suggests, the fact that she was 'brought up . . . by white folks' (54). Indeed, Stein is explicit that Rose's upbringing in the home of 'white folks' has not changed her nature but simply given her airs (she 'had strong the sense of proper conduct' and does not see herself as 'common') because 'her white training had only made for habits, not for nature', whereas Melanctha's 'white blood' has given her capacities that Rose seemingly cannot attain (55). This appears at first glance to run counter to the progressive faith in environment. When considered in the context of the concomitant belief in acquired characteristics, however, Rose's desire for 'good conduct' and 'decency' and her success in being 'regularly married' point to the possibility of future generations envisioned in her husband Sam's small-town American imaginary: 'to have a little house and to live regular and to work hard and to come home to his dinner . . . by and by . . . to have some children all his own to be good to' (157). This resonates strongly with the gradualist approach of the American reform cause and synchronises neatly with Baker's thoughts on the best strategy for successful African American citizenship. Baker's answer to the problem of the 'color line', in the true spirit of progressivism, is reformist rather than revolutionary. He engages with the work of the two key figures in African American civil rights at the time, W. E. B. Du Bois and Booker T. Washington, arguing that, 'there must always be men like Dr. DuBois [sic] who agitate for rights; their service is an important one, but at the present time it would seem that the thing most needed was the teaching of such men as Dr. Washington, emphasising duties and responsibilities, urging the Negro to prepare himself for his rights' (*Following the Color Line*, 304). The emphasis on the 'development' of 'the Negro', grounded in an ideology of racial hierarchy, enables Baker to dismiss Du Bois's rejection of white supremacist terms and embrace Washington's call for gradual assimilation. Baker's belief in racial naturalism stands in for political argument: just as his vision is blurred by the lens of racial hierarchy so that he both sees and does not see the 'forces . . . that are at work', so a pseudo-scientific ideology of race deflects his attention from the investigation of social conditions and the political reality that underpins them.

The aporia that emerges as a result of the emphasis on racial hierarchy shows itself in a number of places in *Following the Color Line*. Significantly, it is most conspicuous in Baker's discussions of 'the mulatto'. At crucial points in his exploration, Baker comes close to understanding that the construction of this figure challenges the very logic of race. In the opening remarks of the chapter, 'The Mulatto: The Problem of Race Mixture', Baker admits he finds himself 'face to face with a curious and seemingly absurd question: "What is a Negro?"'. Baker, in endeavouring to answer that question, throws up again and again the impossibility of answering it, first in his understanding of 'how large a proportion of the so-called Negro race in this country is not really Negro at all, but mulatto or mixed blood' (153), and second in his belief that African Americans are racially distinct from 'the native African' in that they are 'far superior' (154). His expression of the white supremacist constructions of race that ground these ideas are undermined as he articulates them. If African Americans are not 'negro' because of their 'blood', and if they are not 'negro' because they are not geographically or culturally 'African', then it is impossible to determine what the signifier either contains or delimits. Baker attempts to use both the construct of 'blood' – or 'nature' – and the idea of a 'native' locale – or 'environment' – to anchor his racialisation, and, in doing so, he reveals the inadequacy of these ideas in identifying race, and, therefore, the slippage of the master-signifier in itself. Baker ends with the frustrated outburst: 'What is this race? The spirit and the ideals are not Negro: for the people are not Negro . . . in the sense that the inhabitants of the jungles of Africa are Negroes . . . But neither are they white!' (156–157).

The preoccupation with race as such serves to occlude and mystify Baker's earnest attempt to get to grips with the issue he sets out to explore, the 'exact present conditions and relationships of the Negro in American life' (vii). This effect is crystalized in the following passage on the relative merits of 'the black man' and 'the mulatto' from the chapter on 'race mixture':

> The very first mulatto, a preacher in Atlanta, with whom I raised the question, surprised me by denying that the mulatto was in any degree potentially superior to the real Negro: that if the black man were given the same advantages and environment as the mulatto, he would do as well, that the prominence of the mulatto is the result of the superior advantages he has long enjoyed, being the house servant in slavery times, with opportunities for education and discipline that the black man never possessed... In other words, the prejudice of white people has forced all coloured people, light or dark, together, and has awakened in many ostracised men and women who are nearly white a spirit which expresses itself in the passionate defence of everything that is Negro (*Following the Color Line*, 156).

The preacher whose views he solicits points out the definitive role of cultural attitudes and social conditions in determining the relative status of the two groups, a clear and coherent challenge to the narrative of racial hierarchy, yet Baker's conclusion, his interpretation 'in other words' of an argument that needs no interpretation, is that 'the prejudice of white people has forced all coloured people, light or dark, together'. Rather than attending to the preacher's statement about the cultural and social origins of both racialisation and racial hierarchy, Baker, instead, deploys it in order to return to the question of race to solve the problem 'What is a Negro?' by suggesting that Americans who are 'nearly white' identify as 'negro' and so complicate the category themselves. The implication is that those with 'white blood', although they may be 'superior', are cast, and allow themselves to be cast, in the type of the 'negro'. In this way, the puzzle is solved without troubling the category of race as such: the problem is one of interpretation rather than with the category itself. That Baker cannot think outside the paradigm of racial hierarchy is not surprising, but the ways in which his investigation repeatedly reveals the illogicality of race reflects both the seriousness, however flawed, of his attempt to explore 'present conditions' and the deeply ingrained nature of the paradigm itself.

What Baker's study shows is that the figure of 'the mulatto' both secures and problematises the discourse of racialisation, and this, as I suggest above, is also key to understanding Stein's representation of Melanctha in relation to progressive discourse. Melanctha's dissonant chord contrasts with the ability of other characters to situate themselves in the available configurations of class and race, whether in terms of the 'decent enough' but 'rough' labourer class, or of the 'regular living' of the 'better' strata of the working class and emerging professional class of African Americans. In Stein's crude alignment of class and racial characteristics, Melanctha's mixed racialisation at first glance appears to reinforce a taxonomy of race and class. Melanctha is unable to settle and moves restlessly from one position to another: from Rose's friendship to the relationship with Jeff, then with Jem and back to Rose, finally rejected by and rejecting all of those potential locations in the system and so bearing out her opening lament, in which 'the thought of how all her world was made, filled the complex, desiring Melanctha with despair' so that 'She wandered, often, how she could go on living when she was so blue' (*Three Lives*, 55). The 'complex', 'subtle' indeterminacy of her racial identity, resonating with Baker's cry, 'What is this race?' means she does not belong in the social world Stein maps, representing, therefore, an aberration that reveals the apparent ontological necessity of race identity.

Like Baker's account, however, Stein's presentation of Melanctha also profoundly troubles the stability of race precisely because she does exist and is, indeed, central in Stein's realist account of black lives in Bridgepoint: Melanctha's failure or refusal to fit in is the subject of the text. The initial cycle of 'wandering' and 'escape' from her 'daylight . . . talk with rough men', shifting, 'when the darkness covered everything' to her conversations with 'a clerk or young shipping agent' represents, in itself, a recursive, oscillating dissatisfaction (66). Later, this cycle gives way, in her 'wandering' with Jane Harden, to one in which she abandons the 'rougher men' and 'express agents' in favour of 'men in business, commercial travelers, and even men above these', but these are, themselves, subsequently relinquished as Melanctha and Jane 'began to wander, more to be together than to see men' (68). Eventually, even these superseding cycles are renounced when Melanctha understands that she wants 'something realer . . . something that would move her very deeply' (70–71). She appears to find 'real meaning' in the relationship with Jeff Campbell, but this is in turn abandoned when her capacity for 'real courage' (112) and 'real feeling' (123) begins to chafe against

Jeff's insistence on 'living regular' (113) and 'thinking everything all over' (123).

As each of these phases gives way to another, the text returns to the reiterative, deepening refrain. After the end of Melanctha's relationship with Jeff, the formula is reconfigured to blankly manifest the origin of her failure to locate herself:

> Melanctha with her white blood and attraction and her desire for a right position was perhaps never to be really regularly married. Sometimes the thought of how all the world was made filled the complex, desiring Melanctha with despair. She wandered often how she could go on living when she was so blue. Sometimes Melanctha thought she would just kill herself (*Three Lives*, 144).

Stein is interested in the figure who cannot survive because she cannot be comprehended within the confines of social conditions as they are. What Stein emphasises through her 'wandering', in the cycles of abandonment, and in her rejection of Jeff's stabilising regularity, is the lack of a social or cultural space for Melanctha to occupy. The repeated refrain continually foregrounds this disjunction, and her inability to kill herself starkly underscores her absence in the system: she fails to make herself intelligible even in the decision on her own life or death, on her own existence. Significantly, the subtitle of the story, the only example of this formal device in *Three Lives*, is 'Each One as She May', a note that subtly asserts the relationship between the individual and her environment and reflects the constraints this relationship imposes. The modal 'may' expresses both the notion of possibility (what the individual might or might not do) and the idea of permission or opportunity (what the situation allows or enables the individual to do), thus drawing attention to the interaction of individual will and external conditions. On these terms, Melanctha's failure and her death are the result of the lack of opportunity or permission for her to exist. In that sense, like Baker's 'mulatto', Stein's emphasis on Melanctha foregrounds the category that dislocates the system of racial hierarchy and the social stratification it underwrites.

As we have seen, there are many similarities in the ways Stein and Baker frame their narratives of African-American lives, specifically their categorisations of race, their correlation of superficial features – themselves imposed in that process of categorisation – with particular abilities and tendencies, and the aporia that emerges out of their figure of the 'mulatto' when they try to map a taxonomy of race onto a notionally systematic social environment. Both Stein and Baker narrate race through a progressivist construction of the interaction between inherited traits and environmental conditions, and both also point to a notion of progress or future-oriented development for African Americans. In Baker's text, the answer lies in the acquisition of skills and knowledge within the circuit of African-American self-improvement. In Stein's, through the examples of Jeff, who 'behaved right' and will 'live regular' and 'work hard', 'for himself and for all the colored people' (*Three Lives*, 141) and Rose, whose husband 'do so good now with his working' (159), we are given an image of accumulating respect, dignity and agency in the context of an American imaginary of decent 'colored' living. Baker overtly advocates the gradualist 'duties and responsibilities' approach in which African Americans keep their heads down, stick to their own, and prepare themselves for the rights and responsibilities of citizenship in American democracy, and this approach also seems to be favoured in Stein's depiction.

Thus, *Three Lives* sustains the progressive gaze that examines American life, from an evolutionary perspective, in terms of race and species, following the logic that had Stein's psychology professor, friend, and champion Hugo Munsterberg, himself an influential voice in the popular American magazines of the 1900s, declare that 'the human race in America has begun to differentiate into a species which is anthropologically distinct'.[44] In his examination of the American 'species', however, Munsterberg makes it clear that African Americans are also 'distinct', suggesting that 'It must be left to anthropology to find out whether the negro race is actually capable of such complete development as the Caucasian race has come to after thousands of years of steady labour and progress' (170–171). Although Munsterberg's racism is more overt and extreme than the ostensibly more careful account of a committed progressive journalist like Baker, he, too, comes to the same answer to the 'negro question', that the African-American population 'is honest, healthy, and fit social material, which only needs to be trained in order to become valuable to the whole community' and which 'First of all . . . ought to learn . . . a manual trade', and, chiming with Stein's presentation of the futures of decent hard work mapped out for Jeff and Rose, 'modestly to identify his race with the destinies of the white nation by real, honest, thoughtful, true, and industrious labour' (181–182).

While Stein, like Munsterberg, does not necessarily view African Americans as Americans, as progressive author it is her duty to extend literary representation to all Americans and to document an American typology in order to understand the evolution of the diversity of national citizens. Although, in this regard, Stein might be viewed as exemplary of what Munsterberg terms the American middle-class woman's political and cultural 'self-assertion' (558), a phenomenon about which he is highly ambivalent, hers is a paradoxical endeavour in which, rather than straightforwardly opening the way for greater cultural participation, authorship confers power over the 'reality' of class and race others.[45] As author, Stein includes her 'low-life' subjects in order to broaden representation, and her experimental realism is an attempt to make her representation more 'true', but by the same token they are the subjects of a literary experimentation that seeks to probe, explicate, contain and account for them. Stein's residual attachment to American realism and its affiliated genres and to the reformist ideas for which they are so often the vehicle in this period, particularly as produced in American magazines, is clearly still important for her authorship at this stage. The character sketch, social documentary and the realist short story in this context bespeak an understanding of authorship as progressive activism engaged in identifying and examining racial types and social problems and calling for reform.

Problematising Progressive Discourse

Ultimately, however, Stein's text points in a quite different direction. While she might be posing the same progressivist question of how to manage American democracy by examining the relations between 'nature' and 'environment' to understand and improve the full range of 'races' that make up the demos, *Three Lives* in fact refuses, from the outset, to advocate the reformer's solution of systematisation and institutionalisation. Stein's scepticism about the techniques of progressive social reform lurks in the background of all three stories, with particular attention to institutions associated with health and education. In 'The Good Anna', the protagonist is rendered 'patient, almost docile' by her first hospitalisation, and the 'slow recovery of her working strength' is 'soon worked and worried well away' (*Three Lives*, 16), suggesting both the oppressive, dulling function of institutions and their inability to effect real or lasting change either in the social world beyond their reach or in the deeper organising structures of individual natures. Mrs Lehntmann, a 'woman other women loved' and the 'only romance Anna ever knew' (33), is an unofficial midwife working outside the bounds of regulatory practice. As Daylanne English points out, 'Mrs Lehntmann's female idyll is disrupted by a male physician in a narrative reenactment of the actual institutional contest then taking place between the native U.S. doctor and the immigrant midwife' in which 'the advent of the male medical professional obscures, at least partially, the woman's diagnostic gaze'.[46] Mrs Lehntmann's unregulated, subversive practice of 'deliver[ing] young girls who were in trouble' frees young women from the institutional consequences of bearing an illegitimate child, hinted at in references to the "'sylum' from which Mrs Lehntmann saves the 'dear little boy' she keeps to bring up herself (25). In 'Melanctha', the 'colored college' (67) where she was educated and the 'colored school' she has taught in cannot mould or contain Jane Harden, who is dismissed from both 'on account of her bad conduct' (68), details that add to Stein's narrative that social institutions fail to account for or manifest complex natures. Jeff Campbell, helped by the white family who were his parents' employers (and by whom they were presumably enslaved), also 'went to a colored college' where he 'studied hard' and 'learnt to be a doctor' (73), but early on in their relationship, Stein makes it clear that this is not what makes him significant for Melanctha: 'He was a doctor who had just begun to practice. He would most likely do well in the future, but it was not this that concerned Melanctha'. Rather, Melanctha desires him simply because he is 'good and strong and gentle' (71), thus attending to his apparently innate traits as opposed to their manifestation in his social role, and particularly not as they are expressed in his interaction with institutions and norms. The refrain that characterises Jeff's interaction with his social environment consists of variations on 'working hard', 'decent living', 'being good and careful and always honest' (80), 'never wanting to be always having new things' and, in particular, 'living regular' (105), a phrase that appears without variation in each example. The repeated iteration of Jeff's mode of being emphasises his tendency to social conformity, with the persistent assertion of 'living regular' encoding and deepening his normative stance, not just for himself, but also for 'all the colored people' (105). The stability of this position is briefly challenged in his relationship with Melanctha, but it is reaffirmed at the moment when the relationship finally ends. In its ultimate occurrence, 'Jeff Campbell loved to think now he was strong again to be quiet, and to live regular, and to do everything the way he wanted it to be right for himself and all the colored people' (141), Stein marks the reassertion of his normativity as requiring Melanctha's erasure. Jeff's approach to his own life and to that of 'all the colored people' is textbook progressivism, insisting on regularisation and normalisation, the careful tending of boundaries and categories, and the development of expertise. Thus, Jeff embodies the reformist approach to social problems, and a critique of that approach emerges in his failed relationship with Stein's 'wandering', subversive, unassimilable protagonist Melanctha.

If we accept the prevailing view, initiated by Leon Katz in the 1960s, that in Melanctha, Jane and Jeff, Stein rewrites the lesbian love triangle of her youth depicted more overtly in the unpublished Q.E.D., then it is important to situate Stein in the ordering of these series of cyphers to understand her view of progressivism in 1906. Linda Wagner-Martin argues that 'although the dialogue between Jeff and Melanctha has been described as typical of conversations between Gertrude and May Bookstaver, with Stein presented by Jeff Campbell and Bookstaver by Melanctha, Gertrude portrayed herself, too, in the character of Melanctha'. It is in this slippage of Stein's depiction of herself that her struggle with progressive ideas can be traced.[47]

Mapped against Stein's ties to the progressive milieu, Jeff's medical training, his 'racial uplift' narrative, his discourse of 'living regular' and his insistence on the value of 'thinking it all over' and 'remembering right' (123), point to Stein's own education at Johns Hopkins School of Medicine in Baltimore, and to the influence of progressive ideas on her worldview and, indeed, on her epistemology.[48] As Wagner-Martin suggests, however, Stein's presentation of Melanctha can also be glossed as identification. By 1906, Stein herself has, in a series of restless trips to and around Europe, 'wandered' out of the American social stratum which held her in a particular position, moving, also, away from the institutional discipline of her medical training and toward the open field of her experiments with literary authorship. Moreover, the problem at the heart of Jeff and Melanctha's relationship pivots around a dispute about the relative merits of two ways of being. On the one hand, Stein outlines Jeff's tendency for 'thinking everything all over' which lead to the 'fits of remembering' that result in moments when he 'threw [Melanctha] off' and made her 'suffer' (123). On the other, she sketches Melanctha's 'real feeling every moment' which, Melanctha argues, 'does seem to me like real remembering', a mode of direct experience that is not transfigured in memory by 'thinking it all over' after the fact. Given Stein's dedication to the mapping of processes and the durational attention to experience that she would later call 'the continuous present', perhaps most powerfully manifested in *The Making of Americans*, this is not just, as Wagner-Martin argues, 'a classical philosophical discourse between reason and emotion', it is a dispute about the relative value of analytical categorisation and creative flow, and therefore a discourse (however crudely conceived), between science and art.[49]

Importantly, Stein also maps this binary onto Jeff and Melanctha's conflicting positions on the race question. Whereas Jeff wants 'to see the colored people being good and careful and always honest and living always just as regular as can be' and likes 'everything to be good, and quiet' because he thinks 'that is the best way for all us colored people' (80), Melanctha values what she calls the 'real courage' to 'run around and not care nothing about what happens, and always be game in any kind of trouble' (112), characterised by Jeff thus: 'you think you got a right to go where you got no business, and you say, I am so brave, nothing can hurt me' (122). In the context of contemporary civil rights debates, I would argue that this corresponds loosely to those two major movements that had emerged in this period, led by Booker T. Washington and W. E. B. Du Bois respectively, that, as we have seen, were being categorised and debated among white progressives. Munsterberg's approving characterisation of Washington's approach, as 'a quieter road' focused on 'the slow and steady enlightenment of the masses' and the 'slow work of uplifting their people' has striking echoes in Jeff's refrain, whereas Munsterberg's representation of Du Bois's demands for 'the right of independent existence' is refracted in Melanctha's search for independence, her rejection of social norms and her essential refusal to stay in her place. Melanctha's rejection also voices the radical's impatience with a gradualist, assimilationist approach: she is 'not strong enough inside her to stand any more of his slow way of doing' (110). In the choice between reformist and radical positions, these oscillating identifications are more likely to reflect Stein's ambivalence about progressive answers to social problems than her advocacy of Du Bois's radicalism, for which there is no evidence at any point in her life. Rather, Stein uses this text to complicate, challenge and finally dispel her previous identification as a scientist and, alongside that, as a progressive, and to begin her move, through a parallel struggle with realism, into the unmapped territory of avant-garde authorship.

Alongside her portrayals of Jeff and Melanctha, Stein begins to develop a critique of progressive regulation and institutionalisation through her representations of her protagonists' final moments. Her *Three Lives* are ultimately three deaths, following the narrative construction of the text that initially prompted Stein's 'histories', Flaubert's 1877 triptych *Trois Contes*.[50] Whereas Flaubert's deaths – of the servant Felicite, the medieval saint Julian the Hospitalier, and John the Baptist – are presented as moments of transcendence, Stein's deaths are baldly told and contain no trace of Flaubert's beatification. What characterises the final moments of Stein's protagonists, and of her narratives, is a medicalisation that strips them of agency and identity. The three women are subsumed and erased in the clinical coldness of the public institution, an effect created by the stark factuality of Stein's language. The depiction of Anna's death repeats 'hospital' and 'operation' in a grimly limited litany that is reiterated from a number of narrative perspectives, first in the free indirect reporting of the doctor's instruction, then twice through the omniscient narrative voice, and finally in the direct reporting of Mrs Drehten's letter to Anna's ex-employer Mathilda, the Stein-figure in the story who had gone 'far away to a new country' (48). With this repetition, all modes of discourse and all positions on the story of Anna's death are saturated with the language of the institution. The free indirect discourse of the initial iteration, 'He said she must go to his hospital and there he would operate upon her', foregrounds the domination of the doctor figure, with the modals 'must', and 'would', the possessive 'his' and the emphasis on active male subject and passive female object demonstrating Anna's powerlessness. Similarly, Melanctha's death emphasises her lack of control, both because she 'never really killed herself' (162), but dies of consumption, a disease, in direct contrast to the final and absolute agency of suicide, characterised by a gradual wasting and diminution, and because, taken to a 'home for poor consumptives', she ceases the wandering prompted by her 'complex, desiring' (55) nature and her failure to 'live regular', and 'stayed until she died' (162) in an institution that finally defines her as a social problem.

In the death of her final protagonist, Lena, Stein develops her presentation of the regulation and management of biological processes reflected in the other two deaths through the figure of Herman Kreder. Lena dies in childbirth in a hospital, with the narrative comment, 'nobody knew just how it has happened to her' echoing the other deaths in its intimation of the impersonal affectlessness of the institution. She had, however, already been dwindling in the face of her husband Herman's aggressive efficiency, and in this sense the coldness of the institution is an extension of his domestic discipline. Herman 'never really cared much about his wife, Lena', rather, the 'only things Herman ever really cared for were his babies', until eventually, as Lena becomes 'more and more lifeless' he 'saw to their eating right and their washing and he dressed them every morning', taking control of all areas of work and family life until 'he began to work all day in his own home so that he could have his children always in the same room with him' (191). Herman's dedicated and systematic care, indicated at the outset in the characterisation 'Herman all his life only wanted to live regular and quiet . . . and to do the same way every day like every other with his working' (186), manifests as a form of violence that emerges fully with Lena's death in the final lines of the narrative:

> Herman Kreder now always lived very happy, very gentle, very quiet, very well content alone with his three children. He never had a woman any more to be all the time around him . . . Herman Kreder was very well content now and he always lived very regular and peaceful, and with every day just like the next one, always alone now with his three good, gentle children (192).

Echoing Jeff Campbell's desire to be 'quiet' and 'regular', this description of Herman's methodical form of life is brutal in its erasure of Lena, whose death goes unnoticed except as a relief, merely clearing the way for Herman to take full control. It also taps into Stein's earlier representation of Jeff's contentment once the complication of Melanctha's 'real living' has been removed from his purview. The story ends with Herman's wholesale control over all aspects of life and in particular his attentive management of his children's bodies. As well as managing their eating, washing and dressing, he also 'taught them the right way to do things' and 'put them to their sleeping' until he is 'every minute with them', (191) and this is integrated into the working day through the efficiency created when he decides to do 'all his work in his own house' (192). With Stein's decision to shift this story to the end of the sequence, *Three Lives* culminates in an image of absolute, systematic and efficient paternal control of space, time, labour and bodies that implies a critique of the progressive attention to the supervision and management of bodies and of its regulatory answers to social problems.

Herman's comprehensive administration of his children's lives and his emphasis on the 'regular and peaceful' organisation that makes 'every day just like the next one' also gestures toward progressive methodologies responding to the zeal to create the new human reflected in Washington Gladden's call for a 'new kind of man and woman'. The impetus to create this 'new kind' is present in much progressive rhetoric, exemplified in the slogan 'Produce Great Persons, the Rest Follows' and, indeed, forms the basis of what Roosevelt calls 'the great work of reconstruction'.[51] The vision of a wide-ranging management of human life included Frederick Winslow Taylor's techniques for the scientific management of workers, in which, 'each man must learn how to give up his own particular way of doing things, adapt his methods to the new standards, and grow accustomed to receiving and obeying directions covering details, large and small, which in the past have been left to his individual judgement'.[52] Herman's detailed directions to his children, his desire for 'every day to be like the next one', and his increasing drive for efficiency present us with the nightmare of the Taylorist family. In the final paragraph, the narrator notes, 'Herman always was alone, and he always worked alone, until his little ones were big enough to help him' (192): Herman's fatherhood is a Taylorist training programme designed to reproduce himself.

With this plank of American reformist thinking in mind, another significant aspect of *Three Lives* can also be understood as important to Stein's ambivalent confrontation with her progressive roots. Throughout the text, Stein expresses in a variety of ways a horror of biological reproduction. Lena's births, rendering her increasingly 'lifeless', diminish, silence and finally kill her. 'Melanctha' begins with the coldly meaningless death of Rose's baby, whose birth is presented in the most degraded terms, and whose death, apparently the result of Rose's 'careless and negligent and selfish' neglect, is quickly forgotten because 'these things came so often in the negro world' (54). In 'The Good Anna', Mrs Lehntman's midwifery helps 'young girls who were in trouble' (31) to be released from the consequences of reproduction. Indeed, Anna's ultimate rift with Mrs Lehntman is prompted when the midwife decides to keep a 'cute little boy' she has delivered (25). Reproduction is fraught with 'trouble' in working-class communities, both in its processes and its repercussions. On one level this representation can be read, as Daylanne English argues, as retaining strong traces of eugenicist ideology while at the same time expressing 'reservations about medical and eugenic prescriptions' that 'emerge as feminist, although not antiracist, in all three women's lives' (*Unnatural Selections*, 110). As Stein struggles to reject progressive thinking, she problematises the reforms it advocates and initiates, but she does not divest herself fully of the eugenicist discourse that underpins it, and this inflects her representation of reproduction among working-class immigrants and African Americans as both grotesque and catastrophic.

An odd addition to the panic generated by the possibility of reproduction, however, indicates that this feature of the text has further set of values for Stein. In 'The Good Anna', the narrative thread emerges early on of Anna's persistent and recursive attempts to prevent procreation. This first asserts itself not in the realm of human reproduction, but in relation to her dogs, introduced with her castigation of 'the youngest and the favorite dog', Peter, and in the narrative comment 'The good Anna had high ideals for canine chastity' (2). At first an apparently simple narrative trope to extend Anna's characterisation, the stories of 'bad Peter' take on a greater significance because of their repetition, because of the parallels the narrative draws between these 'transgressions' (7) and those of Sallie, the under servant, and because of the main narrative strand which has Anna engaged in a 'romance' with Mrs Lehntman, who helps girls 'in trouble', and whose 'first gift' to Anna is 'best of all dogs, little Baby' (15). In *Three Lives*, babies ultimately only cause trouble, including the dog 'Baby' that Lehntman bestows on Anna, a proxy child of their union which deepens an attachment that eventually leads to 'Anna's troubles' in the 'Dark days' after their 'romance' ends (34). Anna's concern, and the concern of the text, is with reproduction *as such* rather than the reproduction of particular 'types' or, indeed, particular species. When Stein problematises the new human in her presentation of Lena and Herman Kreder she is not just problematising the reformist drive towards a large-scale administrative management of human reproduction: she is also problematising procreation itself.

In this context, I would argue, the character who stands in for Stein in 'The Good Anna', Miss Mathilda, is presented as occupying a space outside the relentlessness of these life processes and thus achieving a freedom beyond their inevitable cycles. In Stein's presentation, Miss Mathilda is separated from the 'trouble': Anna's watchful eye keeps the danger of procreation at bay in a battle that takes place in the underworld of the servants and animals where Mathilda rarely descends. Anna's overdetermined ban, her anxiety to keep Mathilda's territory clear of copulation, also draws attention to the fact that, more broadly, Mathilda has nothing to do with reproduction. She is not married or involved in a romantic relationship, there is no mention of her parents or siblings and nor, indeed, is there any indication of her origins. Given the emphasis on family, 'stock', genetic inheritance and ethnic identity in *Three Lives*, this is a significant omission. Mathilda's relationships with her 'happy crew' of friends lie outside the family order that constrains and limits many of the characters in *Three Lives*. The depiction of their collective rambling:

> Miss Mathilda loved to go out on joyous, country tramps ... stretching free and far with joyful comrades, over rolling hills and cornfields glorious in the setting sun, and dogwood white and shining underneath the moon and clear stars over head, and brilliant air and tingling blood (9).

emphasises the liberating egalitarianism these looser comradeships afford. Indeed, the key characteristic of Mathilda is her liberty, expressed in all areas of her existence. She is not bound to her location; neither to Bridgepoint, which she leaves every summer 'across the ocean to be gone for several months' (6), or to anywhere else, as she 'often changed her home, and found new places where she went to live' (48). She is not tied to Anna because 'When Anna had first come to Miss Mathilda she had known that it might only be for a few years, for Miss Mathilda was given to much wandering', a precondition of their relationship that contributes to Anna's adoration of her 'cherished Miss Mathilda' (48) and to the latitude she allows her 'careless' mistress. This carelessness in itself is also a signifier of her freedom, exemplified in her 'careless way of wearing always her old clothes' (9) and her easy-going resistance to Anna's exhortation that she buy a new dress, both of which assert her rejection of feminine norms and social expectations.

Most significantly, Mathilda's freedom is strongly associated with art, a connection expressed in her tendency, predicated on the liberty of both her wandering and her profligacy, to 'come home with a bit of porcelain, a new etching and sometimes even an oil painting on her arm' (8) and in the shift in narrative style to a sensual, highly visual form to present her 'joyous country tramps'. Stein, as author, refracts herself in Mathilda, the figure of the creative artist in the text who expresses her creativity through her art collection and through her representation of landscape populated by a loose collective of like-minded 'comrades'. The parallel with Stein is also evident in Mathilda's trips 'across the ocean' and her absence from Bridgepoint by the end of the text, evoking Stein's European travels and her move to Paris into an artworld of liberated 'comrades' in which, as collector and as writer, she has begun to develop her authorship. Reading this vision of the artist critically, one could argue that, in situating the author outside the biological and social realities of the working-class 'others' she depicts, Stein gives herself a special right to document them that is simply a reframing of the privilege of the middle-class progressive American woman. This position is exemplified in the narrative observation in 'The Good Anna' that 'It is wonderful how poor people love to take advice from people who are friendly and above them, from people who read in books and are good' (44). Here the text appears to celebrate Mathilda's feel for the poor, her apparent ability to cross class boundaries as Jane Addams did, to offer accurate insights into working-class lives, echoing the function of the progressive 'settlement houses' in poor districts to enter and seek to improve the realm of the working-class immigrant. Thus, she claims a greater, deeper knowledge of the interior, and her readers, amateur social anthropologists, go in with her.

I would argue, however, that Stein's presentation of the artist is complicated and ultimately challenged by her identification with Melanctha. The designation of Melanctha as artist is indicated through the character's defence of creative forces in favour of Jeff's 'regular' logic of science, and of direct experience over categorical knowledge, but it is also, significantly, expressed in the parallels Stein constructs between Mathilda and Melanctha. The most evident of these, the shared tendency for 'wandering', has been noted by a number of critics: as we have seen, Mathilda 'was often given to much wandering' (48) and Melanctha 'wandered widely' (63).[53] This wandering in itself signifies in both characters, as we have seen, a desire for independence and a restless refusal or failure to adopt or adapt to specific social norms. Melanctha does not take her place in a racialised social order, Mathilda rejects the feminine norms of middle-class family life and social expectations. Looking more closely, there are striking parallels in Stein's presentation of the rambling of Mathilda and her comrades and the wandering of Jeff and Melanctha:

> 'They were very happy all that day in their wandering . . . They sat in the bright fields and they were happy, they wandered in the woods and they were happy . . . Jeff . . . loved all the colors in the trees and on the ground . . . Jeff loved everything that moved and that was still, and that had color, and beauty, and real being . . . Jeff loved very much this day when they were wandering . . . [Melanctha] felt joy in all his being' (100).

Here, the repetition of 'wandering' reconfigures in abstracted form the more traditionally visual representation of Mathilda's 'joyous country tramps, stretching free and far', while the colourful evocation of 'cornfields, glorious in the setting sun', 'dogwood white and shining', and 'brilliant air' in Mathilda's lyrical depiction is also condensed and reduced in the repetition of 'color'. These abstractions, along with the repetition of 'being', connect a more radical artistic rendering with Melanctha's fervour for the 'real experience' in which Jeff, following her, now participates, a connection that elucidates 'wandering' as a mode of being that is the mode of the artist.

The fact that both Jeff and Melanctha engage in this appreciation of direct experience enabled by the 'wandering' that has, throughout the story, signified Melanctha's untethering from the social order, suggests a transfiguration of life, involving the shedding of the social self, that anyone can achieve, and in which the artist is defined as a position outside the system of biological and social categories that is occupied precisely in the refusal to assimilate. Stein uses the figures of Mathilda and Melanctha to situate the creative artist outside the constraints of biological processes and their associated and often painfully ill-fitting social constructs. Creating rather than procreating, throwing off the bands of genetic and ethnic inheritance, the artist is the author of herself. Importantly, this mode of autogenesis also sets the artist beyond the reach of American progressive social evolutionary regulation that Stein is, literally, politically and creatively, leaving behind.

Three Lives in the American Press

The complex relationship of *Three Lives* to American progressivism is reflected in the raft of responses in the contemporary mainstream press. Influential and widely read newspapers of all political persuasions such as the *New York Sun*, the *Brooklyn Daily Eagle*, and the *Kansas City Star*, all major publications for their regions and beyond, engaged with Stein's text in ways that both register its signification as progressive realism and amplify its ambivalence. Although perhaps prompted by the promotional dustjacket description of the text as 'a most extraordinary piece of realism', a genuine perception of *Three Lives* as realism is evident in all of the reviews, and each of them engage in sincere explorations of what this means for the text.[54] Most significantly, the realist genre is invariably associated in the reviews with a conception of authorship as political activism serving the reformist cause. Accompanying these designations are alternatively admiring, mocking, or angrily bewildered responses to the strangeness of the text, generally attached to a vague sense of foreign unconventionality or eccentricity that is at times more precisely pinned to a bizarre European avant-garde. Most of the reviews, however, read *Three Lives* as realism because of its subject matter and its concern for and sympathy with the daily lives of working-class and African-American women, reflecting in great measure the contemporary delineation of literary culture in Moody et al.'s *A First View of English and American Literature*, not least the view that, in writing with 'popular appeal', concerns of form are 'unimportant compared with those of subject matter' (383). In this regard, it is the apparently progressive intent of the text to understand and include these subjects that preoccupies the majority of the reviews and through which they identify Stein as author. Indeed, and importantly, discussions of the realist mode are much more likely to involve the designation of Stein as author, whereas the unorthodox formal qualities of the text are more often ascribed to the figure of the artist.

As well as seeing the text as 'a masterpiece of realism', the *Kansas City Star* views it as a 'character study', reflecting the nature of the text and the contemporary ubiquity of this mode in mainstream literary culture.[55] The language this review uses also confirms the widespread views of race and pseudo-scientific beliefs about evolutionary theory that *Three Lives* reflects and sustains. Jeff Campbell is described in the review as 'the very best type evolved in the race, a young physician', reflecting both Stein's presentation of racial categories and types and the progressivist ideas about genetic heredity and evolution circulating in the mainstream literary and political cultures intersecting in American papers and magazines (24). This collocation of realism and progressive ideology is repeated across the reviews, inflected with alternately affirming, dismissive or hostile attitudes to the apparent social activist motives of Stein's realism. The *Brooklyn Daily Eagle* describes *Three Lives* as 'an extraordinary piece of realism' and associates its generic characteristics with a 'level' head and 'warm' heart that denote 'real human sympathy'.[56] Similarly, *The Boston Globe* calls it 'in some respects a remarkable piece of realism' that offers 'a serious picture of life' attending to 'humble characters, their thoughts and their tragedies'.[57] For the reviewer in the *Chicago Record-Herald*, *Three Lives* is an 'imaginative understanding of the simple, mystic, humble lives of the women of whom the author writes' which is 'unlike the work of Henry James' in that it presents 'obscure, humble, vague, flowing, undefined life' rather than a 'tense, active, intellectual world', but it nonetheless works 'by an analogous method' that ensures 'people are as truly shown as are James' people'.[58] Exemplifying the distinction that Moody et al. make between American realists, that Eastern writers attend to 'the well-to-do members of a conservative society', whereas Western writers portray 'every kind of citizen' (509), this comparison puts Stein firmly in the realist mode of more socially conscious authors such as Harte and Twain. In these reviewers' representations of *Three Lives*, realism can express and generate 'real' sympathy precisely because of its simultaneous observational facticity and emotional charge. The conclusion of the *Brooklyn Daily Eagle* review, that Stein's work is 'intensely human in all its appeals' (10), foregrounds the moral and ethical function of literature and connects the text to the recent history of American realism that, as Moody et al. put it, in 'passing through a period of national self-consciousness' portrays 'the life of the whole community' and attends to 'questions of social conduct' to promote 'civic righteousness' (510).

Less favourable reviews nonetheless maintain the emphasis on the realist genre of the text and attribute to this mode the social activism of the progressive cause. The *New York Sun*, again gesturing to the popular format of the character sketch, describes the *Lives* as 'sketches of the psychology of domestics from the settlement worker's point of view', an interpretation that situates Stein firmly in the ranks of the progressive women who established and ran the settlement houses in poorer urban districts.[59] The reviewer's lack of sympathy for either the progressive cause or the lives of working-class women mean that the text is praised for the realism of its 'keen ... observation' and 'truth' but not for its attention to social conditions, described as the 'sordid side of the women's lives' (5). This is echoed in the *Pittsburgh Daily Post*, which accepts that 'realism is the keynote of the work' but dismisses the subject matter as the 'sordid, unpretty existence of a trio of lowly women' and the 'vacancy and monotony' of their minds.[60] The *Washington Herald* expresses similar views, designating the text as a 'peculiar exposition of the art of character delineation' that attends to 'minds of low caliber and meagre cultivation'.[61] This reviewer adds that, 'if she should attempt the same things with minds of a higher caliber, the result might be more entertaining', chiming in with the *Sun*'s argument that the text 'could have been made bright and cheerful with equal truth, if the author had preferred to tell about other realities' (*Sun*, 5) and suggesting an allegiance to the Jamesian realism that, as Moody et al. point out, tends toward 'excluding the harsh and common types' (509).

Despite their differences of opinion, however, a hierarchical typology of mental function and capacity set in the context of a pseudo-scientific garbling of evolutionary biology extends across the reviews, whatever their judgement of the text. The *Pittsburgh Daily Post* considers Stein's style as the rendering of what 'may be regarded as typical of the brain processes of the characters sought to be depicted', in an alignment of type and brain function in the working-class characters Stein, as anthropological author, has 'sought' (7). *The Nation* has the text as Stein's attempt to 'follow unrelentingly the blind mental and temperamental gropings of three humble souls wittingly or unwittingly at odds with life', presenting an image of lives lived out in the darkness of ignorance, in thrall to conditions over which they have no control, with the additional imputation that they have not adapted well enough to master their environments.[62] The *Chicago Record-Herald*, contrasting Stein's depiction of 'obscure, humble, vague, flowing, undefined life' with James's 'tense, active, intellectual world', suggests once again the vague and undefined 'groping' of creatures who, unlike James's middle-class characters, have not yet evolved intellectually, who are not involved in the process of worldbuilding, and who merely live (Curnutt, 12). The most enthusiastic review, in the *Kansas City Star*, also employs the same trope of darkness or blindness when it describes the subjects as 'humble human lives groping in bewilderment' and as 'humanity groping in the mists of existence' (24). Here, the imagery presents a primordial scene of formless existence that reiterates the position of the author as anthropologist, engaged in the close observation and documentation of her evolutionarily underdeveloped subjects. In this example, as is also hinted in the others, the designation of the 'human' takes on a troubling signification that corroborates Arendt's post-war problematising of rights. In this period before human rights, to be identified as merely human is to be set outside the remit of democratic rights whose object is the citizen. The formulation in this review reveals the unifying principle of these responses to *Three Lives*: that these characters are human, and they live, but that this position, whether it elicits sympathy or disgust, offers no agency and confers no rights. Indeed, as Potter and Stonebridge remind us,

> Arendt . . . famously described how pity can be the most lethal of moral actors: 'Pity taken as the spring of virtue, has proved to possess a greater capacity for cruelty than cruelty itself.' Once the suffering of others becomes the cause of action, all sorts of terror can follow.[63]

The pity expressed in the admiring reviews, far from being the reverse of the aversion in the more sceptical ones, is grounded in the same belief that the characters depicted are merely human.

The author, on the other hand, is granted full privileges. A striking expression of Stein's right to write occurs in the *Brooklyn Daily Eagle* reviewer's admiration of her agency and power: 'she has the right of way and uses it and brings things to pass'. With its stern warning to the reader, 'do not quarrel with the author', the review insists that 'she knows why she writes and what', ascribing to Stein the absolute right of an authorial integrity derived from her knowledge and mastery of her subject matter: the lives and minds of the rightless human others she defines (10). The trope of author as master is hinted at in the reviewers' discussions of Stein's subjects and their quasi-anthropological treatment and augmented, in this and other reviews, by the overt ratification of her authorial rights, not least in the sustained repetition of the term itself. *The Boston Globe* argues that 'The author, Gertrude Stein, has given expression to. . .her own way of seeing the world' and that we are presented with 'the author's conception of her humble characters, their thoughts and their tragedies' (9). *The Nation* admires the almost brutal force it imputes to Stein's commitment to 'follow unrelentingly' those 'blind mental and temperamental gropings' of her subjects. This review also legitimizes Stein's authorial right by predicting that 'From Miss Stein, if she can consent to clarify her method, much may be expected' and in comparisons with other literary traditions – her work has 'sense of urgent life which one gets more commonly in Russian literature than elsewhere' – and other authors – she writes like 'a Browning escaped from the bonds of verse' (Wagner-Martin, 371).

There are a few exceptions to this emphasis on Stein's authorial status that reveal the other discourse currents these mainstream considerations of her authorship engage. One of these is the longer article on Stein, 'American Authoress Who Scorns Fashions', first published in the *Pittsburgh Post-Gazette* and subsequently syndicated across a host of other papers, including the *Kansas City Star* and the *Vancouver Province*.[64] This piece, appearing in the following news cycle and capitalising on the interest *Three Lives* had generated, is a sensationalist feature on Stein and her life in Paris that attends more to her social life and habits of dress than to her writing. The association with Paris – she is 'a familiar figure in the Latin Quarter' – exoticises Stein's unusual writing, an expression of her 'utter disdain of conventionalities', as something foreign.[65] The article connects Stein to French literature and art by suggesting that *Three Lives* is 'Zolaesque' and in its derisively double-edged account of Stein's association with Matisse: 'This talented woman was one of the first to discover great merit in that revolutionary and eccentric painter, Henri Matisse. Perhaps no painter has ever been so held up to the ridicule of the public'. Concluding with the disingenuous speculation 'one wonders if the reserved American taste will rebel', the piece situates Stein outside American literary culture and presents her writing as the equally ridiculous product of an eccentric 'authoress' rather than a serious American author. The emphasis on her social life also serves to diminish her authorship, with the subheading, 'Despite Her Eccentricities She Has a Host of Friends Among Paris Intellectuals' simultaneously depicting her as a crackpot and raising American suspicions of high-mindedness. The suggestion that a 'little coterie of old friends . . . eagerly awaited this first production' undermines her literary work as an insignificant and amateurish contribution and adds to the construction of both her aloof intellectualism and her outsider status.

The commentary on her sartorial style foregrounds her gender and simultaneously hints at degeneracy, a feminisation that is, significantly, marked in the insistent repetition of the designation 'authoress', a term not used in any of the reviews. The headline 'American Authoress Who Scorns Fashions' is accompanied with a photograph of Stein in the Jardin des Tuileries, captioned 'Miss Stein, Who Scorns Fashions' and the subheadings 'Miss Stein Always Wears Corduroy Dresses and She Abjures Corsets' and 'SANDALS ONLY FOOTWEAR'. These reiterations reflect and amplify the emphasis on her personality and her gender as opposed to her authorship, trivialising her work and drawing attention to her body. In the main text, the assertion that 'The homely axiom "Laugh and grow fat" certainly applies to Miss Stein' extends the reader's interest from her corduroy outfit to the body beneath. This is compounded by the sensational revelation that, 'the corset, that modern invention for the suppression of unruly flesh, is an unknown article in the simple wardrobe of the fearless Miss Stein'. The unruliness of Stein's flesh, reiterated in the bullying mockery 'her avoirdupois is of the spreading kind' is allied with her fearlessness, her unconventionality and her 'spontaneous laughter', cynically described as 'infectious . . . for the time being, no matter what small worries were uppermost at the time of the meeting', to construct, insist upon and punish a feminised corporeal seepage of the uncontainable, the undisciplined and the immoderate. While the initial reviews tend to accept Stein's authorship, this feature, syndicated widely and therefore distributing its construction of Stein to a broad American (and, indeed, Canadian) audience, presents her as an inappropriate subject for legitimate author status, as a weird and aberrant exotic who has no place in American literary culture. That this image of Stein is revived, perhaps even partly recycled, as we shall see, in the 1914 press responses to *Tender Buttons*, reflects the power of this discourse of the body in constructing Stein as biological object rather than authorial subject. The *Post-Gazette* article deploys the discourse of biological formlessness, of a feminised 'life' without discipline or mastery, that the reviews attribute to the characters in Stein's *Lives*. While the initial reviews of Stein's text denote her as author in contrast to the 'undefined' objects of her expert authorial gaze, the feature denies the validity of her author status by moving her to the other side of the equation. The way both the reviews and the feature deploy the conception of authorship, therefore, sustains the paradigm in which a feminised and inferior other determined by biology is the object of authorship rather than the authorial subject.

In the most positive reviews, however, a third term emerges that resonates with Stein's depiction of the potential escape from biological constraint: the figure of the artist. Although they initially define her as an author, both the *Kansas City Star* and the *Chicago Record-Herald* identify the originality of Stein's form as the work of an artist. The association of originality with the figure of the artist is insisted upon in the *Star*'s recursive collocation, in which Stein is 'a literary artist of such originality' and a 'new and original artist come into the field of fiction' whose work is notable for the 'originality of its narrative form' (24). The *Record-Herald* explores this designation on more complex terms, arguing that the 'style' of *Three Lives* is 'artistically justified' despite at first seeming 'crudely inartistic' (Curnutt, 12). For both these reviews, approaching the text as a work of art means appreciating its form rather than expecting a transparent communication of subject matter, the mark of popular realism as defined in Moody's textbook. Concluding that 'the place of such as work as this is always obscure when first examined. It is certainly worth considering as a curiosity; doubtless also as an artist's story; possibly much more than this', the *Record-Herald* situates the originality of the work in its status as 'an artist's story' rather than an act of authorship (Curnutt, 12). Breaking the bands of realist fiction as Mathilda and Melanctha are liberated from biological processes and social constructs by their creative 'wandering', Stein becomes an artist rather than an author, and so slips free of the paradigm of progressive realist authorship as mastery of merely human others.

Notes

1. For a detailed argument vis-à-vis Stein's rejection of progressivism, see Sean McCann, *A Pinnacle of Feeling: American Literature and Presidential Government* (Princeton, NJ: Princeton University Press, 2008), chapter 1. For a discussion of Stein's struggles with progressive arguments for women's rights during her university days, see Jody Cardinal, 'Gertrude Stein and College Education for Women: Early Activism and Its Modernist Legacy', in *Modernist Women Writers and American Social Engagement*, ed. Jody Cardinal, Deirdre E. Egan-Ryan and Julia Lisella (Lanham, MD: Rowman & Littlefield, 2019), 91–114.
2. The classic arguments for the influence of the avant-garde are Jayne L. Walker, *The Making of a Modernist: Gertrude Stein from Three Lives to Tender Buttons* (Amherst: University of Massachusetts Press, 1984) and Harriet Scott Chessman, *The Public Is Invited to Dance: Representation, the Body, and Dialogue in Gertrude Stein* (Stanford, CA: Stanford University Press, 1989).
3. See, for example, Brenda Wineapple, *Sister Brother: Gertrude and Leo Stein* (London: Bloomsbury, 1996), 269–270, 282–283 and 298–299; and Linda Wagner-Martin, *Favored Strangers: Gertrude Stein and Her Family* (New Brunswick, NJ: Rutgers University Press, 1997), 87.
4. For example, Alice M. Walker, *Historic Hadley: A Story of the Making of a Famous Massachusetts Town*, (New York: Grafton, 1906); Henry McCoy Norris, *Ancestry and descendants of Lieutenant Jonathan and Tamesin (Barker) Norris of Maine* (New York: Grafton, 1906); David Lear Buckman, *Old Steamboat Days on the Hudson River* (New York: Grafton, 1907); and Byron Barnes Horton, *Horton Family Year Book* (New York: Grafton, 1908). The press also published some fiction and verse. Included among Grafton's publications in the 1900s was a science-fiction novel, Edward Austin Johnson, *Light Ahead for the Negro* (New York: Grafton, 1904), written by a successful lawyer and civil rights activist, Dean of Shaw University and the first African American member of the New York state legislature. The novel is narrated from the point of view of a white Yale graduate who, knocked unconscious on a journey to help solve the 'negro problem' in the South, wakes up in 2006 to find the 'problem' has been solved by a new system of education. Stein's text thus also keeps company with reformist utopian fiction serving as important social critique and setting out serious solutions through a speculative, future-oriented imaginary.

5. Sean McCann documents her experience in his excellent chapter on Stein: 'her experience was typical of the Progressive intellectuals. As a student at Cambridge and Baltimore, she experienced first hand the rapid rise of the research university and the enthusiasm for expert knowledge it produced. . .she worked in the hottest fields of the newly professionalizing sciences. . .she knew well a number of young people who were involved in both the growing political movements to reshape American institutions and the closely related social-scientific theories that would often be called on to justify those changes': McCann, *A Pinnacle of Feeling*, 37.
6. Friends included Hutchins Hapgood, who would later support the publication and promotion of her second publication, *Tender Buttons*. See Chapter 2 below.
7. For Stein's list of submissions, see Ulla Dydo, *Gertrude Stein: The Language That Rises: 1923–1934* (Evanston, IL: Northwestern University Press, 2008), 15. Duffield was first choice, followed by Bobbs Merril then *McClure's*. Stein later (1910) had *McClure's* as her first choice for 'Ada', followed by *The American Magazine*, founded in 1906 by a group of *McClure's* journalists.
8. Letter from Flora Holly to Gertrude Stein, 3 January 1907, reprinted in Donald Gallup, *The Flowers of Friendship: Letters Written to Gertrude Stein* (New York: Octagon Books, 1979), 39.
9. In a very diluted and often hackneyed form. These tales tend toward the residual 'romantic' aspects in Melville's work. For a discussion of Melville and realism, see Sanford E. Marovitz, 'Melville among the Realists: W. D. Howells and the Writing of "Billy Budd"', *American Literary Realism*, Vol. 34, No. 1 (Fall 2001), 29–46.
10. The series ran in nineteen parts over two years, beginning with, an editorial announcement in November 1902. See 'Miss Tarbell's History of Standard Oil', *McClure's Magazine*, Vol. 19, No. 6 (November 1902), 588–592. The whole series was published shortly after completion as Ida M. Tarbell, *The History of the Standard Oil Company*, 2 vols (New York: McClure, Phillips, 1904).
11. In a speech given in April 1906. See Theodore Roosevelt, 'The Man with the Muck-Rake', in *The Works of Theodore Roosevelt: American Problems*, National Edition, Vol. 16 (New York: Charles Scribner's Sons, 1926), 415–424 (415).
12. Norris and Crane also served as correspondents for *McClure's* in the Spanish–American war.
13. Jack London, 'The Unexpected', *McClure's Magazine*, Vol. 27, No. 4 (August 1906), 368–382 (368 n.).
14. William Vaughn Moody, Robert Morss Lovett and Percy H. Boynton, *A First View of English and American Literature* (New York: Scribner's, 1905), 383. Note that this is the revised edition of the 1902 publication.
15. James was a Harvard Professor from 1872 to 1907, during which time he founded the Psychology Department. He regularly taught at the Radcliffe Annex. See William James, *The Letters of William James*, Vol. 2, ed. Henry James (Boston, MA: Atlantic Monthly Press, 1920), 4.
16. Letter from Pitts Duffield to Gertrude Stein, 14 August 1906, reprinted in Gallup, 34.
17. For a sense of their general remit in this period, Duffield & Company published

Henrik Ibsen (letters, 1905), Elinor Glyn (1907), W. Somerset Maugham (1909) H. G. Wells (1909, 1910), D. H. Lawrence (1910), Edmond Rostand (1910), reprints of 'old-spelling' Shakespeare (1907, 1908), Nathaniel Hawthorne (1910) and Palgrave's *Golden Treasury* (1911).
18. Letter from Flora Holly to Gertrude Stein, 3 January 1907, reprinted in Gallup, 38.
19. Letter from F. H. Hitchcock to Gertrude Stein, 9 April 1909, reprinted in Gallup, 43.
20. See Dydo, *Gertrude Stein*, 14; 105–106.
21. See Ellery Sedgwick, *The Atlantic Monthly 1857–1909: Yankee Humanism at High Tide and Ebb* (Amherst: University of Massachusetts Press, 1994).
22. Josiah Flynt and Francis Walton, *The Powers That Prey* (New York: McClure, Phillips, 1900), x, ix.
23. Robert Thacker, '"It's Through Myself That I Knew and Felt Her": S. S. McClure's "My Autobiography" and the Development of Willa Cather's Autobiographical Realism', *American Literary Realism*, Vol. 33, No. 2 (2001), 123–142 (124).
24. Stein's abiding investment in American magazines and her penchant for *McClure's* is indicated in a recent article on one of her early portraits, with this image of a lively discussion in Paris, some time in autumn 1907, of a series critiquing Christian Science: 'One evening at 27 rue de Fleurus, he overheard a discussion of a series of extremely critical articles of Christian Science and Mary Baker Eddy written by Georgine Milmine and running in *McClure's Magazine*. The guests at the Stein studio joined in the ridicule of Eddy's ideas.' Rolf Lundén 'Translating Back: Re-embodying Gertrude Stein's "A Man"', *English Studies*, Vol. 101, No. 2 (2020), 174–196 (193).
25. See Ray Stannard Baker, 'Admiral Sampson. A Character Sketch', *McClure's Magazine*, Vol. 13, No. 5 (September 1899), 388–397; William Allen White, 'Hanna. A Character Sketch', *McClure's Magazine*, Vol. 16, No. 1 (November 1900), 56–64; William Allen White, 'Croker. An Analysis of the Man and an Explanation of His Power', *McClure's Magazine*, Vol. 16, No. 4 (February 1901), 317–326; Rollo Ogden, 'Governor Odell of New York. A Man of Business in Politics', *McClure's Magazine*, Vol. 17, No. 3 (July 1901) 283–287; Ray Stannard Baker, 'J. Pierpont Morgan', *McClure's Magazine*, Vol. 17, No. 6 (October 1901), 507–518; and Ida M. Tarbell, 'John D. Rockefeller. A Character Study', *McClure's Magazine*, Vol. 25, No. 3 (July 1905), 227–249.
26. Baker, 'J. Pierpont Morgan', 509.
27. Tarbell, 'John D. Rockefeller', 228.
28. White, 'Croker', 321.
29. Baker, 'Admiral Sampson', 388, 389.
30. White became a Progressive leader in Kansas and helped President Roosevelt form the Progressive Party in 1912. At this stage, however, his sympathies to his earlier, more conservative, politics had not quite been withdrawn. White would later present Hanna as less significant a player. See Edward G. Agran, *'Too Good a Town': William Allen White, Community, and the Rhetoric of Middle America* (Fayetteville: University of Arkansas Press, 1998), 71–72.
31. The challenge from biologists can be seen in the 'Spencer-Weismann

Controversy', a debate between Spencer and German evolutionary biologist August Weismann. For a contemporary summary, see P. Mitchell, 'The Spencer–Weismann Controversy', *Nature*, Vol. 49 (February 1894), 373–374. Note, however, that this was also a point of contention for William James, who took issue with Spencer increasingly vocally in the first years of the twentieth century. See, for example, his retrospective consideration shortly after Spencer's death: William James, 'Herbert Spencer', *Atlantic Monthly*, Vol. 94 (July 1904), 99–108.
32. White, 'Hanna', 60.
33. Washington Gladden, *The New Idolatry and Other Discussions* (New York: McClure, Phillips & Company, 1905), 211. Note that this is published by S. S. McClure, proprietor of *McClure's Magazine*.
34. Gertrude Stein, *Three Lives*, ed. Andrew Moore (New York: Mondial, 2007), vi. All further citations are from this edition.
35. Daylanne English, whose excellent study I will discuss later in this chapter, presents a compelling recent argument for this: 'She was, then, both witnessing and contributing to new forms of medical and literary discourse. Her original title for *Three Lives*, *Three Histories*, suggests that the three lives might function as fictional medical histories, as charts. Generic hybrids, they occupy a discursive space between modern medical and literary authority – partaking of and, at times, resisting both. Suggestively, as physician-author, Stein frequently exerts the greatest clinical authority precisely where she appears most formally experimental, with African American and immigrant women the subjects, perhaps even the victims, of some of her most radical early experiments': Daylanne K. English, *Unnatural Selections: Eugenics in American Modernism and the Harlem Renaissance* (Chapel Hill: University of North Carolina Press, 2005), 99–100.
36. Stein, *Three Lives*, ed. Moore, 1.
37. McCann argues that, 'in nearly every respect, the world painted by *Three Lives* is antagonistic to the deepest hopes of Stein's reformist contemporaries. Not only are the unchanging rhythms of each protagonist's personality clarified, as Katz notes, by their inevitable and recurrent conflict with other, incompatible personalities. In keeping with that view, the environment in which Stein sets her characters reads like a point-by-point rejoinder to the social theory of Progressive reform. Stein's characters are not only fatally confined to their own repeating personal rhythms; they live in a world of impermanent, individualistic relations that lacks any intimation of public institutions, social bonds, or common culture' (*Pinnacle of Feeling*, 48–49).
38. See, for example, Marianne DeKoven, *A Different Language: Gertrude Stein's Experimental Writing* (Madison: University of Wisconsin Press, 1983) and Lisa Cole Ruddick, *Reading Gertrude Stein: Body, Text, Gnosis* (Ithaca, NY: Cornell University Press, 1990).
39. Carl Schurz, 'Can the South Solve the Negro Problem?' *McClure's Magazine*, Vol. 22, No. 3 (January 1904), 259–275 is a comprehensive account by an experienced and sympathetic politician arguing for full democratic rights for African Americans; Thomas Nelson Page, 'Slavery and the Old Relation between the Southern Whites and Blacks', *McClure's Magazine*, Vol. 22, No. 5 (March 1904), 548–554, offers a highly romanticised misrepresentation, in keeping with his

novels depicting the old South as an 'Arcady'. On this, see, for example, Fred Arthur Bailey, 'Thomas Nelson Page and the Patrician Cult of the Old South', *International Social Science Review*, Vol. 72, No. 3/4 (1997), 110–121.
40. *McClure's*, Vol. 22, No. 4 (February 1904), 4.
41. T. Jenkins Hains, 'Beneath the "Bulldog's" Bilge', *McClure's Magazine*, Vol. 25, No. 4 (August 1905), 348–354 (348). Henry C. Rowland, 'Oil and Water' *McClure's Magazine*, Vol. 25, No. 6 (October 1905), 649–660 (649).
42. Stein was also a reader of this publication, as evidenced, for example, in her submission of 'Ada' in 1910. See n.7 above.
43. Ray Stannard Baker, *Following the Color Line: An Account of Negro Citizenship in the American Democracy* (New York: Doubleday Page, 1908), 123.
44. Hugo Münsterberg, *The Americans* (Boston, MA: McClure, Phillips & Company, 1904), 23. See Rena Sanderson, 'Gender and Modernity in Transnational Perspective: Hugo Münsterberg and the American Woman', *Prospects: An Annual of American Cultural Studies*, Vol. 23 (1998), 285–313 (286): 'In addition to his academic writings, however, Munsterberg also published, during the first decade-and-a-half of the 20th century, a virtual torrent of social and cultural criticism. His descriptions and critiques of American life are most fully developed in five English-language books: *American Traits from the Point of View of a German* (1901), *The Americans* (1904), *American Problems from the Point of View of a Psychologist* (1910), *American Patriotism and Other Social Studies* (1913), and *Psychology and Social Sanity* (1914). With the exception of *The Americans*, these books are collections of essays, most of which first appeared in high circulation magazines such as *Good Housekeeping, Ladies' Home Journal, McClure's Magazine, Saturday Evening Post, Atlantic Monthly, Metropolitan Magazine,* and *Popular Science Monthly*. Though his popular writings on American life were disdained by some of his academic colleagues, his observations attracted substantial and respectful attention from the public and from the press.'
45. Munsterberg notes the 'labour which [American] women perform in the interests of the church or school, of public welfare, social reform, music, art, popular education, care of the sick, beautification and sanitation of cities, every day and everywhere' and terms it 'a powerful inborn idealism' (570), but, in his final analysis, he argues that 'If the entire culture of the nation is womanized, it will be in the end weak and without decisive influence on the progress of the world' (586).
46. English, *Unnatural Selections*, 110.
47. Wagner-Martin, *Favored Strangers*, 79.
48. For a discussion of Stein's resistance to 'uplift' literature, see Corinne E. Blackmer, 'African Masks and the Arts of Passing in Gertrude Stein's "Melanctha" and Nella Larsen's "Passing"', *Journal of the History of Sexuality*, Vol. 4, No. 2, Special Issue, Part 1: Lesbian and Gay Histories (October 1993), 230–263.
49. Wagner-Martin, *Favored Strangers*, 79. Stein's conception of the 'continuous present' is fully formulated in her 1926 lecture, published as Gertrude Stein, *Composition as Explanation* (London: Hogarth Press, 1926). See Chapter 3 below for a full discussion.
50. For a full and illuminating discussion of the significance of Flaubert for Stein's

narrative, see Ulla Haselstein, 'A New Kind of Realism: Flaubert's *Trois Contes* and Stein's *Three Lives*', *Comparative Literature*, Vol. 61, No. 4 (Fall 2009), 388–399.
51. See Michael McGerr, *A Fierce Discontent: The Rise and Fall of the Progressive Movement in America* (New York: Free Press, 2003), 100.
52. Frederick Winslow Taylor, *Shop Management* (New York: Harper and Brothers, [1903] 1911), 137.
53. Often linked to Stein's fugitive identity with the figure of the 'wandering Jew', originally posited in Leon Katz, 'The First Making of The Making of Americans: A Study Based on Gertrude Stein's Notebooks and Early Version of Her Novel (1902–1908)', PhD dissertation, Columbia University, 1963. See, more recently, Will, *Unlikely Collaboration*, 33. For a helpful overview, see Yeonsik Jung, 'Why Is Melanctha Black?: Gertrude Stein, Physiognomy, and the Jewish Question', *Canadian Review of American Studies*, Vol. 49, No. 2 (Summer 2019), 139–159.
54. The *New York Sun* review points this out: 25 December 1909, 5.
55. *Kansas City Star*, 30 January 1910, 24.
56. *Brooklyn Daily Eagle*, 2 March 1910, 10.
57. *The Boston Globe*, 18 December 1909, 9.
58. *Chicago Record-Herald*, 22 January 1910, reprinted in Kirk Curnutt, *The Critical Response to Gertrude Stein* (Westport, CT: Greenwood Press, 2000), 12.
59. *New York Sun*, 25 December 1909, 5.
60. *Pittsburgh Daily Post*, 17 January 1910, 7.
61. *Washington Herald*, 12 December 1909, reprinted in Curnutt, 9.
62. *The Nation*, 20 January 1910, reprinted in Gertrude Stein, *Three Lives* (Bedford Cultural Editions), ed. Linda Wagner-Martin (New York: Bedford, 1999), 371.
63. Potter and Stonebridge, 'Writing and Rights', 7.
64. *Pittsburgh Post-Gazette*, 30 January 1910, 29; *Kansas City Star*, 30 January 1910, 24; *Vancouver Province*, 8 February 1910, 16. Karen Leick also notes that this piece was reprinted in 'a Baltimore paper', in the New York City press and in the *San Francisco Chronicle* (Leick, 29).
65. *Pittsburgh Post-Gazette*, 30 January 1910, 29. All quotes are from this page.

CHAPTER 2

Authorship and Community in Stein's Pre-war Portraits and *Tender Buttons*

Stein and the New Art

By the 1910s, Stein's break from progressivism and its prose genres seemed complete. The publications of her literary portraits of Matisse and Picasso in 1912 and of Mabel Dodge in 1913, and the appearance of her collection *Tender Buttons* in 1914, mark her turn away from American realism and its subject matter.[1] In these texts, Stein develops new methods of formal experimentation in which, significantly, the artists around her and the new art they are producing are themselves her subjects. Thus, Stein's exploration of the figure of the artist and the nature of art practice, begun in *Three Lives*, broadens and deepens in the following decade. Despite her shift in emphasis, however, Stein was still very much attached to a vision of a popular American audience for her work. The portraits of Matisse, Picasso and Dodge were published in the American avant-garde journal, *Camera Work*, but they were also promoted at the sensational 1913 International Exhibition of Modern Art at the New York Armory. The exhibition attracted huge crowds and its impact was amplified by extravagant responses in the popular press, many of which identified Stein as literary exemplar of the new art. *Tender Buttons*, published by the private New York press, Claire Marie, caused a second surge of interest and outrage in the mainstream American papers. These publications are Stein's public interventions into what we can now identify as a nascent period in the development of American modernism, and, because of their fevered reception in the mainstream press, both events featured strongly in the public perception of modernism in the US and cemented Stein's reputation as the American author of the new art.

This complex stage of modernism, as it blossomed across a network of centres in European capitals, is marked primarily by a diversity of alternative formulations that attempt to redefine the work of art, both literary and visual. The gathering of writers and artists around new conceptions and theories of art generated the group culture that became a defining feature of the European artistic and literary scene in the 1900s and 1910s. This new culture attracted the attention of artists in the US, as we can see in this 1912 letter from the American painter Marsden Hartley to the photographer and editor of *Camera Work*, Alfred Stieglitz:

> Here one finds more cliques and groups than could be imagined – and such groups for instance as the Fergusson–Estelle Rice group which exploits itself in *Rhythm*. In one of the last numbers of *Rhythm* is a treatise on Gaugin's influence in which Kandinsky is talked of among others. He is evidently one of Gaugin's pupils and is I believe a modern light in Berlin and Munich. He has lately brought out a new magazine called *Der Blaue Reiter* which I shall look up – very likely they talk of modernism – and God knows they talk much about everything here.[2]

Visiting Paris for the first time, Hartley, like many other American artists interested in developments in the European art world, had crossed the Atlantic to absorb its influences. During his stay he became friendly with Stein, to whom he had been introduced by Stieglitz, often visiting her at the Rue de Fleurus. His comments here recognise that the new art at this point, and thus the context for Stein's literary production, is characterised by a complex inter-European network of 'cliques and groups'.[3] As the letter also intimates, group culture is developed and sustained in a raft of new publications. The magazine *Rhythm* mentioned here prompts Hartley to trace its allegiance with the Munich-based Expressionist magazine *Der Blaue Reiter*, but it also competed with a proliferating number of modernist publications, from *Poetry* to the *Egoist* to *BLAST*, involved in the generation and distribution of new ideas about art alongside an explosion of provocative exhibitions, talking points that begin in Britain with Roger Fry's 1910 exhibition at the Grafton Galleries, *Manet and the Post-Impressionists*, and his 1912 *Second Post-Impressionist Exhibition*, with perhaps the most notorious example being the 1915 Vorticist exhibition at London's Doré Galleries.[4] Importantly, these publications and events overtly posited a collective practice legitimised through the manifesto and the group that had significant ramifications for the role of the author or artist, the nature and position of the reader or viewer, and the relations between work, author and audience.

The production and promotion of Stein's highly unusual portraits of artists and participants in the modernist scene and of her literary experiments in *Tender Buttons* must be read as active engagements in this radical reassessment of conceptions of the artist and the author and in the attempts to broaden participation that, I will argue, accompany it. Stein gains much from the status conferred on her texts as products of a recognisable persona involved with a significant group, and the work she produces in this period is important in part as a vehicle for signifying her alliances in the fluorescence of group activity that characterised the European avant-garde of the 1900s and 1910s. Rather than simply serving as a method of self-promotion, however, I would argue that, in the texts published, circulated and championed in the US during the early phase of American modernism, these relationships and their display are significant for Stein's artistic development, for her sense of her own role as an author and for the messages they send about authorship and cultural participation. The direction that her writing takes in this period is shaped in profound ways by her group associations, and she also actively engages in collective forms of cultural production as an important corollary to the writing itself.

Stein's relationship to the progressive movement was, as we have seen, complex and fluctuating. Tracing Stein's journey from her promising start as a student immersed in the progressive milieu of the 1890s colleges Radcliffe and Johns Hopkins to her overt rejection of reformist ideals of social evolution and national collectivism in the mid-1900s, Sean McCann sharply contrasts the politics her work seems to reflect with progressive beliefs and policies:

If Progressive social theory had hoped to amend the individualistic bias of liberal democracy by finding a basis for a deeper social contract in the laws of cultural history, Stein, rejecting that possibility, leaned drastically in the opposite direction, establishing her own literary mission on the premise that agreement of any kind was impossible.[5]

I would argue, however, that these portraits show that Stein was also attempting to find a way to square the circle of liberalism's 'individualistic bias'. Rather than representing 'a radically antisocial individualism' that is posed '[a]gainst the soft collectivism of Progressive evolution' (49), not only do the portraits make their meaning through the collective endeavour of the Armory Show, the texts themselves work through the problem of the individual and the community in ways that have important ramifications for conceptions of authorship and retain traces of Stein's early progressive immersion.

For Stein, the desire for a meaningful group identity is strongly linked to the desire to escape existing categories of subjecthood that had accompanied both her move to Europe in 1904 and her move away from traditional literary forms in *The Making of Americans*, completed in 1911. This is exemplified in a striking passage from the opening section of the novel, a text which both performs and tracks the transformation of her work to an experimental writing practice:

> Brother singulars, we are misplaced in a generation that knows not Joseph. We flee before the disapproval of our cousins, the courageous condescension of our friends who gallantly sometimes agree to walk the streets with us, from all them who never in any way can understand why such ways and not the others are dear to us, we fly to the kindly comfort of an older world accustomed to take all manner of strange forms into its bosom.[6]

This passage is from the section of the novel written in 1903 in the midst of her series of journeys between America and Europe, and it reflects the impulse which led to Stein's decision to move to Europe permanently in June 1904. It is an urgent act of self-identification and reflects a keen sense of the necessity for the group as a context in which such a 'singular' identity can be enabled. The narrative at this point has moved abruptly from a third-person contemplative digression on the notion of 'vital singularity' to a direct address to the reader. The rhetorical foregrounding of the interpellation 'Brother singulars' ascribes such a singularity to the reader as well, who is thus identified as a type who presents a 'danger' to the 'bourgeois mind' which has only 'a little of the fervour for diversity' and can only countenance 'a strain of singularity that yet keeps within the limits of conventional respectability'. The reader is therefore unconventional, dangerous and 'queer', and is claimed in brotherhood with Stein. The necessity of group formation is, in this representation, impelled by a desire to establish a culture out of brotherhoods between those who feel themselves to be 'singular', those American 'brothers' Stein imagines who reject what they perceive to be a stifling dominant culture that is already developing oppressively paternalistic answers to the problem of the liberal individual. Stein's impatience with progressivism's tendency toward regulation and middle-class normativity does not equate to a rejection of the possibilities of community. On the contrary, the modernist development of new methods, media and locations for collective production that proved so formative for Stein's authorship in the 1910s was a context to which she was already singularly open.

This chapter explores the extent to which Stein's work in this period might be understood as a democratic practice by first examining the textual experimentation in and promotion of the portraits, Stein's emblematic genre in this period. These works refer to individual figures, but they are also depictions of their moments, and in rendering those scenes, the portraits trace the networks of affiliation in which Stein embeds herself. They broadcast her own participation, but they also represent a historiography that maps her field and documents the emergence of a collective movement intent on the transformation of cultural life. Stein's portraits and the methods of their publication and circulation stake her claim on a break not just with conventional forms but with the whole apparatus that holds in place the traditional status of and relations between the author, the audience and the work. These texts engage in ambitious attempts to intervene in their cultural moment, participating in the project to create an audience for new kinds of literary and artistic production. Stein's attention to the networks that are making spaces for these interventions is a significant aspect of her work, something that is particularly evident in these portraits and their publication contexts. In remaking artists, audiences and modes of engagement, Stein's work endeavours, like much of the literary and artistic production of her time, to make new authorial forms available.

Camera Work, 1912

Stein's portraits are firmly linked to the Armory Show by a special edition of Alfred Stieglitz's journal *Camera Work*, by the promotion and coverage of the Show in *Arts and Decoration* and by the interventions in these and other contexts of the American heiress Mabel Dodge. In August 1912, as the International Exhibition of Modern Art due to be installed at the New York Armory was being prepared, Stieglitz, whose pioneering Gallery at 291 Fifth Avenue had been exhibiting modernist work since 1907, produced a special edition of his magazine *Camera Work* dedicated to Stein's portraits of Matisse and Picasso as exemplary of 'the Post-Impressionist spirit'.[7] His use of the term 'Post-Impressionist' follows its coinage in Britain by Roger Fry for his exhibitions at the Grafton Galleries, and sets the work of Stein, Picasso and Matisse in this context to signal their representativeness of the new art.[8] Stieglitz was very much aware of the arrangements underway for the Armory Show, having put many young artists in touch with the organising committee and agreed to lend works by Matisse and Picasso.[9] The special edition paved the way for the Show by raising the profile of these practitioners and their affiliation. Following that, Dodge used Stein to exemplify the new art in her article in the March 1913 special exhibition number of the journal *Arts and Decoration*, which she personally distributed at the Show. In June 1913, another special number of *Camera Work* reviewing the Armory Show emphasised Stein's affiliations by opening with her 'Portrait of Mabel Dodge at the Villa Curonia', which Dodge had already circulated among her New York acquaintances. Disseminated in these contexts, Stein's portraits signify a transatlantic modernist group and provide an American connection to the European modernist movements. This is not wholly a result of either Stieglitz's composition, Dodge's article, or her links to the Armory

Show, however: Stein's portraits represent a new genre which enables her to offer a portrait of herself as an artist working within a 'modernist' or 'Post-Impressionist' group attempting to create and sustain a new context for the production and reception of their work. In the 1912 special number of *Camera Work*, the significance of Stein's role in the group of Post-Impressionist artists is heightened by Stieglitz's introduction:

> And it is precisely because, in these articles by Miss Stein, the Post-Impressionist spirit is found expressing itself in literary form that we thus lay them before the readers of CAMERA WORK in a specially prepared and supplemental number.[10]

The emphasis on the presentation of her texts to *Camera Work*'s American audience – one which had begun to engage with the new visual art but had little experience of the literary works – has the quality of a theatrical flourish. Stieglitz presents Stein's portraits as important exemplars of the movement he identifies and Stein herself as a crucial component in a significant group. The dramatic staging of group interventions proliferates in this period. Comparable in Britain to the 'organised disturbance' of Wyndham Lewis and Ezra Pound's *Blast* alongside the 1915 exhibition at the Doré Gallery, the 1912 special edition of *Camera Work* presented the grouping of Stein, Matisse and Picasso as a powerful collective entity intervening in the usual run of the magazine, in the scene of American culture and, indeed, in the conceptualisation of the category of 'Post-Impressionism'.[11] Associated with the Armory Show, Stein's work is the 'literary form' of the movement and as such is read as an emanation of the 'Post-Impressionist spirit' rather than a discrete work of an individual author.

The Portrait Form

In her essay on Picasso and Stein, Jane Bowers argues that Stein's self-identification as a new kind of author is clarified in her experience of over ninety sittings for Picasso's portrait of her, completed in 1906.[12] It was during this time that Stein began writing her own portraits of artists and writers on the Paris scene. It is highly significant that, after Picasso's painting of her, Stein begins to use the portrait form to signify other practitioners she identifies with: not just 'Picasso' and 'Matisse' (written in 1909), but also 'Manguin: A Painter' (1909), 'Nadelman' (1911), 'A Portrait of One. Harry Phelan Gibb', 'Guillaume Apollinaire', 'One. Carl Van Vechten', 'Braque', 'Marsden Hartley' and 'Monsieur Vollard et Cezanne' (all 1913). Previous 'portraits' had either attended to fictional figures, for example in the earlier form of *Three Lives*, or had dealt with personal relationships, such as 'Ada' the portrait of Alice B. Toklas 'written in the winter of 1908–9', which Janet Flanner claims 'was her first' true portrait.[13] In the works written and published between 1909 and 1915 and with a striking proliferation in 1913, Stein develops a new genre which dramatises her relationships with other practitioners and gestures towards their collective endeavour. Picasso's portrait of Stein and her subsequent portrait of him complicate the roles of patron and practitioner, artist and subject in a series of experiments that broaden questions of form out through genre and mode, and into experimentation with the whole apparatus of relations. This is further developed in her portrait of the wealthy American heiress Mabel Dodge. The 'Portrait of Mabel Dodge at the Villa Curonia', a prominent addition to the promotion of Stein's work at the Armory Show, shifts the focus from artist to patron, and, as I will explain later, further emphasises and complicates those relations.

Stein's appropriation of the portrait genre from visual art into her literary production is significant. Sitting for Picasso's portrait of her was an experience of collective meaning-making that seemed to enable Stein to begin writing in earnest. Stein is ostensibly, as the subject of Picasso's portrait, an investor in the painter's work, a patron. The difficulty in the execution of the painting (which involved over ninety sittings), the emphasis on process, the status of this work as one which marks a crucial break from representational art, and the uncomfortably mask-like quality of the image itself, however, are all aspects which serve to overtly disrupt the painting's function as patron portrait. This genre, a feature of visual art since the Renaissance, is complicated in Picasso's painting in a way to which Stein, as an art collector, must have been sensitive.[14] The painting stands, not as a representation of Stein, but as a signifier of the problematising of representation as such. Rather than reiterating the position of the patron according to the conventional function of this mode, the painting dramatises a resistance to representation in which the patron refuses to be represented, destabilising the artist's position as master of representation, the patron's position as the passive object under the artist's gaze, and the whole set of relations the artist/patron nexus hold in place. In other words, Stein becomes engaged in a practice of experimentation that radically challenges the artist's authorship.

In producing portraits of Picasso and Matisse three years later, Stein puts herself on the other side of the frame, further troubling the patron and practitioner roles, the status of the author and the cultural places they occupy. Lawrence Rainey emphasises the necessity of patronage in creating a culture for the production and reception of modernist work, but I would argue that Stein's complication represents the desire to reimagine that paradigm.[15] Until that point, as Bowers shows us, Stein had been identified primarily alongside her brother Leo as sponsor of and investor in the new art.[16] Stein's portraits of these artists are not just signifiers of her movement out of Leo's shadow, however: they also enable her to problematise her role and her position in the art world. This is a collective experiment not just with technique but with cultural configurations, with the place and role of art and its relationship to social institutions. Stein's portraits at this point are portraits of other artists and as such they mirror the practice of painters who began to use like-minded artists as models because their work was not accepted by the traditional patron.[17] In writing portraits of other artists on the scene, Stein also positions herself as a writer within a group of experimental artists rather than simply as a patron investing in the art from outside the group. The portraits also achieve another very significant function: they fix Stein to a group identity, but one which is fluctuating and open to revision. They form a transient canon of 'brother singulars'. The temporary status of this collective is emphasised both by the portraits' unfinished quality and by the genre itself, which presents individuals in a series, connected by Stein's treatment of them in a self-conscious dramatisation of their assembly. Echoing the arrangement and rearrangement of paintings on her atelier wall, the collection represented by her portraits is a composition – an act of creative curation which effaces the distinction between patronage and practice and generates a fluid assembly.

The Portraits of Picasso and Matisse

Both 'Picasso' and 'Matisse' appear at first to be portraits of two individuals and representations of their behaviour or character. 'Picasso' opens with the lines:

> One whom some were certainly following was one who was completely charming. One whom some were certainly following was one who was charming. One whom some were following was one who was completely charming. One whom some were following was one who was certainly completely charming.[18]

The repeated references to Picasso's charm and the emphasis on his followers seem to reflect his characteristics as an individual and his effect on those around him. Rather than representing his work and its importance, it looks like a portrait of Picasso's personal potency. The repetition of 'charming' identifies the most striking feature of his character and offers a sense of the experience of being in his company. An insistence on his individuality is created by the repeated grammatical foregrounding of 'one' and the repetition of 'who'. The first paragraph of 'Matisse' also attends to his personal qualities and experiences, using the repetition of 'one' and 'he' but evoking a more hesitant and sensitive approach and presenting a more introverted and isolated character. The sentences replicate an internal process in which Matisse personally comes to an acceptance of himself, characterised simply as the development of certainty about 'what he was doing' that contrasts with Picasso's confidence and popularity:

> One was quite certain that for a long part of his being one being living he had been trying to be certain that he was wrong in doing what he was doing and then when he could not come to be certain that he had been wrong in doing what he had been doing, when he had completely convinced himself that he would not come to be certain that he had been

wrong in doing what he had been doing he was really certain then that he was a great one and he certainly was a great one. Certainly every one could be certain of this thing that this one is a great one.[19]

Matisse's personal development is embodied in Stein's text as an oscillating drift, a gradual coming-to-terms with his own value. The paragraph is made up of two sentences, the first of which is long and repetitive, figuring the gradual change in the artist's consciousness, from 'trying to be certain that he was wrong in what he was doing', to being 'really certain then that he was a great one'. The second is rather shorter, clarifying the position reached at the end of this part of the process as one in which 'Certainly everyone could be certain of this thing that this one is a great one'.

This second sentence in 'Matisse', however, marks a shift in emphasis. With its reference to 'everyone', it suggests that these judgements about value are made not by the individual but by others around him. In this sentence, in which 'everyone could be certain', the gathering of the group around this conviction has a crucial role. The movement into certainty is engendered by the coordination of a set of related positions that validate the individual's activity, and this appears to be a necessary condition for 'what he was doing' to take on its full meaning. The second sentence therefore looks much more like the representation of a response to Matisse's art and the formation of a consensus about the artist's activity and its value. Similarly, the second paragraph in 'Picasso' shifts the emphasis from the personal qualities of the subject of the portrait to a group's response to the subject's activity: 'Some were certainly following and were certain that the one they were then following was one working and was one bringing out of himself then something'. Picasso is 'working' and, rather than being something, he is bringing something 'out of himself'. Shifting from the grammatical foregrounding in the first paragraph of the individual subject of the portrait ('one') to the foregrounding in the second paragraph of the group ('some') who were following him, the emphasis moves, as it does in 'Matisse', from an image of the artist to a representation of the responses to his work.

The second paragraph of 'Matisse', clarifying the reference to 'everybody' in the first paragraph, develops the representation of the group around Matisse's work: 'Some said of him, when anybody believed in him they did not then believe in any other one. Certainly some said this of him'. The first sentence performs two functions. First, it indicates the division of opinion on Matisse's art into those who are grouped around it and those who are not. Second, it proposes that accepting the kind of art it represents is an act of faith that rejects other forms, a narrative of rupture and opposition that signifies a conscious recognition of the necessity for the new art to generate new contexts in which it can be meaningfully received. In 'Matisse', however, Stein complicates this because she uses the notion of certainty ironically to figure a new understanding of all these cultural values as in fact unstable and shifting. The continued repetition of the adjective 'certain' and the adverb 'certainly' from the opening passage and throughout the text draws the attention again and again to the instability of such convictions about the value of a work of art and emphasises the contingent nature of these judgements. Certainty becomes a transitory position, a provisional conviction around which consensus gathers, foregrounding the role of the group in defining and holding a set of attitudes on a shifting cultural field.

In both the portraits, certainty merely signifies a position around which consensus has gathered. The portrait of Picasso also places emphasis on the group in establishing new cultural values. The modulations represented by the repetitive, oscillating and accretive uses of language and syntax in 'Matisse' are also present in 'Picasso' and come to embody the processes through which groups are assembling around these new ideas about art. 'Picasso', like 'Matisse', uses references to certainty in order to evoke a scene of fluctuation and instability in which the group – the 'some' who were 'following' Picasso – gather and shift around his work, that which he is 'bringing out of himself'.

> Some were certainly following and were certain that the one they were then following was one working and was one bringing out of himself then something. Some were certainly following and were certain that the one they were then following was one bringing out of himself then something that was coming to be a heavy thing, a solid thing and a complete thing.
> One whom some were certainly following was one working and

certainly was one bringing something out of himself then and was one who had been all his living had been one having something coming out of him.

Something had been coming out of him, certainly it had been coming out of him, certainly it was something, certainly it had been coming out of him and it had meaning, a charming meaning, a solid meaning, a struggling meaning, a clear meaning (4).

The repetition of 'certainly' and 'completely' to describe both Picasso and his followers in the opening paragraphs, as with 'Matisse', at first appears to offer a sense of that which is reliable and constant, particularly in combination with the other signifiers of stability and fixedness used to describe Picasso's work such as 'heavy' and 'solid'. This is complicated, however, by the indeterminacy of both the 'something' these adjectives describe and the references to less stable qualities such as 'charming' and 'struggling' in the description of Picasso's work as having contradictory qualities: 'a charming meaning, a solid meaning, a struggling meaning, a clear meaning'. The instability of these adjectives is also a function of the fact that they are formed from the present participle and therefore associate with movement and transience. The alternation between charm and solidity, clarity and struggle intimates that this kind of oscillation and the ambiguity it throws up is, in itself, what characterises both Picasso's work and cultural responses to it.

This shifting or drifting of the group from one unstable certainty to another is clearly reflected in the final paragraph of 'Matisse':

Some were certainly wanting to be doing what this one was doing that is were wanting to be ones clearly expressing something. Some of such of them did not go on in being ones wanting to be doing what this one was doing that is in being ones clearly expressing something. Some went on being ones wanting to be doing what this one was doing that is, being ones clearly expressing something. Certainly this one was one who was a great man. Any one could be certain of this thing. Every one would come to be certain of this thing. This one was one, some were quite certain, one greatly expressing something being struggling. This one was one, some were quite certain, one not greatly expressing something being struggling (2).

The repetition of the nebulous pronoun 'some' and the references to 'Any one' and 'Every one' has individual subjectivity and group culture inextricably bound together. Moreover, the mode of the text itself with its web-like form and its shifting accretions and definitions defies linearity and emphasises instead the convolutions in the process of moving from A to B. Indeed, the final sentences do not constitute an arrival. In closing the portrait with opposing positions, Stein suspends Matisse himself in the drift. This sustains the oscillating rhythms of the syntax without allowing a conclusion, emphasising the tension generated by Matisse's work. This final inconclusive wrangle places Matisse's work in a persistent equivocal position, not fully accepted but accepted by some, an expression of the status of his work at that very moment in history.

In both portraits, the ambiguity of these artists' work and the attendant ambivalence of its reception are articulated in the word 'struggling'. Ostensibly, this proposes an image of the struggling artist – a marginal figure denied entry to the pantheon and whose work is yet to be valued for its true worth. Stein's use of this word, however, complicates the picture of the artist's individual struggle from the margins into the mainstream, instead emphasising the meaningful complexity of the intervention itself. In 'Matisse' she repeatedly uses the present participle 'struggling' either as a gerund or to modify a noun rather than in conjunction with an auxiliary verb to indicate action. In repeating such phrases as 'the greatness of struggling', and 'he was greatly expressing something struggling', Stein denies the potential of the word 'struggling' to participate in the formation of a verb – to denote action. This, however, is counteracted by the image the word conjures up: that of unceasing movement. What we are presented with is a static image of continuous action. The implication here is that the struggle is a necessary feature of Matisse's work, an idea that is also articulated in the repeated insistence that he is 'expressing something being struggling' (with 'being' and 'struggling' as adjectival participles modifying the noun 'something'). He is not struggling to express, he is expressing the existence of the struggle itself. The context in which the work of art intervenes is not fixed, and this proposes a vision of the cultural field as inherently unstable and the status of the work and the artist as shifting and both defined by and defining the cultural context in its fluctuations. The use of gerunds and the paradox of a repeatedly amended certainty also dissolves the central figure of the artist, who is not a subject taking action but a ripple or a movement in a medium constituted of dispersed energies and flows.

Stein's portraits provide an active and live conceptualisation of these artists as moving nodes in a multiple, heterogeneous and unstable field that is continually being assembled and disassembled, in which they are both forming and formed by the consensus which gives them meaning. Rather than representing a series of private individual experiments located outside the conventional public sphere, or viewing the modernist group as a sealed and self-reflexive entity divorced from the existing cultural context, these early portraits signify the dispersal of authorship into series of forces and energies generated by multiple forms and shifting centres of activity.

Stein's interest in the rhythms of collective behaviour is reflected in her contemporaneous works such as the matching pair of unpublished meditations on the culture of shopping, 'Bon Marché Weather' and 'Flirting at the Bon Marché' (1911). This section taken from the latter text exemplifies Stein's broader interest in the language of crowds:

> These go shopping. They go shopping and it always was a thing they were rightly doing. Now everything is changing. Certainly everything is changing. They go shopping, they are being in a different way of living. Everything is changing.
>
> Why is everything changing. Everything is changing because the place where they shop is a place where every one is needing to be finding that there are ways of living that are not dreary ones, ways of living that are not sad ones, ways of living that are not dull ones, ways of living that are not tedious ones.[20]

Her fascination with collective behaviour is evident here in her use of plural pronouns to denote the cultural and psychological impact of the Parisian department store. The text marks these collective changes and adjustments and maps a dynamic reciprocity of behaviour and psyche, tracing the effects of this modern experience and the feelings it generates in ways that also suggest the patterns of the crowd as they move through the space of the store.[21] Like these portraits of crowds, Stein's portraits of Matisse and Picasso capture the moving forces of the collective and the new relations they initiate. They attend to the communal energy that creates the art internationalised by the movement of writers and artists across Europe and now between Europe and the US and reflect the flows, compositions and decompositions of cultural forces that so interested her.

Eric Schocket argues that the form of the work that Stein produced before *Tender Buttons* reflects, 'a totalizing, managerial structure and epistemology' and reveals a desire to '[align] her writing with the process of production, with the new "conception of assembly"' of the Taylorist industrial methods that went hand-in-hand with the increasingly technocratic approach of the progressives.[22] One can see how in these texts the repetitions and accumulations over time might well be interpreted as counterparts to Taylorist time-and-motion studies. The portraits of Matisse and Picasso, however, represent flows of movement that are precisely *not* managed, reflecting an attention to free and random fluctuations rather than an attempt to discipline them. While one might identify progressive traces in Stein's 'scientific' methods, seeing the portraits as clinical observations of cultural phenomena, their insistence on the unmanageable, unregulated movement of creative production and reception makes it hard to see how they exemplify an approval of a technocratic, managerial style of government. Moreover, with this reading of Stein's portraits I think we can also nuance McCann's argument that 'For Stein, as for the Progressives . . . the fact that individual freedom and collective self-government seemed to be at odds . . . needed to be overcome in the expression of popular sovereignty' (65) and his conclusion that Stein's response is a 'radically antisocial individualism'. The experiments in the portraits, along with her activity around them, are aspects of an endeavour to find new forms of collective self-government that rework the older liberal conception of individual freedom and this is what the loose collective represented in these portraits embodies.

The 'Portrait of Mabel Dodge at the Villa Curonia'

The 1913 portrait of Mabel Dodge, a wealthy patron and promoter of modernist art and writing, further complicates Stein's position. Neither a personal rendering of an intimate relationship, nor a fictional or unidentified subject, nor a portrait of an artist, the 'Portrait of Mabel Dodge at the Villa Curonia' ostensibly appears to operate more along the lines of artists' portraits of Ambroise Vollard. The Parisian art dealer, whose patronage was crucial for the dissemination of French Post-Impressionist works, was depicted in portraits by, among others, Cezanne (1899), Bonnard (1904), Renoir (1908), and Picasso (1910).[23] The portraits of this figure are clearly opportunities to express respect, even homage, but they also often typify the painters' work at that moment, subjecting the image of the promoter to radical formal experimentation in a way which emphasises his support for their endeavours as 'refusés'. The Steins knew Vollard well and bought paintings from him (indeed, Stein's portrait of him attests to this) and, with her interest in Cezanne's work and her friendship with Picasso, Stein must have been aware of these representations of Vollard as dealer, promoter and patron. Although Dodge in many ways performs the same role for Stein, there are differences in the execution of Stein's portrait, in the role it confers on Mabel Dodge and in the function it is assigned which make it once again an example of her complication of the relative status and institutional roles of the artist, the promoter, the patron and the work of art. Alex Goody argues that, although 'The "Portrait of Mabel Dodge" is neither a typical nor exceptional "example" of Stein's modernist becoming', it is 'as an event' in fact 'incredibly productive'.[24] The portrait is indeed productive because of the way it promotes Stein's image as a practitioner of the new art. I would also identify a much more significant role for this portrait, however: this text once again problematises the relationship between author, portrait, subject and patron in a way which performs another fruitful destabilising of those categories. I would also argue that this destabilisation is expressed again in the way the text is disseminated.

First, it is significant that, as Goody suggests, the portrait is not 'exceptional'. Unlike the portraits of Vollard – Cezanne's extraordinary mask-like face, Picasso's extreme deconstruction of the image – Stein's portrait of Dodge in many ways seems less 'experimental' than any of her other portraits of this period. The portrait can be read, as Dodge suggests in her article on the portrait, as 'a series of impressions' which produce 'a coherent totality'.[25] The opening sentence 'The days are wonderful and the nights are wonderful and the life is pleasant', presents in conventional terms the experience of a holiday in a beautiful place, suggesting directly Stein's own experience of staying at the Villa Curonia, Dodge's Florentine home.[26] The repetition of the phrase 'So much breathing' in the third paragraph gives the impression of a meditative space, the references to objects and spaces in the Villa such as 'the hall', 'blankets', 'A bottle', 'the bed', 'a garden', 'the vase', provide a drifting sense of place, and the distinctive line 'This is this bliss' expresses the sensual pleasure of a restful holiday (465–467). Read like this, the text is much more denotational than Stein's other portraits, offering an example of what Dodge calls 'impressionistic writing'.[27] This portrait, then, is rather pretty and pleasing, a portrait of Dodge as a rather languid influence who does not urge innovative experimentation and instead prompts a response more reminiscent of Impressionism than of Post-Impressionism.

So, unlike the experimentation which appears to be prompted in the various depictions of Vollard, in the 'Portrait of Mabel Dodge' the subject is not represented in the work as a figure who cultivates a radical response. The portrait of Dodge also lacks the urgent driving repetitions of Stein's portraits of Matisse and Picasso. She does not appear as a substantial force in the text, contrasting sharply both with the treatment in the artists' portraits of Vollard and with the shifting and gathering of forces around Matisse and Picasso in Stein's portraits of them. Indeed, the text is as much a portrait of the Villa Curonia as it is of Mabel Dodge. A fifteenth-century Medici palace, the Villa is a signifier of Dodge's position as patron, locating her in the space inhabited by the wealthiest and most influential patrons of the Renaissance. The portrait, however, appears to diminish the power this position might confer: the text depicts a rather bland space filled with gentle distractions. There is an emphasis on expressions of lack which occurs in the continual use of negations that characterise the text: 'They did not darken', 'It had not all the meaning', 'This is not heartening', 'It is not inundated', 'There is the climate which is not existing' (465). The association of Mabel Dodge and the Villa with lack and deficiency is also signified more explicitly in the lines, 'There can be that lack of any quivering' (466) and 'An open object is establishing the loss that there was when the vase was not inside the place' (467), and in references to reduction and nothingness such as 'vanishing', 'evaporating', 'lessening', 'disappearing', and 'absence' (465-466). Similarly, the disembodied narrative seems to offer observations, but these appear generalised and indiscriminate, recording a state of affairs in a disjointed series of indeterminate declaratives. Most of the sentences in the text are existential, very often beginning with the phrase 'There is'. This phrase denotes a static condition, expressing simply the notion of existence or, in the negative examples, non-existence. Moreover, it is a device for leaving the subject position vacant of content. The existential 'there' – and the empty 'it' which Stein also uses often in this text – do not refer to any object or entity: they represent dummy subject forms which enable Stein as observer to disappear. They also suggest a condition or state in time and space which, repeated throughout the text, provides a focus on the Villa and on the state of things as they are. This gathers iteration in the final paragraph: 'There is all there is when there has all there has where there is what there is' (468). In this sentence, the existential 'there' repeats to emptiness because the corresponding state or condition is not named. The Villa becomes a space of empty nothingness observed from nowhere.

In a letter inviting her to return to the Villa in July 1913, Dodge encourages Stein to take up the position of writer-in-residence at the Villa, her function to document the kind of transgressive activity Dodge finds so thrilling: 'Please come down here soon – the house is full of pianists, painters, pederasts, prostitutes, and peasants. Great material'.[28] Dodge wants Stein to observe the bohemian goings-on at the Villa and to record them for a breathless posterity. Dodge's letter imagines fixed roles for herself, Stein, the subjects of Stein's art and the audience for it. Stein's portrait of Dodge, however, has already resisted these categories and challenged the very paradigm which constructs them. In its execution the subject of the portrait herself disappears, replaced by generalised activity, and rather than having Dodge as a node around which energy gathers, the portrait suggests instead a dispersal or seepage of energies. An uncertainty about the relative status of the artist and the patron is also generated by the absence of the artist's own observing subject-position. This plurality denies the homage to an individual patron whose actions have a definitive effect on the value and reception of the modernist artwork. The figures of patron, artist and audience are dissolved in a series of indefinite states and activities. The patron, therefore, does not have a special status, and the roles of patron, artist, subject and audience are not fixed or determined.

The blurring of these distinctions is also reflected in the way the text is produced, promoted and distributed. Dodge had 300 copies of the 'Portrait of Mabel Dodge' printed and bound in Florentine wallpaper with a lavish floral pattern of large and colourful blooms, and she personally touted them around New York at the time of the Armory Show. This action at once performs two opposing functions. Dodge's manifestation of the text presents Stein's work as a decorative object in a way that makes it more acceptable and emphasises Dodge's connection to Florence, to art history and perhaps even to a Renaissance notion of the patron. The portrait's distribution to coincide with the Armory Show, however, which, as Dodge put it in a letter to Stein was the 'wonderful great show' to which 'All the moderns [are] sending over', is a signifier of its modernity.[29] Dodge's letters to Stein reveal the activity of her patronage: 'Already people tell me that everywhere, on account of my judicious scattering of the Portrait everyone is saying "Who is Gertrude Stein? Who is Mabel Dodge at the Villa Curonia?"'[30] Dodge's 'judicious' activity places Stein's text firmly in the context of the controversial works of art on display in order to identify both Stein – and Dodge herself – with the explosion of modernism onto the American scene. The text is also given further status by Dodge's article, which was published in the March edition of the magazine *Arts and Decoration* and sold at the Armory Show.[31] It is Stein's association with these groups and their controversial experiments which is promoted by Dodge's activities, and Stein's practice is therefore meaningful because of this context. Dodge's article aligns the portrait directly with the works of art in the show, asserting that 'Gertrude Stein is doing with words what Picasso is doing with paint', her work representing the 'new manifestation in esthetics'. As in Stieglitz's presentation, Stein's work exemplifies the 'Post-Impressionist spirit', the realisation of a spontaneous aesthetic activity unattributable to individual agency (6).

Stein's text, however, is not simply the literary equivalent of visual art's experiments in technique. The construction by Dodge of the text as an object, its distribution around the Armory Show and the promotion of its association with Picasso's portrait of Stein make it a result of all these activities. It is made by Stein, by Dodge, by Picasso and by the Armory Show. The significance of dispersed activity embodied and reflected in the portrait itself is therefore reiterated in its modes of production and distribution. Stein's response to Dodge's promotion: 'I am completely delighted with your performances', is telling in that it presents Dodge as an actor in the spectacle of modernism.[32] The serial production of the 'Portrait of Mabel Dodge' and Dodge's refashioning of the text as a valuable material object which is reproducible and can be distributed as part of the spectacle provided by the Armory Show means that it is an artefact and an event collectively produced by a group of 'brother singulars'.

The Armory Show: Promotion, Reception and Progressive Politics

The reconsideration of authorship that derives from the new formulations of the nature and role of the artwork has a complex relationship to contemporaneous discourses of democracy. Moving from debates within an emergent modernist literary culture to the broader public discourse of newspapers and magazines, discussions of the new art were, from the outset, concerned with the politics of alternative forms of authorship, the possibilities of novel modes of engagement and the potential for modernist art to develop new audiences. This set of concerns shaped the US reception of modernism, whose arrival in the popular consciousness via reports of the Armory Show in the mainstream press coincided with a number of significant events in American politics. In the promotion of the Armory Show and the subsequent tour of the exhibition to Chicago and Boston, the avant-garde work challenging established modes and relations that Stein simultaneously engages in and depicts was presented in ways that productively tuned into the political climate of the day. It was, moreover, received in significant quarters of the American press as a contribution to political debates not just about the rise of the radical political movements with which the early-century avant-garde was widely associated, but also about more mainstream issues in progressive-era American domestic policy.

The year 1913 was a high point in the American progressive movement. The International Exhibition of Modern Art at the New York Armory, organised by the American Association of Painters and Sculptors, opened on February 17th, just a few months after the presidential election – contested by both the popular contenders on progressive tickets – and a matter of days before the Democrat Woodrow Wilson was sworn in after his victory over the Republican incumbent William Taft. Mainstream American politics in the 1910s was dominated by reformist ideals, and the popular policies of the main contenders both reflected and shaped the political mood, responding to the widespread concern that powerful corporations and monopolies and the 'special interests' of the business lobby were controlling the nation; that, in Wilson's words, 'The government, which was designed for the people, has got into the hands of bosses and their employers' and 'An invisible empire has been set up above the forms of democracy'.[33] The progressive measures to wrest control from this powerful class had to tread a line between the radical politics of the burgeoning international socialist and anarchist responses to these 'invisible empire[s]' gaining traction in the US, the statist approach of a large-scale national project to challenge the vast power of monopoly capitalism, and a popular reverence for the first principles of the constitution that situates power in the sovereign individual.

Strikingly, ex-President Theodore Roosevelt, who took second place in the election on the platform of his newly formed National Progressive Party, visited the Armory Show on the day of Wilson's inauguration, before writing a piece on the Show for *Outlook*, a Christian magazine with liberal and progressive leanings. His review, 'A Layman's Views of an Art Exhibition', speaks of the value of the exhibition in 'showing to our people in this manner the art forces which of late have been at work in Europe' which, he judges, are 'forces which cannot be ignored'.[34] Roosevelt had long been involved in the movement to develop American culture and enable popular understanding of and access to the arts, having a role in promoting the expansion in museums and educational institutions that he saw as important in America's advancement in line with the contemporary theories of social evolution that formed an important plank of progressive ideology.[35] His *Outlook* article denounces the European 'lunatic fringe' but accepts the radicalism they reflect as an inevitable 'penalty' in 'any forward movement', and argues that their energy, while not 'good' art, has 'helped any number of American artists to do work that is original and serious' (720). His enthusiasm for the Show also hints at the broad engagement the exhibition elicits, and he draws attention to this in the title of the piece and in his concluding statement, 'All I am trying to do is point out why a layman is grateful to those who arranged this exhibition' (720). The figure of the layman Roosevelt conjures bespeaks the Show's openness to broad participation, a feature that even Roosevelt, patron of the cultural establishment the exhibition explicitly confronts and critiques, appreciates as a significant aspect of its effect. Roosevelt's article reveals the progressive interest in the European developments that are beginning to influence American culture and adds to the varied attempts by promoters and reviewers to understand the value of modernism for a reformist agenda.

Roosevelt's attitude to radicalism has significant parallels in Wilson's successful policy platform, in which he set out a reframing of American democracy that recognised and validated the forms of collective and radical politics at work in the US at the time. The local activism of the progressive meeting and small-town socialism were treated carefully and with respect in his campaign speeches, a move that reflects their potential as meaningful forms of modern democracy while also attempting to contain and direct their energies. This is testament to the prevalence of these forms of organising in the American political sphere in this period. Wilson's overt recalibration of democracy as a mass project rather than a series of individual contracts shifts the emphasis from the centrality of the liberal subject to a national cooperative project envisioned in part as a series of interconnecting collectives protected and supported by a vast national structure. Roosevelt's attitude to the Armory Show reflects the prevailing progressive approach to the 'lunatic fringe' of radicalism in the methods of assimilating and directing what are perceived as dangerously extremist revolutionary energies to vitalise a project of national evolution (718).

Roosevelt's intervention is just one striking example of the way in which, in both its promotion and its reception, The Armory Show and the constellation of events, publications and discourses that came before and after it are involved in the public discussions of this political scene. In many representations, the collective form of the Show's cultural production in itself creates the power of the event, and this is often interpreted as an essential aspect of the new art. The cooperative endeavour that produces this cultural moment is often represented in terms that hint at parallels between authorship and citizenship, and between the modernist group and the forms of democratic association, presentations that tap into the progressive enthusiasm for a vision of the evolution and revolution of a new American democracy of collectivity and cooperation. The Armory Show was critical in the American responses to Stein's work and authorship in the 1910s, and this is true not simply because she was already associated with the radical European practices and groups, but because her portraits of Matisse, Picasso and Dodge came into focus as the exemplary literary expression of modernism in the promotion of the Show itself.

The material promoting the Armory Show and the responses to the exhibition in the various sections of the American press have been well documented.[36] What I want to consider here is the ways in which the Show is understood in relation to contemporary debates about the role of art in the formulation of American democracy set out by the incoming President and consolidated by the definitive ascendancy of progressive politics. Both *Camera Work* and *Arts and Decoration* were important vehicles for the promotion of the exhibition and for discussions of its significance among America's small but growing avant-garde, and beyond this narrow scene the sensation caused by the exhibition gave the new art the full attention of the popular press. In both the avant-garde publications and the mass media, responses to the modernist movement as it was represented in the Armory Show were inflected with writers' views about the progressive vision of American democracy.

Arts and Decoration and *Camera Work* produced special editions devoted to the exhibition. The cover of the March edition of *Arts and Decoration* is emblazoned with the pine tree emblem and motto ('The New Spirit') of the International Exhibition of Modern Art, signalling the appropriation of the journal for the promotion and discussion of the Show. The emblem itself, echoing flag designs from the American Revolutionary War, indicates a liberation from an oppressive past and presents the new art as a political intervention that harks back to the Declaration of Independence. The attitude to revolution expressed in many of the essays in the journal, however, reflects the reformist stance of mainstream progressivism, as represented in Wilson's programme and in Roosevelt's article. This is apparent in the opening 'Explanatory Statement' from Arthur B. Davies, President of the American Association of Painters and Sculptors:

> This is not an institution but an association. It is composed of persons of varying tastes and predilections, who are agreed on one thing, that the time has arrived for giving the public here the opportunity to see for themselves the results of new influences at work in other countries in an art way.
>
> In getting together the works of the European Moderns, the Society has embarked on no propaganda. It proposes to enter on no controversy with any institution. Its sole object is to put the paintings, sculptures, and so on, on exhibition so that the intelligent may judge for themselves by themselves.[37]

Several features of Davies's statement reflect a position on revolutionary art indicative of the influence of progressive ideals, and these are frequently asserted in other articles in the journal. The first, as we can see here, is the emphasis on a loose association of like-minded individuals, or a cooperative of smaller groups rather than an institution. This rejection of the overbearing institution echoes the feeling of Americans at the time, captured and capitalised on in Wilson's campaign, that large corporations and monopolies are controlling economic and social life. Like Wilson's campaign, however, Davies's statement also attempts to tread a line between the institution and the radical revolutionary faction, offering the alternative of the 'association', a loose coalition that simultaneously rejects the potentially monopolistic institutional model and avoids the 'propaganda' and 'controversy' of revolutionary activity. The openness of the association and the call for 'the intelligent' to 'judge for themselves by themselves' reflects a broad invitation for both American artists and the public to participate in the production and development of a new American art with its own particular version of European radicalism.

The loose unity of the group and the attitude of cooperation are asserted throughout the journal, for example in Frederick James Gregg's 'The Attitude of the Americans'. Gregg, a writer and art critic for the *New York Evening Sun* and public relations representative for the exhibition, emphasises that the American artists involved in the exhibition have 'worked together harmoniously for what they regard as a great public purpose', to 'obtain a certain definite unity which was never lost sight of'.[38] This middle way, with its assertion of harmony and unity for a common purpose reflects Wilson's campaign rhetoric, in which revolutionary energies and radical groups are harnessed to form a national cooperative project capable of taking on big business and monopoly interests.[39] This stance is echoed and implicitly associated with the progressive agenda in John Quinn's 'Modern Art from a Layman's Point of View'.[40] Asserting that 'life means growth, and should mean progress' (156), Quinn, a lawyer, collector and patron of modernist art and an important advocate for the Association, attacks the customs laws that protect the interests of an established and hidebound art trade, and stands up for the 'collectors of modest means' (158), framing the potential for the new art to broaden participation not just in the production and appreciation of the new art but also in its acquisition.[41]

Davies's representation of the standpoint of the association also reflects the preoccupation in the journal with the development of a distinctively American form of modern art. Quinn, for example, condemns mainstream American art with its 'effete sentiment' (155), 'cheap confectionery' (156) and its resistance to innovation, an opinion echoed across the journal. This view is repeated in the assertion by William J. Glackens, chairman of the domestic committee, that 'the much-lauded American energy has been displayed everywhere but in our art' and 'We have not yet arrived at a national art'.[42] The arguments that Glackens offers reflect a belief in the evolutionary social science that underpins progressive ideas of the nation exemplified in Woodrow Wilson's campaign demand that, 'in an era when . . . "evolution," is the scientific word', the progressive government be permitted to 'interpret the Constitution according to the Darwinian principle' in recognition of 'the fact that a nation is a living thing and not a machine' (Wilson, 48). These currents can be traced in Glackens's insistence that 'Art, like humanity. . . has an ancestry' and a 'family tree' (Anonymous, 'The American Section', 159), that 'the truly national art, must be the result of growth' (160) and that the conservative tendency in American art is 'Perhaps . . . a reflection of the racial characteristic come down to us from Anglo-Saxon forefathers' (160). His view that 'It may be that the country, going through the process of building, has not had time for art' but that if Americans 'inoculate the energy shown elsewhere into our art . . . I should not be surprised if we led the world' (162), connects the state of American art to a national story that has the flavour of progressive narratives of evolution. The arguments, therefore, that American artists produce work that might be taken for examples of what Gregg later calls 'arrested development' (Gregg, 166) has the development of the artist tied to a national story of American collective identity. Here, again, the injection or channelling of energies reflects a model of the nation as a body subject to internal and external forces and flows. In these narratives, the vitality of European modernism has the potential to redirect the circulation of American energy and stimulate healthy growth.

These representations and discussions of the meaning of the exhibition for an American national art are accompanied by Mabel Dodge's essay on Stein, 'Speculations, or Post-Impressionism in Prose', the final piece in the special number. The article is prefaced with a dramatic editor's note signalling the necessity for American culture to recognise and understand the new art and pronouncing Stein 'the only woman in the world who has put the spirit of post-impressionism into prose' and Dodge 'the only woman in America who fully understands it'.[43] The emphasis on the exceptional status of Stein's writing and Dodge's knowledge are tied here to gender and nationality in a way that, while gently hinting at

America's slow progress, also reflects a civic pride in the intimation that America produces women who work at the cutting edge of a male-dominated cultural scene. The assertion that Stein's prose is exemplary of the spirit of a modernism whose influence 'consciously or unconsciously, is being felt in every phase of expression' (172) also reiterates the argument put forward in *Camera Work*, consolidating Stein's reputation as, paradoxically, a singularly definitive embodiment, the exceptional author who represents a whole movement. This trope figures strongly in the article itself, not just in Dodge's repeated association of Stein and Picasso in variations on the insistence that 'Stein is doing with words what Picasso is doing with paint', but also in her representations of Stein's writing process as a form of transmission, a 'new manifestation in esthetics', a channelling of the energies of modernity in which 'art . . . pursues the artist' (172). This vision of Stein's authorial function as a pure conduit for the art echoes Stieglitz's representation. In Dodge's conception of Stein's authorship, however, the progressive ideology of social evolution once more seems to inflect an American response to the development of the new art. In Dodge's assertion that, 'All the labor of evolution is condensed into this one fact, of the vitality of the individual making way for the many', the individual author contributes to the evolution of the human species in a biological formulation that draws on a concept of vitality she associates with 'Bergsonism' (174) to promote a narrative of cultural evolution that repeats the tropes of energy and flow in the other article.

The evolutionary trope is also important in the essay 'Audiator et Altera Pars: Some Plain Sense on the Modern Art Movement', published in the *Camera Work* Special Number of June 1913, a detailed exposition of the significance of the exhibition by Oscar Bluemner, an exhibitor at the Show and an artist championed by Stieglitz.[44] This edition also reprinted Dodge's article on Stein, Stein's portrait of Dodge, and Picasso's portrait of Stein, a veritable hall of mirrors refracting Stein's authorship as a set of dynamic relations that decentres the authorial position and depicts a model of meaning-making as participation. The Bluemner essay also insists on the participatory character of modernist art, and these two key elements – the cultural evolution of America and the collective generation of meaning – come together to form an argument for the progressive possibilities of modernism. Arguing that the new art represents 'the progressive spirit of European culture . . . in which the United States is fully a generation behind', Bluemner insists that America is not progressive enough, that in the matter of art, 'our free democracy is far more self-satisfied and unprogressive than tradition-hampered Europe' (25), and that 'the new art is a link in the chain of logical evolution' (30) that America must follow. Echoing the condemnation of the art trade we have seen elsewhere, for Bluemner the democratisation of art, from a situation in which art is 'a commodity for the vanities and speculations of the rich' to one in which it is 'the pulse-beat of a people having the money and ambition to express itself and its aspirations, in a language of its own' (25) is a key aspect of its progressive potential. Significantly, Bluemner responds directly to Roosevelt's *Outlook* essay to argue for the democratic value of the art represented in the exhibition, suggesting that 'Mr. Roosevelt is not quite sure; his mind, like the public mind in general, is not so fully biased as that of the critic "authorities"', and that the '"layman's view"' upon which Roosevelt stakes his claim, 'takes us to the art works – and to the new in them, – while the orthodox would have the people flee it as the devil' (31). This argument for the 'layman's' direct and unmediated engagement with the work is, for him, the crux of its progressive potential. For Bluemner, the work 'cannot be experienced without a certain effort and collaboration with the artist on the part of the spectator' (37), a view that reflects the feeling in Stein's portraits that this art is made by a community of participants. The potential for collective meaning-making is foregrounded and the layman spectator put centre-stage as the key figure in the evolution of a new democratic American art.

The Reception of the Armory Show

Although a swathe of popular press accounts of the exhibition were characterised by mockery and derision, often expressed in cartoons and doggerel but also in the responses of art critics such as Kenyon Cox and Royal Cortissoz, there was also much serious consideration of its implications, and, indeed, examples of critical writing that crossed the boundary between popular and avant-garde publications.[45] The work of Hutchins Hapgood is a prominent instance of this.[46] Straddling the avant-garde and popular press, with his articles on Stein, on exhibitions at 291 and on the Armory Show in the *New York Globe* reprinted in *Camera Work*, Hapgood was a committed anarchist whose position in relation to progressive politics and to American democracy are made explicit in relation to the new art.[47] In many ways, Hapgood was exactly the kind of force Wilson wanted to harness. Hapgood's piece on Stein, 'A New Form of Literature', was first published in the *New York Globe* in September 1912 and reprinted in *Camera Work* that November.[48] The article emphasises the unconventionality of Stein's writing, its disregard for formal modes and for 'authority or authorities', drawing out its revolutionary qualities and reflecting Hapgood's other writing on the revolutionary possibilities of the new art, such as his essay, 'Authority in Art' in the *New York Globe*, which critiqued the inherent authoritarianism of the academy system and argued for artists' freedom to self-organise.[49] Like the other commentators, Hapgood also foregrounds both Stein's Americanness and her exceptionality:

> There is an American woman now living in Paris who is, I think, the only American living who is trying to do in writing what Picasso and Matisse and others are trying to do in plastic art. Her name is Gertrude Stein. ('A New Form of Literature', 42)

Similarly, he also associates her repeatedly with these artists and reiterates the communal energies that generate her practice, asserting that 'Miss Stein has been familiar for years with the work of Picasso and Matisse, and this work has sunk very deep into her imagination' (45). For Hapgood, Stein's 'new form of literature', however, represents the radical rather than the progressive potential for American art to take up the revolutionary work of the avant-garde by overturning convention, rejecting authority and creating new forms of collective art.

These views are expressed more forcefully in two successive articles on exhibitions at 291 and on the Armory Show. In 'Art and Unrest', Hapgood parallels the work exhibited at 291 with the US political scene, as an 'interesting moment in the art development of America' that coincides with 'a most interesting moment in the political, industrial, and social development of America'.⁵⁰ He reframes the '"unrest"' in culture and in society as a 'condition of vital growth' and a 'beneficent agitation', arguing that 'Post-Impressionism is as disturbing in one field as the I. W. W. is in another' (43). This positions modernist art firmly with the cause of the revolutionary struggles Wilson was keen to co-opt into his large-scale government programme in order to avoid the 'agitation in art, as well as in labor, politics, and the whole field of our social life' of the kind Hapgood enthusiastically embraces (44).⁵¹ These ideas are repeated in Hapgood's piece on the Armory Show, reprinted in the same edition of *Camera Work*.⁵² Indeed, here, his insistence that 'Breaking rules in favor of fundamental law is the process of all real reform' argues for the necessity of disruption, agitation and rebellion, and suggests the inefficacy of the managed or 'silent' revolution of progressive reformism (45). Hapgood's discussion of the Armory Show, couched in these revolutionary terms, also expresses enthusiasm for the kind of participation the art enables. His depiction of the crowds of visitors, 'the eager, vital faces, the range of types, the curiosity, and the intelligence' interprets in them a new, more 'vital' form of engagement in both culture and society and suggests the levelling effect of the work. More than this, the active involvement of the spectators in the meaning of the art, intimated in many of the discussions and embodied in Stein's portraits, is comprehended in Hapgood's article as its primary effect. His description, 'the people merged into the pictures, as it were, communicated with them, argued with them, compared life notes with them', reflects a form of participation in which the viewer confronts the work from a position of agency, develops a personal response in communication with it, and is actively involved in the generation of communal meaning. For Hapgood, this relationship of reciprocity and mutuality between the works, the viewers as individuals and the community represented by the crowd at the exhibition 'made one trust democracy' (45). Thus, modernist cultural production seems to offer a version of democracy that both radicals and progressives can live with.

Despite the organisers' seemingly reformist leanings, the association of the exhibition with radical politics is not confined to the view from Hapgood's anarchist perspective, as we have seen in

Roosevelt's condemnation of the 'European extremists' (718). The popular weekly *Life* magazine, whose pages provided such a rich picture of the 1919 moment of Stein's engagement with Wilson's post-First-World-War policies, also understood it on those terms.[53] The editorial for the 13 March 1913 number is unequivocal about this, calling it 'a great show, a little shy in the matter of art, but a wonderful exposition of politics' in which 'we see compendiously the temper of the times, the prevailing revolt from technique and the whole apparatus of modern life, and the insistent demand for expression without knowing how and without caring what'.[54] The understanding of the exhibition as exemplifying the upheaval and political agitation of the time connects the 'refusé' character it sees in the rejection of conventional 'technique' to attempts to overturn the whole 'apparatus' of the social order. Significantly, the editorial's review of the exhibition is framed by a report on Wilson's inauguration and the establishment of his new cabinet, and is co-opted as a means to impress on its readership the magazine's enthusiasm for the new administration and its promise to overhaul the national apparatus in order to create a massive new flexible system to manage and regulate modern economic and social forces. Consistently Democrat and supportive of Wilson from the outset, the magazine's editorial stance here includes a reference to Roosevelt's failed re-election campaign that draws a parallel between what they see as his extreme brand of liberalism, associated with the direct democracy measures he advocated, and the radicalism of the Armory Show, claiming that the 'passion for liberty and the contempt for human experience' in the art on display is reminiscent of 'the reverberating clamors of a Bull Moose convention'.

The analogy between the 'revolt from technique' and political struggle is broadened out to include a global story of agitations aiming to 'chuck all the existing apparatus of life out of doors'. Exhorting the reader to 'Look at it all over the world!' the editorial lists 'China, Turkey, Mexico, Japan, Russia, Spain, England, Ibsenized Scandinavia, Christian Science, feminism, woman suffrage, socialism, syndicalism, the referendum, the initiative and all the recalls!' This picture of international upheaval begins with China, narrows to domestic politics and includes the calls for extension of the franchise and for direct democracy measures, and presents all of these as aspects of a tendency that is dangerous and destructive without the rational system Wilson proposes. Arguing that 'of course there is something in it, and though it is not art, it may be a kind of new birth that will lead to art' and that 'the world needs from time to time to be born again', the concession made to this 'new birth' is deployed in a move that very much resonates with Wilson's attempts to channel and regulate the extra-governmental political activities of socialists and the women's movement. For the editorial, the exhibition offers an important lesson to Wilson's new cabinet 'that men cannot live by apparatus, but are bound to revolt from it from time to time' but that 'to ease it up is far better, saves time and tears and reconstruction, for apparatus there must be, else knowledge stagnates, learning hides, and grass grows in the streets' because 'without technique there is no art, nor liberty without order, nor business without industrial machinery, nor prosperity without security'. The analogy of technique and apparatus, modernist art and social unrest enables a powerful and simple argument for a technocratic style of government of the kind Wilson was indeed proposing. This parallel is brought to a neat conclusion that reiterates the arguments for a centralised system of government in Wilson's campaign programme: 'Mr. Wilson is no Matisse. He knows technique and knows its value; and about our governmental apparatus nobody knows more or seems better qualified to stand over its readjustment to life'. Promoting a reformist ideology and putting the President at the head of a massive national apparatus that will manage the threatening forces of modernity through minutely-balanced adjustments, the editorial reinforces the central tenets of Wilson's new government: a centralised national system that assimilates and contains political radicalism and a model of regulation that emphasises the protection of rights against dangerous forces both within and outside the national body in a paradigm of national evolution.

These examples of responses in more mainstream publications are instructive because they reveal how far the Armory Show is what promoters and commentators want it to be. Where there is common ground is in the way these responses value how the show adds to a public understanding of art and draws the public into cultural debates. What is certain, however, is that the perceived vitality of modernist art and, in the form of Gertrude Stein's writing, modernist literature, might inject into American art was understood by radicals and progressives alike as important to the development of American national culture. More interesting is the way progressive ideas underpinned not just the favourable mainstream responses but much of the promotion of the exhibition in avant-garde circles. Whether reformist or revolutionary, the emphasis is on the co-production of meaning predicated on new modes of authorship and engagement that enable the participation of the 'layman' in the cooperative evolution of a new American art. There is pressure, however, on the assessment of what constitutes participation, what is considered accessible, and what forms of agency the work should offer. There is also a tension between reformist's suspicion of these disruptive forces and their desire to assimilate the energies that produce the art and the mobile, communal and ad hoc new modes of production and authorship embodied in Stein's portraits.

Tender Buttons and Images of Authorship

The progressive ideals of cooperation, community and social evolution that view the nation-state as a body made up of energies and flows of influences to be contained and regulated are, however, shadowed by a set of troubling preoccupations and mechanisms. This darker counterpart, hints of which coloured attitudes to the exhibition, became more pervasive in the reception of Stein's second intervention in the development of American modernism, the publication of *Tender Buttons* in June 1914. While responses to the Exhibition of Modern Art and to Stein's portraits and her promotion as literary exemplar of modernist art shaded through a range of views, from outrage through scepticism and ambivalence to recognition and enthusiasm, *Tender Buttons* prompted much more extreme and widespread condemnation.

   The reviews of *Tender Buttons* deploy a range of tropes that extend a charge of fraud to imply that Stein is not an authentic author. The political resonance of this imputation, I would argue, reveals the more troubling ramifications of American progressivism's emphasis on regulation and protection in a model of managed social evolution. Before examining these implications in more detail, I want to turn first to the text itself and to its significant precursor, the 1911 piece *G.M.P.*, to consider how far the writing and how far its promotion and circulation might have contributed to the problems reviewers had in accepting the intelligibility of Stein's authorship. Several important elements are at play here. First, *Tender Buttons* must be understood as a continuation of the collective project signified by the Stein–Matisse–Picasso triad, part of a communal endeavour to rethink perceptual and conceptual norms and conventions, and as such it offers a profound challenge to the notion of individual authorship. The association of Stein with European group culture is foregrounded in many of the reviews of *Tender Buttons*, and this has a twofold function, both to pin her firmly to a category and to cast aspersions on the sincerity of her authorship. Indeed, the insistence in the press that Stein's work is 'cubist', while it works to discredit Stein, also elides the presence of Matisse in the work in order to stabilise its provenance, representing an attempt to manage the categorisation of the text within an identifiable classification through which it can be marked as extreme, absurd and/ or dangerous. Second, the indeterminacy of *Tender Buttons*, along with its unprecedented confluence of an intense intimacy and a decentred narrative subjectivity, signifies for many reviewers the absence of a legible authorial intent. This provokes, time and again, attempts to concretise an authorial figure upon which to ground the text, very often in order, paradoxically, to disparage that figure as a fraud. Finally, *Tender Buttons*'s apparent purposelessness, its lack of development, its failure to produce a result despite seeming to provide a form of accounting or documentation of objects and locations, appears to exasperate beyond measure the proponents of a culture grounded in pragmatist ideals of evolution and progress.

    The association of Stein with the group culture of European modernism prevails across the board in newspaper reviews. Don Marquis, a popular humorous commentator with a regular column in the *New York Sun*, refers to Stein as 'the champion scrambler – brain, egg, or word – of Futurist literature', the *Chicago Tribune* connects her to 'Signor Marinetti, the far distant futurist', while the *Boston Evening Transcript* presents her as 'widely known in Europe and one of the foci of the futurist circles in Paris' and 'part of a movement which is mightily interesting Europe'.⁵⁵ Outside the major centres associated with the exhibition, the *Minneapolis (Minnesota) Bellman* characterises her as '"cubist" of literature, futurist of words, and self-advertiser of pseudo-intellectual antics' (163), and the *Pittsburgh Sun* offers the tongue-in-cheek complaint that 'We are unduly disappointed in this book. We had been informed that it was futuristic, cubiste, unconventional'.⁵⁶ These characterisations are occasionally used to reflect seriously on the relevance of her work for contemporary art, but they are usually the source of mockery and derision, and present *Tender Buttons* as a literary example of 'extremist' art that is at once laughable and elitist, a high-brow foreign trick on the average American. References to group culture are also often accompanied by assertions that they represent cultural anarchism, for example when the *Boston Evening Transcript* argues that *Tender Buttons* reflects 'the contemporary anarchy of art in the form of literature' (18) or when the *Cleveland Leader* suggests her 'words are used with a freedom that is anarchistic' (160).⁵⁷ Like the parallels between the work exhibited at the Amory Show and anarchism, the group is presented as a threat to the social order, a disruptive and potentially dangerous intrusion arriving in force. In most of these representations, whichever form they take, Stein's affiliation with modernist groups tends to be used to discredit her work as the product of a deceptive and dangerous trend, however, risible, that is attempting to infiltrate American culture.

The collective mode of authorship represented by *Tender Buttons* does indeed have its provenance in the group culture that many reviewers, however reductively, reference in their responses. The development of this project can be traced from the portraits of Matisse and Picasso through the fugitive text *G.M.P.*, written in 1911 but unpublished until 1930, both in its representation of the group culture that picks up the theme of the portraits and in its documenting of Stein's shift from the repetitive mobile accretions of the portraits to the denser syntactic units of *Tender Buttons*.⁵⁸ The significance of the communal project is evident in the title of *G.M.P.*, a combination of their three initials that presents as a single monogram. The first half of the text is taken up with depictions of the scene of the new cultural endeavour, representations of unnamed individuals in shifting patterns of activity, working in the context of a developing milieu and generating swirls of interest and recognition. References to individual expressions and endeavours, from 'he is expressing and he is expressing, he is expressing' (203), to 'he was one saying what he was saying and intending to be saying what he was knowing he was saying', (205) and from 'he did use the complete way of showing leading being staying' (213) to 'He accomplished it all' are interspersed with repeated references to 'they', suggesting a group of practitioners 'Working then they were producing saying what they were knowing they were saying' (211) and 'working and all working they have hanging what they put where it is' (216), and to a broader cultural scene of 'succeeding', 'exhibiting', and 'selling' (214). These representations indicate the individual endeavours of those involved in the project but without identifying them individually. Traces of the portrait of Matisse do seem to be retained in the 'suffering' and 'worrying' (215) of one of the figures, and of Picasso in the 'leading' (216) and the 'complete way of feeling' (229) of another. The work of each artist also appears to be reflected in the two modes intimated in 'One making something is making a vigorous brilliant completed ragged covered thing. One making something is making a completed, heavy, brilliant, vigorous, startling, adjoining thing' (214), with Matisse the colourist producing dense yet unfinished surfaces ('completed ragged covered') and Picasso working with the planes and geometries of experience ('startling, adjoining'). The indeterminacy of attribution, however, implies a scene of experimentation where individual actions progress a general project and so both are and are not the crucial factors. This first half of the texts builds through a series of climaxes reflecting breakthroughs in experimentation such as 'He and continuing, prospering and assorting, varying and meaning, hoping and enlarging, tolerating and turning, he and producing, he and producing, he and seeing, he and feeling' (213) and 'he said he was feeling the absolute transmission of the accumulation of regarding what he was regarding' to a culmination half way though the text with an urgent, pacy cogitation on the relations of 'those three' (229–230) which suggests the GMP triad of the title and therefore the joint project of Gertrude Stein, Matisse and Picasso.

This moment creates a hinge between Stein's previous method and the new mode of experimentation subsequently developed in *Tender Buttons* and returns us to the collective as a community of 'brother singulars'. Insisting that 'Always there are three' Stein introduces the significant formulation 'One and one and one' to indicate the collective individuality of the three as an equilibrium. She further explicates this dynamic with two sets of contradictions between contiguous statements: 'If any one is mentioned, three are not mentioned. One is mentioned, three who are mentioned are mentioned' and 'They have not any union. They do not come to separate' (246), in which the naming of individuals in the 'three' both does and does not represent the triad, and the 'three' are neither separate nor unified. The subsequent declaration 'They are there, everywhere' (246) seems to offer a recapitulation that sustains this paradox as a productive tension: the collective work (the product of 'they') is reflected in the work each one produces (it is 'everywhere'). This formulation is comprehensively expressed in the statement 'Each one has that entire system. Each one is not lonesome' (245), which emphasises their singularity in the foregrounding of 'each one' while also insisting on a common 'system' in which they all participate that stops them being 'lonesome', with its hint of 'not onesome' refracting and undoing the reiteration of 'each one'.

It is at this point in *G.M.P.* that the new method Stein extends and develops in *Tender Buttons* emerges. This second half of *G.M.P.* begins to attend to concentrated moments rather than to the flux of experience as in the previous accretive series. The writing becomes more staccato, presenting shorter, more contained sentences with little repetition beyond the very broad thematic form of things re-emerging, re-asserting, drifting up again across the thirty pages of the section. Here, as in *Tender Buttons*, Stein brings language into focus, attempting to prevent meaning slipping from one word to another, revealing syntactical forms, experimenting with new ways to experience language. The sentences foreground grammatical structures by using familiar syntactical patterns populated with misplaced vocabulary, offering the shape of grammar rather than the content. Grammar is held and attended to in this way, as are the individual words, which often remain unalloyed by appropriate relations of meaning and unmodified by their lack of any obvious relation to the other terms in the sentence. In other words, Stein extends a concentrated project to explore her medium.

This same project, G.M.P. insists, also drives the work of both Picasso and Matisse, and it is a project that might be understood in terms of T. J. Clark's illuminating characterisation:

> 'Modernism had two great wishes. It wanted its audience to be led towards a recognition of the social reality of the sign (away from the comforts of narrative and illusionism, was the claim); but equally it dreamed of turning the sign back to a bedrock of World/Nature/Sensation/Subjectivity which the to and fro of capitalism had all but destroyed.[59]

Stein brings the experimentation of Matisse and Picasso together with her own work, presenting the 'three' as practitioners working with the same 'system' whose work 'everywhere' reflects a common endeavour to critically explore the medium of expression in 'recognition of the social meaning of the sign' and find new modes of engagement with experience to 'turn the sign back into a bedrock of World/Nature/Sensation/Subjectivity'. G.M.P. begins to explore how far the failed, freighted medium of language can be revitalised, freed from the habits of a culture that, as Stein argues later, is not up to date with itself.[60]

Stein's allegiance to the collective nature of this work underpins the experimentation of *Tender Buttons*, whose most immediate features are the structural triptych of 'Objects', 'Food' and 'Rooms' evoking the still life and the interior, significant genres of visual art, and the use of titles that appear to signal what Leonard Diepeveen refers to as 'a central scandal of modernism', the 'gap between title and art work' that addresses 'the nature of perception and mimesis'.[61] Despite the predominant insistence in the reviews on the influence of cubism (and, to a lesser extent, futurism), for example in descriptions of the text as 'A Cubist Treatise' or as 'the literary cubism of the near future' (an insistence that has, indeed, dogged interpretations to the present day), the presence of experiments in *Tender Buttons* that also enjoin the methods of Matisse reflect Stein's fidelity to a communal endeavour in which authorship is not the outcome of a single mind or the expression of an individual position.[62] The presence of Matisse also suggests the absence of a programmatic approach that might situate Stein neatly in one or other of the groups identified by reviewers. While the linguistic

Authorship and Community / 123

fracturing and reassembly encountered in works like 'A Carafe, That is a Blind Glass', 'Mildred's Umbrella', 'A Method of a Cloak', and 'A Table' might well be understood as 'cubist' experimentation, the dense surfaces of text like 'A Substance in a Cushion', might be more productively compared with Matisse's still-life studies and interiors of the period:

> Light blue and the same red with purple makes a change. It shows that there is no mistake. Any pink shows that and very likely it is reasonable. Very likely there should not be a finer fancy present. Some increase means a calamity and this is the best preparation for three and more being together. A little calm is so ordinary and in any case there is sweetness and some of that.
> A seal and matches and a swan and ivy and a suit.
> A closet, a closet does not connect under the bed. The band if it is white and black, the band has a green string. A sight a whole sight and a little groan grinding makes a trimming such a sweet singing trimming and a red thing not a round thing but a white thing, a red thing and a white thing.[63]

Like Matisse's 1911 'Seville Still Life', a depiction of a domestic interior in an arrangement of intense colour and pattern, Stein's text is highly coloured and variegated, saturated with pigments of 'light blue . . . red with purple . . . pink . . . white and black . . . green' and the final reiteration of 'red' and 'white'. In Matisse's painting, each element insists itself and the potential hierarchies of both planar and recessional space are rejected, a technique reflected in Stein's resistance to syntactical and structural features that might permit the resolution of meaning from one phrase or sentence to the next. Each of these statements has equal weight because the potential movements of relationality that might either replace one term with another, create a new category into which the original term might be subsumed, or perform other mechanisms of hierarchisation is disrupted. In 'a little groan grinding makes a trimming', for example, 'makes' proposes an exchange denied by the mismatch of the verb 'grinding' and the noun 'trimming'. In 'A seal and matches and a swan and ivy and a suit', on the other hand, the listing of objects that might add up to a classification at the level above the individual term is disrupted because the components of the list are objects from radically diverse categories. As in the Matisse interior, everything is brought into the foreground, an effect that is amplified in the painting by unpainted patches where the crude texture of the canvas is revealed, creating a dense surface that is simultaneously unfinished. A similar effect is achieved in Stein's text, which is cluttered with nouns that, despite their syntactically logical positions, are not allotted comprehensible functions and so fail to constitute a smooth surface of continuous meaning. Thus, in both works, the multitude of objects crowding to the surface both offers a total experience and insists on a recognition of the work's constructedness that calls attention to the medium as medium. These effects, along with the deployment in both of a naïf style of simple words and crude lines and colours, reflect the collective project to renew the experience of signification. Thus, the collective reconceptualisation intimated in the portraits and G.M.P. is sustained in *Tender Buttons* and represents a communal project that further complicates the status of Stein's authorship beyond the manageable category of cubism invariably deployed in condemnations of the text.

The charge that the text cannot be traced to an authentic single origin also characterises reviewers' responses to the mode of the writing itself. The confusion provoked by *Tender Buttons* is often expressed in a frustrated search for a 'real' author who can provide a source for the text and a story of the writing process, invariably resulting in the construction of an author figure who can then become the target of censure and ridicule. An instructive paradigm of this effect can be found in Don Marquis's satirical doggerel 'Gertrude Stein on the War'.[64] Marquis, writing in October 1914, imagines a conversation between himself and Stein in which he asks for her response to the Great War, now in its opening stages, which he sets in the context of 'The usual well known poems on war'. Her 'replies' take the form of a parodic approximation of *Tender Buttons* in which structurally conventional sentences are loaded with apparently misplaced terms, such as '"What seal brown bobble can be blamed?"' The Stein that Marquis constructs is imagined as a pompous and self-seeking charlatan whose work is peddled as the emanation of occult forces. She is a crackpot mystic, 'Sibyl and Seeress, Priestess, Sphinx', who makes pronouncements 'from out her trance' and whose sense of her own genius is satirised in the image of her holding 'her great brow in her hand'. His insistent questioning and her apparent lack of engagement with the weighty subject of war suggests that Stein's opaque and esoteric work does not do the job of poetry, which is to respond to important human events, as in the first task he sets her, to '"Explain/Why they are fighting on the Aisne"', and to express human feeling, prompted by the question '"But is not war a grief to you?" Here, Stein is a pretentious fraud, her work is not recognisable as poetry, and she is failing to fulfil her duty as a poet. This final point is significant: there is a moral charge here in that her arcane, self-seeking performance indicates an absence of human feeling, and this puts the question of what poetry should offer to society on an ethical footing. This moral outrage frames Stein as an entirely inappropriate national poet, whose task would be to engage with issues of moment to the nation, provide consolation and hope for its citizens, and to memorialise the dead.[65] Marquis's poem creates a multi-purpose image of Stein that simultaneously provides, however absurd the sham, some sense of the provenance of her difficult work, concretises an apparently elusive entity, provides a figure for ridicule and censure, and enables the adoption of a moral stance on her questionable authorship.

These features, often accompanied by disingenuously framed charges that she has an intellectual disability or is mentally ill, recur across the reviews from initial responses to the publication in late May of 1914 through the rest of the year. The attempts to reconstruct a provenance for the work and an explanation of what kind of practice might have produced it proliferate throughout the reviews. They range from suggestions that the work is generated in a state similar to Marquis's sybilline 'trance', such as the *New York City Call*'s conviction that she sits 'in a darkened room, preferably between the silent and mystic hours of midnight and dawn' (Anonymous, 'Gertrude Stein', 15), to conjecture about connections between her writing and her studies in psychology exemplified in the *Boston Evening Transcript*, which uses the information that 'She is a doctor of medicine and a doctor of philosophy, a brilliant scholar formerly at Johns Hopkins and Radcliffe and a student in whom William James took a great interest' (Rogers, 19) to sketch a tentative defence of her work. These endeavours more often than not are also accompanied by the proviso that the work may simply be the result of madness or cognitive impairment, as in the caution in the *New York Evening Sun* that *Tender Buttons* could be a transcription representing 'confusion of speech in catatonic excitement' (Anonymous, 'Gertrude Stein, Plagiary', 17) or in the starker imputations that 'they are among the mysteries fresh from bedlam' (Anonymous, 'Gertrude Stein as Literary Cubist', 130) or that the text 'belongs nowhere but in a madhouse' (Burton in Curnutt, 163).

On the whole, the reviews hover between theories of Stein's authorship associated with psychological disorder (either as experiments with or as expressions of cognitive dysfunction) and the conviction that the practice and the work it produces are the result of fraud: as the *Boston Evening Transcript* admits, 'the first thing to say – and most people say it – is that the woman is either a colossal charlatan or mad' (Rogers, 19). The imputation of fraud is reported as a consistent feature in the *Cleveland Leader*, whose review recycles much of the material from other papers, in its report that 'There are many who assert that with her tongue in her cheek she is having a sardonic joke at the expense of those who take her seriously'.[66] Examples of this stance in other papers include an assertion that it is 'the latest Cubist joke'[67] and the suggestion that Stein is 'a poseur who laughs in her sleeve at the ease with which she fools misguided enthusiasts'.[68] A significant contribution on these lines that does not rely on recycled material is Alfred Kreymborg's *New York Morning Telegraph* article 'Gertrude Stein – Hoax and Hoaxtress: A Study of the Woman Whose "Tender Buttons" Has Furnished New York with a New Kind of Amusement'.[69] Kreymborg presents an ambivalent exploration of *Tender Buttons* and its reception among his peers from the perspective of the salons of the developing American avant-garde scene, framed as an attempt to judge how far Stein's work should be taken seriously that reflects just how much this question is in the air. The cluster of questions towards the end of the article echoes the prevailing scepticism about the authenticity of the text:

> May not the fond lady be playing a joke on the world? Mystification is one of the most delightful, one of the most secretly joyous of pastimes. Who

knows whether she is not laughing up her generous sleeve? And that the folk who visit her of a Saturday evening are not the most intimate side of her fun? (108)

Here as elsewhere, the accusation of fraud is associated with factors that tap into a cultural and political emphasis on American democracy's straight-talking common sense and the ability of the average American to recognise 'bunk'.[70] This attitude is directly appealed to in another Marquis doggerel in a representation of the paroxysms induced by the 'Cubist Bard' in the cry 'Oh Litteratoor! Oh Bunk! Oh Art!'[71] Stein's potential charlatanry is often associated, as it is by both Marquis and Kreymborg, with images of an elitist Parisian coterie that present her as a literary aristocrat with secretive special interests. This image is frequently reflected in reviews, for example in H. L. Mencken's reference to the 'illuminati' (14) and in the presentation of Stein in the *Philadelphia North American* as 'this trouble-making evangel of a new literary dispensation' who 'lives in luxury in Paris, with ample leisure to set conundrums to the reading public' (130).[72] The charge of sham that casts doubt on the authenticity of her authorship also works with these images of an elite group to indicate that this is the work of a secretive cabal rather than an individual author. Further, the repeated emphasis on her Parisian rather than her American affiliation implies that it is a foreign endeavour, that Stein and her acolytes are laughing at Americans from across the Atlantic. The emphasis here, as elsewhere, on Stein's 'leisure', also articulated in Kreymborg's implication that her hoaxing is a 'pastime', adds another important strand to the construction of Stein as an undesirable model of American authorship, carrying the connotations of decadent aristocratic leisure rather than energetic democratic activity, that churn into the mass of recycled newspaper responses. This adds up to a crudely drawn image of true authorship, of which Stein is the obverse, grounded in the sincerity of a singular individual who works hard to fulfil the functions and duties of a real writer.

The intimation that Stein is not an authentic author evidently reflects the problems that those reviewers who had read *Tender Buttons* found in understanding what it was, how it was produced and what it was for, and the conception of Stein's illegitimate authorship circulates forcefully through the reviews in a way that suggests there is much a stake in this idea, even for those many writers who had not read it. The idea that *Tender Buttons* is not a sincere act of authorship is directly expressed in many of the reviews, and it is also reflected in the common practice of quoting at random from the text to illustrate its impenetrability, meaninglessness or absurdity, a practice that also works to imply the apparent randomness of the text itself.[73] The frustrated search for an author expressed in Marquis's cry 'All we know of Gertrude – really – is that she is Gertrude Stein!' can partly be understood as a response to the indeterminacy of the text, in particular, as I suggested earlier, in the construction of a discourse of intimate experience without a reference to an experiencing subject.[74] The atmosphere of intimacy that characterises *Tender Buttons* generates a range of related responses that, again, circulate repetitively in an unusually extended news cycle through the summer and into the autumn of 1914. The *New York City Call*'s 7 June review, reflecting an early and more direct response to the publication of the text which includes extracts from the text for its readers' bemused perusal, provides examples of two significant features recycled in this large volume of newspaper responses.[75] On the one hand, the review emphasises the references to domesticity in the titles to ground a construction of Stein as an amateur whose practice might have the status of a parlour game rather than a work of art. After drawing out the apparent incongruity between the 'warm domesticity' and 'homely topics' (123) of the titles and the difficulty of the content, the review suggests that the pieces in *Tender Buttons* are comparable to light-hearted family pastimes like the game 'Uniquest', the '"Ouija" board', or the 'charade habit' (124). On the other hand, the reviews tend to produce images of Stein that emphasise her physicality, her bodiliness, as in Stein's representation in the same article as 'a mountainous lady, wearing a voluminous (necessarily voluminous) monkish robe of brown, roped – where the waist should be – with a cord' (124). This representation of Stein as occupying the intimate space of the domestic and as a massive physical presence translate the dispersed and indeterminate intimacy of the writing into a manageable image of a conventionally feminised interior occupied by a vast and definitively tangible 'lady'. The urge to construct and locate a concrete and categorisable image of the author is an attribute of almost all of the mass of reviews swirling through the second half of 1914 that, as exemplified in this early example, originates in part as a response to the text itself.

The apparent intimacy suggested by Stein's language has grounded a strand of scholarship that reads *Tender Buttons* as, to some extent, an encrypted representation of her sexual and emotional relationship with Alice B. Toklas, and it has also informed studies that explore the development of Stein's identity as a woman writer and examinations of the status of the domestic sphere in her work.[76] Here, I want to consider the contribution that this feature, however cursorily engaged, might have made to this frequent and apparently urgent imperative in the American reviews to fashion an author figure, and what might be at stake in its construction.

As well as indicating significant genres of visual art, each of the three sections in Stein's triptych deals with an aspect of embodied sensory experience and the relations between the experiencing subject and the object of experience. In 'Objects', this is the visual and tactile experience in the confrontation of the object; in 'Food', the internalisation of the object in its ingestion and absorption; and in 'Rooms', the experience of the subject, as it were, 'in' the object, surrounded by and enclosed in the dimensions of a circumscribed space. In each of these sets of encounters, an acutely intimate experience of those relations is relayed. The feeling of intimacy is generated partly by the consistent references to the domestic quotidian of being among familiar objects, eating, sitting, moving through an interior; partly in the apparent untranslatability of the language in the sense that the articulations are prompted by a specific and immediate engagement with an experience that is lost to the reader; and partly in the oblique but insistent references to the actuality of the intimate life of the body. In the 'Objects' piece, 'A New Cup and Saucer', for example, which consists of the single sentence 'Enthusiastically hurting a clouded yellow bud and saucer, enthusiastically so is the bite in the ribbon', we are given the everyday experience of that domestic world in the acquisition of a new piece of china, reflected in the enthusiasm this small event generates (22). There is also that difficulty in translating the immediate experience of this event: we are offered a set of hints, a taste of the incident, that, in its incompleteness, emphasises the lost original. There are glimpses here of the experience, with the 'clouded yellow bud' hinting at a pattern on porcelain, and the sweetly childlike pun of the 'bud and saucer' reflecting the simple delight in its newness and representing a visual trace in the corresponding shape of cup and bud. These remain as inchoate glimpses, however, because of the undecidability of other aspects of the sentence, such as the 'bite in the ribbon'.[77] Alongside the intimacy of domestic living that one can almost have access to, the references to intense experiences of touch in 'hurting' and 'bite', reflect a submerged life of the body that fails to be assimilated into the simple joys of crockery and so retains, as it were, its sensual 'bite'. This triad of effects is replicated throughout the collection, as we see here in 'Custard' from the 'Food' section:

> Custard is this. It has aches, aches when. Not to be. Not to be narrowly. This makes a whole little hill.
> It is better than a little thing that has mellow real mellow. It is better than lakes whole lakes, it is better than seeding (51).

Snatches of the subject are suggested in the 'mellow real mellow' texture, beneath which also hovers a palimpsest of custardy yellow, and the gusto in 'it is better than lakes whole lakes', which provides an image of an enthusiastically filled bowl, but these are also shadowed by the tints of bodily discomfort indicated by 'It has aches, aches when'. Similarly, in the line from 'Rooms': 'Lying in a conundrum, lying so makes the springs restless, lying so is a reduction, not lying so is arrangeable', the private space of the bedroom is infused with a cerebral and physical experience of a subject lying in bed, with the simultaneous interiority of both cogitation and bodily contact opening out into an abstract contemplation of space that indicates the drifting mind of a morning *au lit*.

In all these examples, and throughout *Tender Buttons*, however, despite the complex indices of intimate life and the flickers of palpable experience, there is no direct indication of the individual subject involved in them. There are no characters and there is no narrator, either first- or third-person, who might be encountering these objects or inhabiting that body. The intimacy of the experience, unfiltered through a fictional subject, therefore, falls back to the author, who can only be constructed in the void around which the accumulated encounters gather. As the fiction falls away, challenging the conception of the individual author creating and sustaining a fictional world from a place outside the work, the question of authorship comes to the fore. The tantalising glimpses of a missing subject involved in confronting, ingesting and inhabiting offers an outline of the 'author' of this experience from inside and out. This structuring of experience without an identifiable sovereign agent breaks the bounds of the subject: it undoes the unit of individuality yet plasters intimate experience all over the place in an excess of indeterminate subjectivity refusing to be a stable origin.

Of course, the newspaper responses are not predicated on such analysis, but this effect is encountered in even a cursory reading of the text. The reviewers' scepticism and frustration are, as we have seen, generally piqued by the undecidability of a text that does not construct a fictional world and seems to convey no information, no action, no ideas and no apparent message. This is typified in the *Bellman*'s commentary on a sample from the text:

> 'Every writer has a right to be judged by her best, and Miss Stein picked this jewel as typical: "A blue coat is guided, guided away, guided and guided away, that is the particular color that is used that length and not any width not even more that a shadow".
>
> I am no tailor, but venture to assert that as a direction for making a coat, this would not do; and as to the interest or felicity we look for in literary composition, it seems to leave something wanting' (Curnutt, 165–166).

This example, in which the writer dramatises a failed search for a purpose, literary or otherwise, for the text, represents a common response to direct quotations from *Tender Buttons*. This is also achieved in many reviews in the form of irony, for example in 'Time to Show a Message', a review in the *Omaha World Herald*, which presents pieces from the text prefaced with mockingly straight-faced proposals for their subject matter, such as the guess that she is 'Venturing into the field of science, statesmanship and government' that introduces a section from 'Glazed Glitter'.[78] The criticism that the text has a lack of obvious purpose is a significant element in the refusals to recognise Stein's authorship. This is compounded by reactions to the apparently misleading factuality of the titles, which, as is suggested in the *New York City Call* 'are on the whole admirably simple and matter-of-fact' (Diepeveen, 123). They seem to indicate something tangible and familiar, but, as the *Call* goes on, 'the Brancusi bust of Mlle. Pogany, popularly known as "The Lady or the Egg," is as plain as the nose, which isn't on the face, compared with Miss Stein's portrait of "Eggs"' (Diepeveen, 123). The titles appear to indicate a coherent project, in the form of representation, documentation or comment on the subjects they refer to, but, as the reviews point out, they do not fulfil any of those aims. Indeed, as the *Bellman* shows, they seem to have no function at all. What frustrates the writer here and elsewhere (and we can see this in Don Marquis's imagined conversation with Stein) is the work's apparent lack of pragmatic value. This significant strand of the dismissal of Stein's authorship across the reviews is also expressed in that practice of quoting 'at random' from the text which is often followed by blank expressions of disbelief. For the reviewers, the text seems to promise something systematic but it refuses to provide it, and, for a culture driven by the vision of collective energy, practical activity and technological and entrepreneurial progress to which Woodrow Wilson so successfully appealed, this is unbearable. These constructions of Stein, however obliquely, inevitably reflect the preoccupations of the mainstream cultural and political milieu. This is entirely evident in the *Omaha World Herald* review, which presents a tongue-in-cheek defence of Stein as a 'notable contribution to the progressive movement', who 'should by all means be indorsed in the next platform on which Colonel Roosevelt runs for president' (Diepeveen, 127). This bit of banter from a strongly Democrat paper with an outsize circulation in the Midwest reflects, as we saw in *Life* magazine's response to the Armory Show, the association of unconventional modernist art with Roosevelt's version of progressivism, portrayed as a rather libertarian individualism associated with direct democracy.

Stein's Aberrant Authorship

These texts – the portraits circulated around the Armory Show, *G.M.P.*, and *Tender Buttons* – reveal a vision of authorship as a process involving diffuse and multiple forces. Stein refuses to let the author coalesce as a single figure, and this, it seems, is the most troublesome aspect of her work for a cultural and political milieu in which the first unit of regulation is the citizen. The practice of group authorship, the dispersal of the authorial position and the indeterminacy of authorial identity trouble this construction and escape its system. Much of the frustration in reviews of *Tender Buttons* is about things not being in their place or escaping definition, and this has its most significant and provocative exemplification in the troublesome effect of the author escaping unitary enumeration and individuation. It is notable that anarchy is the political ideology repeatedly referenced in relation to Stein, despite the significance of socialism and other radical movements in US politics at the time. In these responses, anarchism stands, as Roosevelt also does for Democrat progressives, for the challenge to authority and regulation as such and for the fear of the permeation and proliferation of dangerous, unpredictable forces. The presentations of Stein's body figure her as grotesque and abject, the resistance to her example and the horror expressed at the idea that her work might have some cultural sway reflect a fear of contamination, the emphasis on the seeming purposelessness of her work contribute to the image of a decadent elitism, and the assertions that she is a fraudulent infiltrator from elsewhere hint at a narrative of infection. These constituent aspects in the construction of Stein's author figure present her as a dangerously amorphous, aberrant and degenerate influence, the obverse of the productive, efficient association of sovereign individuals whose energies can be managed to ensure the health and evolution of the national organism. This is the malign counterpart of social evolution, of the ideal of a carefully regulated cooperative community, of the vision of nation as a mobile fluid body of cells and germs. The healthy body of national culture must be protected against dysgenic influence and inoculated against cultural, social and political infection. Care for the national body becomes control of the body, and rights and protections create categories of exclusion. In American print culture, therefore, Stein becomes a signifier of the new artist and author as aberrant and illegitimate, onto which scepticism about and dismissal of the new practices are loaded, and it is here that the figuring of Stein as an inappropriate biological subject for author status is constructed and begins to circulate.

Notes

1. These are publication dates. 'Matisse' and 'Picasso' were written in 1909, the portrait of Dodge and *Tender Buttons* in 1912.
2. Marsden Hartley on Paris, in a letter to Alfred Stieglitz, July 1912, in *My Dear Stieglitz: Letters of Marsden Hartley and Alfred Stieglitz 1912–1915*, ed. J. T. Voorhies (Chapel Hill: University of South Carolina Press, 2002), 19.
3. Over the last two decades scholarship has emphasised the variety in the nature and composition of groups. The introduction to *Modernist Group Dynamics: The Politics and Poetics of Friendship*, for example, puts it thus: 'For decades, the study of literary and Stein and the new art philosophical modernism concerned solitary figures like the flâneur, the exile, and the lonely genius, but recently the group formations that fostered modernist movements have emerged into view. Scholars now recognise how much of modernism took shape in letters and personal encounters, and how collaborative ventures like the salon and the "little magazine" contributed, not incidentally but centrally, to the cultural innovations of the early twentieth century'. *Modernist Group Dynamics: The Politics and Poetics of Friendship*, ed. Fabio A Durão and Dominic Williams (Newcastle upon Tyne: Cambridge Scholars, 2009), vii.
4. Note these examples reference the British context, in keeping with my emphasis on Anglo-American modernism. There are, of course, many more examples of journals, anthologies and events across Europe as far as Russia in the 1900s and 1910s. For a helpful overview, see Milton A. Cohen, '"To stand on the rock of the word 'we'": Appeals, Snares and Impact of Modernist Groups before World War I', in *Modernist Group Dynamics: The Politics and Poetics of Friendship*, ed. Fabio A Durão and Dominic Williams (Newcastle upon Tyne: Cambridge Scholars, 2009), 1–24.
5. McCann, *A Pinnacle of Feeling*, 51.
6. Gertrude Stein, *The Making of Americans* (Funks Grove, IL: Dalkey Archive Press, 1995), 21.
7. Alfred Stieglitz, 'Advertisement', *Camera Work*, No. 13 (July 1912), 1.
8. Fry also had strong connections with the US, having held the position of curator at the Museum of Modern Art in New York from 1905 to 1907.
9. See Milton W. Brown, *The Story of the Armory Show* (Greenwich, NY: Joseph H. Hirshhorn Foundation, 1963), 66 and 75. Correspondence between Stieglitz and Marsden Hartley over the summer of 1912 also provides evidence of his involvement: Stieglitz sent an invitation to Hartley to exhibit. See Marsden

Hartley and Alfred Stieglitz, *My Dear Stieglitz: Letters of Marsden Hartley and Alfred Stieglitz, 1912–1915*, ed. J. T. Voorhies (Chapel Hill: University of South Carolina Press, 2002), 25.
10. Stieglitz, *Camera Work*, No. 13, 1.
11. Wyndham Lewis, *Blasting & Bombardiering* (London: Eyre & Spottiswoode, 1937), 32.
12. Jane Palatini Bowers, 'Experiment in Time and Process of Discovery: Picasso Paints Gertrude Stein; Gertrude Stein Makes Sentences', in *Harvard Library Bulletin* Vol. 5, No. 2 (1994), 5–30. For other discussions of Picasso's portrait of Stein, see, for example, Michael North, *The Dialect of Modernism: Race, Language, and Twentieth-Century Literature* (Oxford: Oxford University Press, 1994) and Michael Levenson, *Modernism* (New Haven, CT: Yale University Press, 2011).
13. Janet Flanner, 'A Frame for Some Portraits', in *'Two' and Other Early Portraits: Volume One of the Yale Edition of the Unpublished Writings of Gertrude Stein* (New Haven, CT: Yale University Press, 1951), ix–xvii (x).
14. See, for example, Louis A. Waldman and Brenda Preyer, 'The Rise of the Patronage Portrait in Late Renaissance Florence: An Enigmatic Portrait of Giovanni Di Paolo Rucellai and Its Role in Family Commemoration', *Mitteilungen des Kunsthistorischen Institutes in Florenz*, Vol. 54 (2010), 133–154, and Jill Burke, *Changing Patrons: Social Identity and the Visual Arts in Renaissance Florence* (Philadelphia: Penn State University Press, 2004).
15. See Lawrence Rainey, *Institutions of Modernism: Literary Elites and Public Culture* (New Haven, CT: Yale University Press, 1998), 39: 'More concretely, what had once been an aristocracy of patron-*salonniers* would now be replaced by an elite of patron-investors. For the Anglo-American avant-garde, the future lay in the new patronage provided by a small group of people such as John Quinn, Harriet Shaw Weaver, Scofield Thayer and James Sibley Watson, Jr.'
16. See Bowers, 16–21.
17. See Gemma Blackshaw, *Facing the Modern, 9 October 2013–12 January 2014* (London: National Gallery, 2013), n.4: 'Few patrons were willing to give a public face to their private lives. Here, fellow artists, family and friends played a vital supporting role. Many of the most audacious experiments in portraiture were made using such sitters'.
18. All references to this text are from Gertrude Stein, 'Picasso', in *Camera Work*, Special Edition (August 1912), 4.
19. All references to this text are from Gertrude Stein, 'Matisse', in *Camera Work*, Special Edition August 1912), 2.
20. Gertrude Stein, *Two: Gertrude Stein and Her Brother and Other Early Portraits* (New Haven, CT: Yale University Press, 1951), 353.
21. See Michael B. Miller, *The Bon Marche: Bourgeois Culture and the Department Store, 1869–1920* (Princeton, NJ: Princeton University Press, 1981), 5: 'In the years before the First World War the Bon Marche was the quintessential big store. It was the world's largest department store, and if its claim to being the world's first was somewhat askew, few people if any were willing to argue'.
22. Eric Schocket, *Vanishing Moments: Class and American Literature* (Ann Arbor: University of Michigan Press, 2006), 167, 179.

23. Stein's own portrait of Vollard adds to this list.
24. Alex Goody, *Modernist Articulations* (London: Palgrave Macmillan), 54.
25. Mabel Dodge, 'Speculations', in *Camera Work*, Special Number (June 1913), 6–9 (8).
26. Gertrude Stein, *Selected Writings*, ed. Carl Van Vechten (New York: Random House, 1946), 465–468 (465). Further references to the edition are given after quotations in the text. Stein and Toklas visited the Villa in autumn 1912. See Patricia R. Everett, *A History of Having a Great Many Times Not Continued to Be Friends: The Correspondence between Mabel Dodge and Gertrude Stein, 1911–1934* (Albuquerque: University of New Mexico Press, 1996), 60.
27. Dodge, 'Speculations', 6.
28. Dodge to Stein, c. July 1913. Everett, 202.
29. Dodge to Stein, c. January 1913. Everett, 152.
30. Dodge to Stein, 27 January 1913. Everett, 163.
31. The article was reprinted in the June 1913 Special Number of Stieglitz's magazine *Camera Work*. References to the text here are taken from this publication. See n.25 above.
32. Stein to Dodge, early February 1913. Everett, 169.
33. Woodrow Wilson and William Bayard Hale, *The New Freedom; a Call for the Emancipation of the Generous Energies of a People* (New York: Doubleday, 1913), 35. On the popularity of Roosevelt and Wilson's Progressive platforms, it is important to note that, despite losing very decisively with 6 states to Wilson's, 40, Roosevelt took 27.4 per cent of the popular vote against Wilson's 41.8 per cent even as he split the Republican vote, which drew only 23 per cent of the popular vote.
34. Theodore Roosevelt, 'A Layman's Views of an Art Exhibition', *The Outlook*, No. 103 (29 March 1913), 718–720 (718).
35. For a fuller contextualisation of Roosevelt's response to the Armory Show in relation to his views on national culture, see Stephen L. Levine, '"Forces which cannot be ignored": Theodore Roosevelt's Reaction to European Modernism', *Revue Française d'Études Américaines*, Vol. 2, No. 116 (2008), 5–19 .
36. The classic account of this is Milton W. Brown, *The Story of the Armory Show* (New York: New York Graphic Society, 1963). See also, more recently, Casey Nelson Blake, Kimberly Orcutt and Marilyn S. Kushner, eds., *The Armory Show at 100: Modernism and Revolution* (New York: Joseph H. Hirshhorn Foundation, 2013).
37. Arthur B. Davies. 'Explanatory Statement: The Aim of The Association of American Painters and Sculptors', *Arts and Decoration*, Vol. 3, No. 5 (6 March 1913), 149.
38. Frederick James Gregg, 'The Attitude of the Americans', *Arts and Decoration*, Vol. 3, No. 5 (6 March 1913), 165–167 (165).
39. Wilson's subsequent treatment of radicals has been the subject of much critique. See, for a recent example, Jacob Kramer, *The New Freedom and the Radicals* (Philadelphia, PA: Temple University Press, 2015).
40. John Quinn, 'Modern Art from a Layman's Point of View', *Arts and Decoration*, Vol. 3, No. 5 (6 March 1913), 156–158.

41. For more on Quinn's involvement in American Modernism, see Judith Zilczer, 'John Quinn and Modern Art Collectors in America, 1913–1924, *American Art Journal*, Vol. 14, No. 1 (1982), 57–71.
42. Anonymous, 'The American Section: The National Art, An Interview with the Chairman of the Domestic Committee, Wm J. Glackens', *Arts and Decoration*, Vol. 3, No. 5 (6 March 1913), 159–164 (159).
43. Mabel Dodge, 'Speculations, or Post-Impressionism in Prose', *Arts and Decoration*, Vol. 3, No. 5 (6 March 1913), 172–174 (172). All subsequent references are from this edition.
44. Oscar Bluemner, 'Audiator et Altera Pars: Some Plain Sense on the Modern Art Movement', *Camera Work*, Special Number (June 1913), 25–37. In 1915, Stieglitz gave Bluemner a one-man exhibition at his '291' gallery.
45. *Camera Work*, for example, reprinted favourable reviews of exhibitions at 291 from the daily and weekly papers.
46. As we have seen, Frederick James Gregg also bridged the popular and the avant-garde. Another notable example is the journalist and art critic Charles H. Caffin, a friend of Stieglitz's who wrote for *Camera Work* as well as for the daily *New York American*.
47. For an interesting discussion of Hapgood's anarchism and modern art, see Allan Antliff, *Anarchist Modernism: Art, Politics, and the First American Avant-Garde* (Chicago: University of Chicago Press, 2001).
48. Hutchins Hapgood, 'A New Form of Literature', *Camera Work*, No. 40 (1 November 1912), 42–45 (45). The *New York Globe* date is cited in the reprint.
49. Hutchins Hapgood, 'Authority in Art', *New York Globe*, 28 January 1912, 10.
50. Hutchins Hapgood, 'Art and Unrest' in the *New York Globe*, reprinted in *Camera Work*, Nos 42–43 (4 June 1913), 43–44.
51. Hapgood was also involved in the Paterson Strike Pageant. See Leslie Fishbein, 'The Paterson Pageant (1913): The Birth of Docudrama as a Weapon in the Class Struggle', *New York History*, Vol. 72, No. 2 (April 1991), 197–233.
52. Hutchins Hapgood, 'The Picture Show', in the *New York Globe*, reprinted in *Camera Work*, Nos 42–43 (4 June 1913), 45–46.
53. See Introduction, 21–27 above.
54. *Life* magazine, Vol. 16, No. 1585 (13 March 1913), 521. Subsequent quotations are from this page.
55. Don Marquis, 'Gertrude Stein's Hints for the Table', *New York Sun*, 14 August 1914 in Curnutt, 233; Anonymous, "What Is Lunch?" *Chicago Tribune*, 12 June 1914 in Leonard Diepeveen, *Mock Modernism: An Anthology of Parodies, Travesties, Frauds, 1910–1935* (Toronto: University of Toronto Press, 2014), 129; Robert Emons Rogers, 'New Outbreaks of Futurism: "Tender Buttons," Curious Experiment of Gertrude Stein in Literary Anarchy', *Boston Evening Transcript*, 11 July 1914 in Curnutt, 18–21 (19, 20).
56. G.V.S., "Tender Buttons," *Pittsburgh Sun*, 17 July 1914 in Diepeveen, 131.
57. Anonymous, 'And She Triumphed on the Tragic Turnip Field!' *Cleveland Leader*, 21 June 1914 in Curnutt, 159–160.
58. G.M.P. was published in 1930 as *Matisse Picasso and Gertrude Stein with Two*

Shorter Stories, the first of Stein and Toklas's self-published Plain Editions, suggesting the significance of this text in Stein's vision of her own authorship. All references are from Gertrude Stein, *Matisse Picasso and Gertrude Stein with Two Shorter Stories* (New York: Dover Publications, 2000).
59. T. J. Clark, *Farewell to an Idea: Episodes from a History of Modernism* (New Haven, CT: Yale University Press, 1999), 9–10.
60. See Gertrude Stein, *Composition as Explanation* (London: Hogarth Press, 1926), 6: 'it is quite certain that nations not actively threatened are at least several generations behind themselves militarily so aesthetically they are more than several generations behind themselves and it is very much too bad'.
61. Gertrude Stein, *Tender Buttons*, ed. Leonard Diepeveen (Peterborough: Broadview, 2018), 16.
62. H. L. Mencken, 'A Cubist Treatise', *Baltimore Sun*, 6 June 1914 in Curnutt, 14–15; 'Gertrude Stein as Literary Cubist', *Philadelphia North American*, 13 June 1914 in Diepeveen, 130. As we can see above, although Stein is also aligned with 'futurism', and there are occasional references to Marinetti, this term was used interchangeably with 'post-impressionism' and, increasingly, 'modernism' to indicate the phenomenon of modern art as a whole, whereas 'cubism' was used to refer more precisely to the work of Picasso, Braque and Duchamp. It is important to note, however, that many reviewers were reusing second-hand material, culled either from other reviews or from the promotional material circulated with the text by the publisher Claire Marie, which introduces her as 'patron saint of the new artists – the Cubists and Futurists' (Diepeveen, 86). See Diepeveen, 12 for this insight. The weaker association of Stein with Matisse may well be the result of this recycling, but it nonetheless shows the tendency for reviewers to pin *Tender Buttons* to a distinct and recognisable group in order to both circumscribe and challenge its unusual and difficult experiments. For the classic interpretation of Stein's cubism, see Randa Dubnick, *The Structure of Obscurity: Gertrude Stein, Language, and Cubism* (Urbana and Chicago: University of Illinois Press, 1984). For a recent example of Stein's writing as cubist, see Chris Coffman's reliance on cubism as a framework for interpreting Stein's texts in her 2018 book *Gertrude Stein's Transmasculinity* (Edinburgh: Edinburgh University Press, 2018).
63. Gertrude Stein, *Tender Buttons*, ed. Seth Perlow (San Francisco: City Lights Books, 2014), 12. Subsequent references are to this edition.
64. Don Marquis, 'Gertrude Stein on the War', *New York Evening Sun*, 2 October 1914 in Diepeveen, 140.
65. Not that America had entered the war at this point, of course, but American citizens had diverse ancestral ties to Europe and the danger was obviously felt.
66. Anonymous, 'And She Triumphed in the Tragic Turnip Field', *Cleveland Leader*, 21 June 1914 in Curnutt, 159–160 (160).
67. The Detroit *Free Press* and Columbus *Dispatch*, quoted in Leick, 45.
68. *Minneapolis (Minnesota) Bellman* in Curnutt, 164.
69. Alfred Kreymborg, 'Gertrude Stein – Hoax and Hoaxtress: A Study of the Woman Whose "Tender Buttons" Has Furnished New York with a New Kind of Amusement', *New York Morning Telegraph*, 7 March 1915 in Diepeveen,

102-109.
70. The prevalence of this term and the attitude it suggests is later reflected in Henry Ford's resonant statement 'history is more or less bunk', attributed to Ford in an interview with *Chicago Tribune* reporter Charles Wheeler. See Charles Wheeler, Interview with Henry Ford, *Chicago Tribune*, 25 May 1916, 10. For a discussion of the legitimacy of this imputation, see Roger Butterfield, 'Henry Ford, the Wayside Inn, and the Problem of "History Is Bunk"', *Proceedings of the Massachusetts Historical Society*. Vol. 77 (1965), 53-66.
71. Don Marquis, 'To G.S. and E.P.', *New York Sun*, 3 October 1914 in Curnutt 235-236, (236). Here, Marquis compares Stein with Ezra Pound.
72. H. L. Mencken, 'A Cubist Treatise', *Baltimore Sun*, 6 June 1914 in Curnutt 14-15; Anonymous, 'Gertrude Stein as Literary Cubist', *Philadelphia North American*, 13 June 1914 in Diepeveen 130-131. This is further intimated as the figure in Marquis's poem 'Summoned her genii to command'. Marquis also produced a series of sketches involving the snobbish salon of a fictional 'Hermione', devotee of Stein. See Leick, 53-58.
73. See *Tender Buttons* (ed. Diepeveen), 15-16 for some helpful comments on this practice. Natalia Cecire also offers an interesting discussion of Stein's 'unreadability' in 'Ways of Not Reading Gertrude Stein' *ELH*, Vol. 82, No. 1 (Spring 2015), 281-312.
74. Don Marquis, 'Gertrude Stein Is Stein, Gertrude: That is All Ye now on Earth, and All Ye Need to Know', *New York Evening Sun*, 14 October 1914 in Curnutt, 238.
75. Anonymous, 'Gertrude Stein', *New York City Call*, 7 June 1914 in Diepeveen 122-124.
76. See, for example, Lisa Cole Ruddick, *Reading Gertrude Stein: Body, Text, Gnosis* (Ithaca, NY: Cornell University Press, 1990).
77. One might also read 'Enthusiastically hurting' as the moment when a new cup is broken and the 'bite in the ribbon' as a visual image of the band of colour around the rim of the cup with a piece missing, but whatever the occasion, these intimations of the body stubbornly remain.
78. Anonymous, 'Time to Show a Message', *Omaha World Herald*, 7 June 1914 in Diepeveen 125-127 (126).

CHAPTER 3

Modernism's Abject: *Geography and Plays* and Stein's Contested Authorship

'Two Cubist Poems. The Peace Conference'

In 1920, Oxford University's student paper, the *Oxford Magazine*, printed Stein's oblique comment on the Paris Peace Conference of 1919–1920, 'Two Cubist Poems. The Peace Conference'.[1] The reference to cubism in the title, whether supplied by Stein or added by the editor, relies on the visibility she had achieved in her association with a community of radical continental European artists. By 1920, however, this was beginning to give way to a period in which her practice was more commonly situated in relation to Anglo-American literary experimentation. Indeed, the fact of this publication by the student magazine of a leading British university reflects a developing interest in her authorship in Britain that included a short lecture tour to read and discuss her work at Oxford and at Cambridge in the summer of 1926. 'Two Cubist Poems. The Peace Conference' also reflects Stein's political stance, being one of a series of critical reflections on Woodrow Wilson's presidency that bespeak her now obdurate opposition to progressivism and to Wilson's perceived internationalism. This publication is also significant because it anticipates her resistance to the type of authority that she begins to attribute to some of the more prominent writers observing with suspicion her role on the scene of literary modernism through the 1920s.

For Stein, the League represents a top-down bureaucracy that extends the management logic of progressive democracy to manufacture a new world order, and what she objects to more and more vocally through this period is the gatekeeping role of expert authority that she often characterises as 'academic' thinking. In the series of works dealing explicitly with the political scene written in and around 1920, this resistance is coupled with an increasing emphasis on a racialised form of national belonging that she sets against a scene of nation-states ordered by a perceived supra-national global elite who calibrate the criteria through which citizens are legitimised. These works reflect Stein's rejection of the America represented by Wilson and the progressives and her interest in what might be described as a more 'organic' America of mass information, production and consumption, unregulated circulation, and the movement of crowds.

While Stein apparently embraced the expanded readership, the proliferation of publications and the possibilities for mass participation emerging since the turn of the century, other modernist writers took a different view. Discursive mechanisms of inclusion and exclusion, anxieties about aesthetic standards and attempts to superintend designations of the author and the literary work in modernist literary culture become more insistent through the 1920s, and these are often expressed in terms that reflect extra-literary fears about the effects of mass democratic participation in Britain and the US. Scepticism about the validity of Stein's authorship became central in 1920s debates about authorial legitimacy among Anglo-American modernist writers. This chapter follows the discourse of Stein's authorship from American accounts of her as the avant-garde author of the radical art before the First World War to discussions among modernist writers in periodicals, essays, monographs and newspapers on the Anglophone European inter-war scene. Stein's reputation as signifier of the bizarre and arcane artistic practices of the early twentieth century came to mean that what was at stake for literary culture in accepting or rejecting her authorship was nothing less than the legitimacy of modernist authorship *per se*.

The extensive debate about the validity of Stein's work was prompted by her growing profile as a modernist author following the publication of *Geography and Plays* in 1922. Redeploying the popular discourse of Stein as illegitimate or aberrant, modernist writers extended these tropes to delimit aesthetic practice and to legitimise particular forms of authorship. In the context of extra-literary anxieties around democracy and rights, many of the louder voices in this literary culture insisted on individual authorship as opposed to collective practice, and on the assertion of a normative model of authorship that enacts the identification and exclusion of those 'others' who had begun to participate in authorship during the pre-war period. The questioning of Stein's right to participate in literary life intersected with contemporary debates about democratic participation that significantly inflected the construction of the figure of the modernist author emerging at the end of the 1920s.

From Cubist to Modernist

As I have suggested, after the First World War and through the early 1920s, Stein's work gained more support in Anglo-American modernist circles, and she became increasingly perceived as an author associated with the scene of literary modernism. The popular representation of Stein as a 'cubist' writer, though it had at times been accompanied with the impression that she was part of the clique around Pound, began to give way to presentations that put her at the heart of modernist literary culture.[2] This is particularly evident in the appearance of her work and discussions of her authorship in *Vanity Fair*. Read in recent scholarship as popularising modernism and contributing to the construction of writers as celebrities, *Vanity Fair*'s interest in modernists as exciting innovators at the cutting edge of the cultural trend extended to Stein, who developed a productive relationship with the magazine though her correspondence with its editor Frank Crowninshield.[3]

Vanity Fair published Stein's work in 1917, 1918, 1919, 1923 and 1924, interspersed with reviews and commentary throughout the period. This included two parodies, the first of which, a 1920 piece by the fictional modernist author 'Paul K. Arthors', reflects the way perceptions of her association with cubism are supplanted by representations of her as an author among modernist authors. The title of the piece 'Cheating the Nature: A Literary Challenge to Opal Whiteley, Patience Worth and Gertrude Stein', has Stein as a stand-in for modernist writing, and puts her in company with other recent American publications viewed as sensational literary frauds.[4] The article is accompanied by an 'Editor's note' that extends the tongue-in-cheek imputation of fraudulence to the broader scene, placing Stein firmly in the context of literary modernism traced in a potted history including 'Alfred Kreymborg and the *Others* group of poets', 'their English *confrères*, Miss Edith Sitwell and the *Wheels* group', the 'London Vorticists' and 'Wyndham Lewis's *Blast*'. This arch and complex mockery, situated in the context of *Vanity Fair*'s consistent support for and discussion of avant-garde work, contributes to the visibility of modernist writers and the impression of the success of these 'literary radicals'. As Hammill and Leick argue, the quality magazines bridged the space between the broadcast reach of newspapers and the tiny circulation of modernist periodicals and anthologies, creating an image of modernist literary production and authorship that developed and extended the popular perception of literary modernism *as* a movement.[5] In this example, Stein is set among other modernist writers in an increasingly recognizable Anglo-American milieu. Indeed, in the title, 'Gertrude Stein' is located as a signifier for modernism as such.

This example, then, points to a new phase in Stein's reception and in the perception and representation of her authorship, in which she herself becomes more involved with other modernist writers and in which she is more frequently associated with them in the press. This shift in Stein's reputation in the early 1920s is reflected in a series of serious reviews and commentaries, particularly those of Sherwood Anderson, Edith Sitwell and Edmund Wilson, that straddle the full range of publication contexts, from the little magazine through the quality magazine to the popular press.[6] The support for her work on the transatlantic literary scene was consolidated in a series of book-length publications, culminating in the 1926 lecture tour of Oxford and Cambridge and the subsequent appearance of her lecture, *Composition as Explanation*, in the Woolfs' Hogarth Essays series.[7]

The Anglo-American Modernist Group

The 1922 publication of *Geography and Plays* in a run of 2,500 was an ambitious intervention in the Anglo-American scene.[8] Its publication initiated, for Stein, a new reassertion of the avant-garde collective in her relationships with, among others, Jane Heap and Margaret Anderson, Alfred Kreymborg, Sylvia Beach, Sherwood Anderson and Ernest Hemingway. Stein's involvement with the surge of American modernists producing work in Chicago and New York and circulating in Paris after the war had resulted in the publication of 'Vacation in Brittany' in the *Little Review* and 'If You Had Three Husbands' and 'Wear' in Kreymborg's journal *Broom*. These connections produced a nexus of mutual legitimisation that began to secure Stein's place in the burgeoning transatlantic scene of literary modernism, exemplified in a circuit of endorsements around *Geography and Plays* that crossed over into the mainstream press. In 1922, the introduction to the collection, written by Sherwood Anderson, was reprinted in the *Little Review* along with Stein's short piece 'Vacation in Brittany' and again in early 1923, in the European edition of the *Chicago Tribune*, where it was accompanied by a review written by Hemingway.[9] This was followed by Stein's review, also in the European *Tribune*, of Hemingway's 1923 *Three Stories and Ten Poems*.[10] This network of alliances means that the promotion of Stein's work broadens through the narrow circulation of the *Little Review* into the front pages of a mainstream newspaper for the American expat community, thus signalling the importance of another triad of modernist practitioners and asserting a culture of American writers in Paris.

The significance of group culture in producing and sustaining innovative work through the first half of the 1920s is reflected in Stein's 1925 review of Kreymborg's autobiography *Troubadour*. Stein's effort, as Edward Burns suggests, presumably reflects her gratitude for Kreymborg's support in the early 1920s, but it also responds to his representation of her authorship in *Troubadour* itself.[11] Kreymborg identifies Stein as the 'most radical of the group' in the avant-garde scene around the pre-war magazine *Rogue* and as the unrecognised originator who had 'quantities of . . . imitators' and was the 'magnet of leading continental artists' at the heart of the Parisian inter-war modernist community.[12] He also aligns her with his own authorship, twice referring to their having in common the 'simultaneous publication of their first books by the Grafton Press' (292). His support for her work through the early 1920s and the recognition he expresses in *Troubadour* reflect an appreciation that redresses his equivocal treatment of her work and her status as author in his review of *Tender Buttons* ten years earlier. Not only does he accept Stein's position, he draws a parallel with her authorship and his in an act of mutuality that is picked up and amplified in Stein's review.

Published in the magazine *Ex Libris,* the journal of the American Library in Paris and another example of a publication aimed at the growing American community in Europe after the war, Stein's review reciprocates Kreymborg's camaraderie in a form that sustains the vision of the collective expressed in *G.M.P.*, but with a new retrospective position that reflects the contemporary status of modernism and the autobiographical function of *Troubadour*:

> There are many histories of us then and now and they are written now and they are often written now. Many histories of us are often written now. Sometimes in the histories of us each one of us is different from the others of us and the one writing the history of himself and us is different in his history of himself and us from us. In this history of us of himself and us Kreymborg makes us makes himself and each one of us different enough so that some one can know us. That is very nice for him and for us and very pleasant for him and for us and very satisfying to him and to us. We are all pleased with him and with us and so we say that he has made a very good description of himself and of each one of us. A history of himself and of each one of us and connections of more than one of us is a very sensitive thing, a sensitive history of himself and of each of us and some who are ones and one. Always this is a good thing.[13]

The repetition of 'us' and 'now' in the opening lines presents the arrival of this modernist chronicle *in medias res* as the paradoxical history of a contemporary group yet to pass into history. This presages the developing proliferation of narratives of modernism that begin to assert accounts of its emergence and stake a claim on its origins. The suggestion here, however, is that each 'one of us' embodies an alternative history of modernism, with the repetition of the plural 'histories' and the emphasis on 'many' also reflecting the instability and subjectivity of history, and so of truth, that opens the field for the many histories of modernism that might be written.

What is important for Stein is not the veracity of Kreymborg's account – for her, the claim to authority is the problem with history – but how far he 'makes himself and each one of us different enough so that some one can know us'. Stein's insistent repetition of this pronoun structures the sentences to present a grammar of the group, marking the history of modernism as the history of a collective endeavour. The emphasis on difference, however, is also reiterated throughout the review, and these techniques frame a conception of authorial recognition that is achieved through both contrast and combination. This configuration signifies, as it did in *G.M.P.*, the distinctiveness of individuals *and* the importance of the group in the construction and maintenance of artistic identity. Stein's representation is consolidated in the final lines, 'A history of himself and of each one of us and connections of more than one of us is a very sensitive thing, a sensitive history of himself and of each of us and some who are ones and one. Always this is a good thing'. Here, the reference to 'connections' is foregrounded both because it is the only word that is not repeated in the text and because of its characterisation as a 'sensitive thing', indicating the fragile yet crucial networks that produce the work of a community involved in a complex and large-scale project to transform culture. In her review, Stein both accepts the multitude of histories that might be written and reinforces her insistence on a communal form of cultural production.

What Stein's review of *Troubadour* reveals, therefore, is that, in 1925, the commitment to a loose group directed by a broad common project still very much frames her conception of her own authorship. It also reflects her understanding of this phase of development, in which writers and artists are beginning to take stock of the advances in art and literature since the turn of the century. Stein indicates that the sensitive topic of a 'history of us' requires an openness to alternative histories and an attentiveness to the dangers of authoritative accounts. Her sensitivity is acute and well-placed. As the idea of a historical movement is initiated, a significant number of texts produced in the late 1920s compete for dominant narratives of the movement, and this battle over 'modernism' is manifested as a battle over the meaning, history and future of 'Gertrude Stein'.

Gertrude Stein, American Modernist

The collection *Geography and Plays* was the first new book Stein had published since the major event of *Tender Buttons* just before the war.[14] Appearing in 1922, the *annus mirabilis* of *Ulysses*, *Jacob's Room* and *The Waste Land*, Stein's *Geography and Plays* marks the beginning of a phase in which her work is heatedly discussed and debated in Anglo-American circles in a highly productive period for literary modernism. The initial promotion of the work by Sherwood Anderson and Ernest Hemingway in the *Little Review* and the Paris *Tribune* was followed by Anderson's review of the collection in *The New Republic* of October 1922, Edith Sitwell's July 1923 review in the *Nation and Athenaeum* and Edmund Wilson's discussion that September in *Vanity Fair*. In 1924 these were accompanied by Mina Loy's *Transatlantic Review* defence of Stein, which focused on *Geography and Plays*. These responses span a range of publication contexts to present Stein as a significant writer who now needs to be taken seriously as both a modernist and an American author.

Sherwood Anderson's introduction to *Geography and Plays*, published alongside Hemingway's review in the *Tribune*, creates a circuit of mutual recognition with a claim to a distinctly American form of innovative writing. As Ulla Dydo points out, Anderson's foreword 'added to her book a prominent name likely to make for sales and critical attention'.[15] Both the introduction and Anderson's *New Republic* review in October of the same year situate Stein as an important American writer in a way that explicitly recuperates her from representations that have her as the literary proponent of a decadent European mode. Anderson's introduction refers to the popular construction of Stein as 'a languid woman lying on a couch, smoking cigarettes, sipping absinthes perhaps and looking out upon the world with tired, disdainful eyes' generated in the 'good deal of fuss and fun being made over [*Tender Buttons*] in American newspapers'.[16] Anderson conjures this image in order to dispel it, and he replaces it with a depiction that assigns to Stein an American identity whose attributes he deliberately contrasts with the dissipated popular press concoction that had shaped his own expectations. Prefaced by a nod to a shared American consciousness in his 'Tom Sawyerish' eagerness to believe the tales he had been told of a European grotesque, Anderson's description of Stein inverts the popular view to present 'a woman of striking vigor, a subtle and powerful mind, a discrimination in the arts such as I have found in no other American born man or woman, and a charmingly brilliant conversationalist' (6).

This alternative Stein is emphatically healthy and strong in both mind and body, possessing qualities of 'discrimination' and brilliance that directly negate the imputations of weakness and indolence in the popular perception. Alongside this, Anderson argues that her authorship is 'the most important pioneer work done in the field of letters in my time', attributing to Stein a clean and earnest work ethic that he associates with the American frontier spirit (6). This characterisation is extended into a defence of her practice as the modest and genuine work of a writer 'who has even forgone the privilege of writing the great American novel' in order to 'go live among the little housekeeping words, the swaggering bullying street-corner words, the honest working, money saving words, and all the other forgotten and neglected citizens of the sacred and half forgotten city' (8). Thus, Stein's authorship is good honest American hard work, a representation that inverts the popular image of the degenerate quasi-aristocratic Europeanised highbrow and presents Stein as the genuine representative and champion of the ordinary American. The emphasis on Stein's American birth provides an insight into Anderson's organicist conception of nationality in which the individual is, as Pericles Lewis puts it 'primarily an emanation of the national "character"'.[17]

This theme is developed further in Anderson's subsequent *New Republic* review, which reconfigures Stein's gender as the strong womanhood of the American pioneer housewife as opposed to the abject feminisation of the decadent popular image. Grounded in an idealisation of American rural traditions, Anderson's Stein stands 'in the great kitchen of my fanciful world', recognizable as the comforting presence of a mother-figure at the heart of a clean-living brick-built American home.[18] The review opens with and sustains the trope of 'a kind of aroma from people' that does much work to replace the stink of 'decay' in Stein's incarnation as European aesthete with the scent of 'green, healthy, growing things' associated with the Stein reimagined as 'an American woman of the old sort'.

Rendering the binary opposition of European decay and American health explicit, Anderson presents his first encounter with Stein as a clean sensory experience, with his assertion that 'she, in her person, represents something sweet and healthy in our American life' and with repeated references to sweetness in smell, taste and sound and in the visual image of 'jars of fruits, jellies and preserves' creating a nexus of sense associations to indicate that she offers a return to something simple and wholesome. His attention to the figure of Stein makes her a whole author, 'the woman in the great kitchen of words, standing there by a table, clean, strong . . . always quietly and smilingly at work', a genuine embodiment of her craft rather than a fraud or a corrupt mystic whose work has an inauthentic or indeterminate relationship to her 'person'.

Anderson's representation also reflects his own relationship to 1920s American democracy and provides a further, and important, insight into his view of nationality. To return to Pericles Lewis's study, Anderson's homespun Stein refracts the conflict 'between liberalism and organic nationalism' that 'pointed to the problem of whether the nation should be understood as a legal and political unit, defined by the voluntary membership in it of individual citizens, or as an ethnic and social unit, defined by the shared culture, history, and (perhaps) biological inheritance that was thrust upon individuals, not chosen by them' (*Modernism, Nationalism*, 6). Signified by the apparently whimsical extension of the pioneer housewife analogy in the suggestion that she 'cares for the handmade goodies and scorns the factory-made foods', Stein's authorship is configured to represent a healthy renewal that unearths something lost in the mass-production of artificial, regulated goods. The food metaphor draws the organic and the wholesome into a relation with each other and places an emphasis on the body as the ground of clean and healthy Americanness. The elevation of the handmade and the homemade rejects the modernity of the factory in favour of something 'intent and earnest' that Anderson associates with the patient duration of an older American mythos Stein channels through her body, her being and her work. Anderson co-opts Stein in a narrative of resistance to industrial modernity and the progressive vision of efficiency, cities, factories and institutions, what Michael McGerr calls 'The confining structures of progressive America' that he argues Anderson kicks against in his own foundational myth, the abrupt rejection of the life of business and the crisis of identity that prefaced his turn to writing in 1912.[19]

Like Kreymborg, Anderson associates Stein's authorship with his own, but here Anderson constructs a deeper, older American identity that, for him, is embodied in individual Americans even as it is eroded in modern life. In the idealisation of domestic labour as analogy for Stein's work, the huge free pioneer kitchen is a mobile space: America exists where Americans are, in a formulation that grounds Americanness even more firmly in the individual as representative of national character. This simultaneously suggests, however, the paradox of a geographical liberation in which Americans can somehow break the bounds of progressive legislation, rejecting the liberal nationalist idea of the citizen as a member of a 'legal and political unit' in favour of a deeper form of national identity irrespective of political borders.[20]

Authorship and Nationalism in *Geography and Plays*

As Stein's first 'selected works', *Geography and Plays* has an important role in representing her oeuvre and exemplifying her authorship. The collection as whole is a densely populated collation of Stein's work from 1908 to 1920 that offers a representative selection of her practice, from the early portraits through the plays to the new, more explicitly political, work written during and after the First World War. In this collection, Stein signals a critique of progressive ideas of nationality in ways that Anderson must have been attuned to. Her version of geography in this collection is to some extent an exploration of creative dislocation, in which America is indeed an abstract and mobile space, the pioneer space of the creative frontier in which, as Emeline Jouve has argued,'the subjects' restlessness forges their identities as "Americans"'.[21] It is also, however, a geography of nation-states, and it is in the texts presenting notions of political geography that Stein engages with ideas of democracy, rights and national belonging.

The title *Geography and Plays* reflects a broad conceptual motivation for the collection as a performance of Stein's authorship as an innovator and as an American. It refers to two ostensibly very different modes and areas of knowledge, indicating a radical experimentation with the categories and forms of discourse that dislocates epistemological classification. The different ways of knowing and being in the world represented by the documenting and cataloguing of physical and political properties of a 'real' world (geography) and the aesthetic creation of a staged world (plays), presents an apparent binary whose boundaries, however, waver even as they are drawn. The comparison of geography with plays begs the question of whether geography simply catalogues spaces or whether, in the manner of a theatrical staging, it creates or constructs them. By the same token, the title also prompts the consideration of whether plays, in identifying and naming space, might be considered a form of geography. These questions also partly motivate the selection and combination of texts. Playing out some of the problematics raised by her title, the selection of a striking number of works on nation and nationality frames political geography as, in fact, the staging of nations. The inclusion of 'France', 'Americans', 'Italians', 'In the Grass (on Spain)', 'England', 'Mallorcan Stories', 'Mexico', 'Land of Nations' and 'Accents in Alsace' presages Stein's position on the staginess, the constructedness, of political geography expressed, as we shall see in the discussion below, in the closing piece 'The Psychology of Nations'. The collection begins with images of restless, vital movement in 'Suzie Asado', a depiction of flamenco dancing that also already hints at an idea of national character and its staging, and it is followed by 'Ada', the narrative of Toklas's move from her family home to live with Stein, a crossing of national borders that is also a crossing out of conventional life. It ends with a meditation on the nature of national identity that recuperates an organicist vision and draws the collection into a formulation of national belonging set against the artificial and mechanistic legality of the liberal nation-state and the political conception of citizenship. This chimes with Anderson's American imaginary and stakes a claim for the Americanness of an author who, at the age of 46, has lived and worked in Europe for almost twenty years.

The title of that final piece, 'The Psychology of Nations', ostensibly indicates a perception of nationality as a psychological state, of nationality itself as a psychological quality, and this is an important thread in the text that reflects Stein's conception of a deep form of national identity. Stein offers the alternative title 'What Are You Looking At', however, which points to another way in which the phrase 'the psychology of nations' can be understood: that an understanding of nation depends on how the subject defines what they are looking at. In this sense, 'psychology' refers to the way the subject processes experience and is grounded in Stein's understanding, roughly put, of psychology as neurology rather than psychiatry, with an emphasis on the functioning of the brain rather than on the psyche.[22] The text presents two alternative modes of 'looking at' or neurologically processing nationality that follows the logic of the collection title. Nationality can be perceived in terms either of 'geography', as a reality of place that deeply shapes psychology, or of 'plays', as the marking out of place ready for the performance of roles in a conscious act of meaning-making. These two forms of categorisation are explored in a series of episodes that establish and reiterate the distinction using various methods.

The whole piece is motivated around references to locations, with an emphasis on 'streets' that explores the relations configured by different conceptualisations of place, a preoccupation that follows the interrogation set up by the collection title: geography and plays are apparently two very different ways of thinking place. The first section envisages a playful sense of place, in which locations create the staging for a series of dances:

> We make a little dance.
> Willie Jewetts dance in the tenth century chateau.
> Soultz Alsace dance on the Boulevard Raspail
> Spanish French dance on the rue de la Boetie
> Russian Flemish dance on the docks.[23]

In these examples, sites are named as the contexts for joyful activity, and the dance seems to register the embodied experience of being in a place. These snapshots have the feel of the end of war, with displaced people celebrating the freedom of the peace. The sustained verb phrases reiterate the sense of movement and life, and the shifting locations and subjects flick past in a playful, mobile geography. This is a muddle of people(s) and places – the American (and very American-sounding) Willie Jewetts in the French chateau, the Alsatians in Paris – suggesting that anyone can be anywhere and still dance out their joyful being. Significantly, however, nationality seems to determine being in a way that place does not. The subjects dancing in three of the sentences are determined only by their nationality, and the incongruity of an American name in relation to an ancient French estate also produces a heightened attention to nationality. Thus, a sense of national identity is the stable thing, while the shifting locations are merely stages for the dance. The idea of nation these sentences represent is indicated in the inclusion of Soultz Alsace, a reference to the region in north-eastern France on the borders of Germany and Switzerland that had passed between French and German hands many times. Significantly, it is the subject of one of Woodrow Wilson's Fourteen Points, instructing that Alsace-Lorraine be returned to French hands to right 'the wrong done to France by Prussia in 1871, which has unsettled the peace of the world for nearly fifty years'.[24] What is interesting about the region is both the liminality of its border proximity and its apparently shifting nationality, which might be thought of as blurring or diluting a sense of nation, and its obdurate specificity, in that Alsatians are famously very protective of their distinctive identity. Thus, a strong sense of ethnic identity emerges precisely from a fragile sense of place, emphasising that an identity founded originally on a locale is held and stabilised in the people rather than reflecting a fundamental stability in the political identity of the region.

The text turns to Wilson in the second section, and develops a critique of the role of politicians in the First World War, Wilson's U-turn on America's entry in 1917, and the settlement represented by the Paris Peace Conference and the League of Nations, figured in the opening lines as a 'picture' of boys playing marbles on the street.

> A little boy was playing marbles with soldiers, he was rolling the balls and knocking down the soldiers.
> Then came a presidential election.
> What did he do. He met boys of every nationality and they played together (416).

The space of the street continues the image evoked in the first section, but rather than providing a context for the dance of being, the street stages the boys' game and the focus zooms out to recast the participants as directors controlling the action of tiny figures. Thus, what they are 'looking at' changes fundamentally with a shift of perspective. The comparison of war to a game of marbles clearly comments on the excessive power of politicians, their distance from the realities of war and their irresponsibility in playing with the lives of millions, and the reference to the presidential election is evidently a critique of Wilson's apparent betrayal of his successful 1916 campaign slogan 'He kept us out of war'.[25] What is staged here is the political geography of war, critiqued in the presentation of politicians as boys playing a game, by the ironic 'All men are intelligent', and by the question at the end of this section, 'How can a little Pole be a baby rusher', which presumably references the Polish–Soviet war of 1919–1920 in a way that sustains an idea of national identity resistant to the potential drawing of new borders (417). These issues, of course, dominated the inter-war period, but what is relevant to this discussion is the way Stein's own perspective on national identity grounds her sense of herself as an American author.

Stein's resistance to the political geography of the liberal nation state is reiterated throughout this text, and it is bound up with the figure of President Wilson, who represents what she sees as a remote and patriarchal political class. The references 'The little boy was tall' (417) and 'the boy is tall' (418) signal a defining feature of Wilson's physique – he was indeed tall – and echo the terms used in her other 1920 political piece 'Woodrow Wilson', published in 1928 in *Useful Knowledge*.[26] The development of this refrain in 'the boy' who 'grows up and has a presidential election', who is 'not necessarily a poor boy' and 'has a memory of permission' connects the boys playing marbles and all the critique that entails to the figure of Wilson as the figure of patriarchal entitlement (418). The text was written, however, in the year of Wilson's retirement from office and the landslide victory of the Republican Party candidate Warren G. Harding over the Democrat Cox, the year that women were able to vote for the first time after the passage of the Nineteenth Amendment into law barely a month before the election. The liberal idea of nation promulgated by the progressives and extended internationally in the Wilsonian foreign policy that aimed to create 'a world safe for democracy' came under enormous pressure in the 1920 election.[27]

The successful Republican campaign under Harding's slogan of a 'return to normalcy' that included 'not submergence in internationality but sustainment of triumphant nationality' filters through to Stein's assessment of how an America released from what she viewed as progressivism's world of rules, in which one can once again 'remember the Fourth of July' (417), might better coincide with her idea of what it means to be American.[28] This is signified by the lines 'I am thinking that the way to have an election is this. You meet in the street. You meet. You have the election' which reads like a yearning for a return to the streets as a place of real action, of being, that might somehow coincide with the democratic process (418). In the final passage, the imperative to 'Settle on another in your seats' points to the necessity to elect a new president, and this is followed by a contemplative tussle over the value and meaning of choosing a president:

> Kisses do not make a king.
> Nor noises a mother.
> Benedictions come before presidents.
> Words mean more (419).

Here, the question of what makes a president is mulled over through the analogies of king and mother, paradigmatic equivalences that define what the president is not. This explores the question by thinking through what makes a mother and what makes a king, both of which, of course, are determined by birth (of the king, of the mother's child), in order to reiterate the fact that the president becomes the president through popular consent, not through birth. Thus, the president is made through the blessing of the people ('benediction') and through the word of the people. In renewing for herself the meaning of the presidency, Stein seems able to accept the democratic process even though it is not 'on the street'. In the final lines the meaning of her own vote – the first time she has had this right – emerges as the significant factor in what might be a coming-to-terms with an America, as she sees it, returning to something she can live with (if not in):

> I speak now of a man who is not a bother.
> How can he not bother.
> He is elected by me.
> When this you see remember me (419).

The 'man who is not a bother', suggests an echo of the Republican 'return to normalcy', and the fact that this man 'is elected by me', indicates a reconciliation with representative democracy in an emphatic declaration of the collective power of the individual vote to create the president. The final line may well be a good way to end the collection, but it also expresses a faith that the president has once more become the people, that Stein can publicly embrace her American identity as an author at a moment when it has become expedient to do so.

Stein's mobility is, of course, a gift bestowed upon her by her American nationality. Her status as cosmopolitan (as opposed to refugee) is firmly underwritten by her American citizenship. These shifting extranational currents were very much in tension with each other, particularly in the inter-war period, as indicated in Lyndsey Stonebridge's discussion of modernist attitudes to statelessness:

> Where the cosmopolitan had been the figure for an earlier moment of modernism, by 1938 it was the refugee who had become, as Giorgio Agamben has put it, a 'new paradigm of historical consciousness'. Even as Virginia Woolf famously declared herself detached from her country on the grounds of her sex, a cosmopolitanism that since Kant had dreamt of a universal humanity framed by a global understanding of rights, was confronted with the calamity of the radically stateless.[29]

The mobility of cosmopolitanism is a position made possible by citizenship, whereas the forced mobilisation of the refugee marks the opposite. While Stein's growing insistence on her American authorship has value for her status and legitimacy as author, the foregrounding of her American citizenship through the 1920s is also a response to the political conditions that *Geography and Plays* recognises.

Edmund Wilson's 1923 *Vanity Fair* review of *Geography and Plays* argues for Stein's significance as an American writer and a modernist, and it also references and revises the earlier versions of Stein as a figure produced in the responses to *Tender Buttons*. The opening paragraph sets out this position, points to the reasons for her neglect and argues for her recuperation as a serious writer:

> There is, perhaps, no other American writer of importance who has been so badly underestimated as Gertrude Stein. And this critical neglect would seem chiefly to be due to an unfortunate accident. The earlier half of Miss Stein's literary work has never really had a fair chance of recognition: it was one of her most advanced and most daring experiments which first attracted public attention. The first most of us heard of Gertrude Stein was when *Tender Buttons* was published in 1914 and was greeted with raucous guffaws as an example of exotic Greenwich Villagism.[30]

The mainstream reaction to *Tender Buttons* and the negative publicity it gathered had, for Wilson, tainted her career, and in presenting the work as 'advanced' and 'daring', he suggests that the public were not ready for it. Wilson's main argument, however, goes deeper than this. The work may have been daring, but it, and her work more generally, has been influenced too much by visual and plastic arts. In his judgement that *Geography and Plays* 'is tantalizing with the suggestion of a fine artist just out of reach', and that 'We have the feeling that we have somehow been cheated out of the masterpieces of a first-rate writer of fiction', Wilson argues Stein should and could be a great writer, but her commitment to the collective project of European avant-garde art has curtailed her development, and, in order to realise her potential as an author she needs to be fully immersed in the world of literary modernism (80). This is significant both because it sustains a vision of experimental, innovative authorship as a communal activity and because it argues that Stein belongs in the company of other modernist writers. It is also highly significant that Wilson, in his invitation for readers to 'Compare the scene in the "pub" in *Ulysses*, in which a somewhat similar use of language is made, with one of Gertrude

Stein's "plays"', proposes the example of Joyce as a writer with whom Stein shares characteristics, and argues that in collaboration with him she might come back to an understanding of 'the conditions under which literary effects have to be produced' (80). The reference to Joyce at the moment when *Ulysses*, with which Wilson clearly expects his readers to be familiar, described by Eliot in *The Dial* as 'the most important expression which the present age has found' and by Wilson himself as 'a work of high genius', has come to prominence, is an argument that Stein, in effect, could and should join wholeheartedly the project of Anglo-American literary modernism.[31]

Indeed, following *Geography and Plays*, Stein's engagement with this increasingly visible and influential literary milieu resulted in the serialisation of *The Making of Americans* in *The Transatlantic Review* and its Contact Press publication, with her status further validated on the Anglo-American Parisian scene by her inclusion in the *Contact Collection of Contemporary Writers* (1925) alongside James Joyce, Djuna Barnes, Ford Madox Ford, Dorothy Richardson and Ezra Pound, and in the US by her appearance in Kreymborg's wide-ranging survey of contemporary American poetry, *American Caravan* (1927).[32] In 1925, 'The Fifteenth of November' was printed in *The New Criterion* under the editorship of T. S. Eliot, and after the lecture tour of Oxford and Cambridge, *Composition as Explanation* was published by the Woolf's Hogarth Press. In 1928, *Useful Knowledge*, a selection of texts with a distinctly American theme, which I discuss in Chapter 4, was published by the New York company Payson and Clarke.[33] This shows how far Stein's work was gaining credibility and acceptance in modernist circles and beyond in the 1920s. The range of publishing models also reflects an unstable yet evolving modernist print culture and indicates the complex relation between coterie cultures and the more established institutions as this network of writers attempts to develop and sustain more stable publication contexts. Stein's publication history reveals the intricacies of the scene at this point, including the uneven transition from the small press towards the less marginal publishing houses. It is at this point, however, when modernist work begins to gather a wider cultural legitimacy, that several writers engage in overt attempts to configure both Stein's work and the kind of authorship they take her to represent as a mistake: indeed, as the mistake of the movement *per se*.

Stein and Eliot: 'The Fifteenth of November'

Stein's portrait of T. S. Eliot, 'The Fifteenth of November', anticipates the potential closure of modernism to a certain kind of authorial subject and offers a representation of the creeping regulatory logic that she felt had subtended her exclusion from Eliot's influential journal *The Criterion*. The text shows how accurately Stein understood the attitude among some modernist writers to her authorship. There is clearly an interest in her work, a sense that it is significant, but there is also hostility from some quarters that translates to a more generalised uncertainty about its value. This is, for Stein, represented by Eliot's hesitations about publishing her in *The Criterion*. As Ulla Dydo has shown, the communication between Stein and Eliot through 1925 and 1926 represents a series of polite snubs which hold Stein in the awkward role of the supplicant.[34] This is reflected in 'The Fifteenth of November', the piece Eliot did finally publish in *The New Criterion* in January 1926. This text identifies and works through these rejections and embodies a critique of the exclusion and marginalisation they represent. Stein inhabits the discourse of the rejection letter, contemplating the register and mode of the genre from within in a series of ironised repetitions. She also explores the binary language of choice and selection, reflecting the processes of inclusion and exclusion that characterise the fluctuating responses to her work in this period.

The first stanza ends with the stark minor sentences, 'To deny twice. Once or twice'. This introduces the theme of rejection and implies, in its dismissive lack of precision, the coldly casual indifference of exclusion.[35] This persists throughout the first half of the text, not least in the fifth stanza: 'The idea is that as for a very good reason anything can be chosen the choice the choice is included' (73). This cynicism about the processes of choice and inclusion is developed in the second stanza with the sense that the rejection of her work is really a refusal to engage with Stein at all:

> On the fifteenth of November in place of what was undoubtedly a reason for finding and in this way the best was found to be white or black and as the best was found out to be nearly as much so as was added. To be pleased with the result (71).

Stein registers that the role of supplicant means the work must please the audience represented by Eliot – or be adjusted to suit it: 'Please please please them' (72), 'less less and more', 'it can be a pleasure' and 'Please please half of it' (73). Repeated contiguously 'please' works as both verb and adverb – pleasing and pleading – and overdetermines the position of the plaintiff. The many repetitions of 'please' and 'pleasure', however, also work as echoes of the etiquette of the letter. 'Please' as an adverb is phatic, empty of denotational meaning, and functions only to convey politeness.

Writing out of and across the form and register of the formal letter, Stein's text draws out the processes of cultural conformity the discourse enacts. The salutation, the valediction and the conventional phrasing of the formal letter, in particular the use of the passive voice, are spun out in repetitions and juxtapositions which begin to take on the 'darker' meanings suggested in the line 'In any accidental case no incident no repetition no darker thoughts can be united again' (71). In the rejection letter, the 'darker thoughts' of the exclusion and erasure represented by that rejection are displaced by the detached passive voice and formal language of conventional politeness. Stein's text works through these conventions to reunite them with the dark thoughts they obscure – that is, the inherent violence of exclusion which the detachment and distance of politeness and formality, in a further act of violence, seeks to disclaim. The process of exclusion is identified in several forms in the text. The lines, 'Entirely a different thing. Entirely a different thing when all of it has been awfully well chosen and thoughtfully corrected', for example, evoke the journal editor's justifications. The imposition of otherness on the rejected work in 'entirely a different thing' is connected to the affirmations of selection which serve simply to reassert the criteria of the selection itself (72). The self-congratulatory 'awfully well chosen' and 'thoughtfully corrected' point out the closed circuit of this process. The adverb, a feature of the formal letter which both intensifies and justifies the letter writer's actions, as shown throughout by Stein's repetitions – 'really', 'actually', 'entirely', 'finally', 'surely' – also serves here to soften the activities of choosing and correction, masking the processes of elimination and deletion they entail.

Through the central section of the text, in a series of repetitions on the relations between 'he' and 'we', Stein locates the function of the passive voice she parodies: to construct the institutional voice that frames and regulates artistic production. The truncated lines and repetitive monosyllables separate this stanza from the rest of the text:

> He said we, and we.
> We said he.
> He said we.
> We said he, and he.
> He said.
> We said.
> We said it. As we said it (72).

The distinctive form of this section also serves to link it with a stanza towards the end of the piece which contains many of the same formal features:

> He said enough.
> Enough said.
> He said enough.
> Enough said.
> Enough said.
> He said enough.
> He said enough.
> Enough said.
> He said enough (74–75).

The first iteration shows how the individual as a functionary of the regulatory process comes to stand in for it – and vice versa. The declarations of the individual ('he') become the declarations of the regulating body ('we'), meaning that the individual speaks for and as that body, appearing to abnegate any personal responsibility or subjective involvement. The individual and the context from which he speaks become interchangeable. Stein's engagement with the contexts for artistic production thus far has been one of intervention. It has been a series of attempts to rethink or reshape functions and relations as an important aspect of her experimentation and in line with much of the activity around her. 'The Fifteenth of November' reflects a response to what she clearly perceives as an institution for the regulation of artistic production that wishes to exclude her.

This is developed in the second representation, which plays with the possibilities of the idiomatic 'enough said' to show once again the violence of exclusion and to link it more explicitly to the processes of the institution. The stanza begins with the phrase 'he said enough' which indicates a functional speech act, the speaker who says enough to achieve his purpose. Communication here is a purposeful activity in which the speaker controls what is said, judging whether it is enough, saying just enough to be understood. In the context of the rejection letter this reflects the editor who politely and carefully makes the exclusion very clear without being explicit or direct – saying enough for the recipient to get the point. Read another way, with 'he said' as a reporting clause, and 'enough' as the utterance (He said, 'Enough'), it also signifies a forceful termination of the speech of another and therefore presents the rejection as an aggressive silencing. The second line, 'Enough said' develops the implications of the first, drawing out the function of the idiom in the processes of exclusion and inclusion. 'Enough said' is a coded communication which activates an engagement in an implicit agreement and shared understanding. Like a wink of complicity, it both indicates and prompts an unspoken collusion. Again, in the context of the rejection, no more needs to be said because there is already an unspoken understanding about who is included and who is excluded. 'Enough said' is a reassurance that what is presupposed still holds true, a reference to something so obvious it does not need to be said. The editor, therefore, rather than making an active choice, simply follows the established line in which the culture of the institution already colludes.

The final stanza of the piece is made up of a single repetitive sentence which diverges significantly from the rest of the text and represents, in a very simple form, an alternative to the exclusion Stein sees in these rejections.

> Not only wool and woolen silk and silken not only silk and silken wool and woolen not only wool and woolen silk and silken not only silk and silken wool and woolen not only wool and woolen silk and silken not only silk and silken not only wool and woolen not only wool and woolen not only silk and silken not only silk and silken not only wool and woolen. (75).

Woven like the textiles which form its content, this sentence uses contrasting threads to represent ideas of value judgement. The exclusiveness and sophistication of silk is juxtaposed with the everyday homespun value of wool, representing in a simple form the distinction made in elitist selection criteria. In a negation of this kind of selectivity, Stein integrates the two potentially antithetical strands by including both of them in her sentence and giving them equal weight. This is achieved in both the repetition of 'not only' and in the form of their repetition, in which they are placed in interchangeable positions in the sentence. Rather than rejecting silk in favour of wool – so rather than rejecting the kinds of choices made by the institution – and rather than setting up another paradigm in which a different set of exclusive value judgements pertain, Stein maintains the openness of a refusal to select. This is also reflected in her initial refusal to select a meaningful title, and the text in its random chance-based subject matter therefore both speaks of and embodies a challenge to that exclusivity. Rather than expressing a rejection of the literary circle for which, in this representation, Eliot serves as gatekeeper, Stein's intervention represents once again an attempt to transform or shape it, to challenge its processes of selection in order that her work is accepted. This is about more than her own exclusion: from Stein's point of view, Eliot and *The Criterion* represent, like President Wilson, the 'school men' of an academic managerial class. For Stein, Eliot's administrative discourse delineates a literary jurisdiction to be superintended and, in the process, delimits and stifles the free flow of cultural production.

Composition as Explanation in the Academy

Stein's critique of the 'academic' cast of these discourses extends, in June of the same year, into the academy itself. Indeed, it is Stein herself who heats up the debate about how the surge of avant-garde innovation might be sustained in a form that resists its installation into rigid structures of validation. In her lecture delivered at Oxford and Cambridge Universities, Stein offers her own vision of a literary history for modernity, contending that the new art should be allowed to transform the whole apparatus of cultural values, so that instead of becoming 'accepted and a classic', in a process of categorisation that makes it 'go dead', it can remain 'irritating annoying stimulating' without being 'refused'.[36] Thus, Stein imagines a movement with a history ('the history of the refused in the arts'), and she imagines a possible future for that movement in a cultural scene it has transformed and continues to transform. Stein's talk intensified a significant conversation whose participants engaged overtly with the concept and history of 'modernism' in a protracted wrangle over the figure of Gertrude Stein.

Stein enters the academic institution at the point at which modernism is beginning to gain recognition: according to the Oxford student papers, on a sweltering summer's day in June, the lecture hall was packed. Stein's lecture is a modernist event in an academic context in which modernism appears to be all the rage. The very excitement generated by Stein's visit, however, indicates that modernism is still perceived as radical. The uncertain state of relations between modernism and the academy in 1926 is signified by that frisson surrounding Stein's visit, which dramatises both the intense interest and the doubt that modernism engenders. Indeed, this uncertainty suggests that modernism is, at this point, far from representing the new establishment. This tension is also indicated on the other side, in Stein's provocative stance, which in turn, rather than indicating a radical rejection of the academy, reflects a complex blend of resistance and fascination.

Stein's ostensible resistance is evident in the lecture itself in her characterisation of the academy:

> Lord Grey remarked that when the generals before the war talked about the war they talked about it as a nineteenth century war although to be fought with twentieth century weapons. That is because war is a thing that decides how it is to be when it is to be done. It is prepared and to that degree it is like all academies it is not a thing made by being made it is a thing prepared (215).

Stein overtly critiques what she sees as the standardising establishment and academic thinking: the academy offers a way of understanding the world which will always be out of date. Her argument parallels the disconnect between the technological reality of the war and the behindhand ('prepared') thinking of the past which framed it with the way in which modern art cannot be grasped by the 'prepared', ready-made categories of the classical and the beautiful. Just as the war could not grasp its own modernity, the 'majority' refuses the authentically modern composition because it cannot recognise how it sees. In presenting a closed system of meaning, something which is 'prepared', the academy, or what, like war, 'is academic', closes down meaning and assimilates what is different into a standardised model which cannot account for the difference represented by the contemporary (215). This is the thinking through which the work of art becomes 'a classic' and no longer 'irritating annoying stimulating'. Stein sees this systematic, regulatory classification as the pre-eminent function of the academy.

Stein enters the academy to critique, and to provoke, and she is successful in doing so, as the student reviews below will show us. It is in the nature of provocation, however, that it reflects interest as well as critique, because provocation is also of course an attempt to goad or provide stimulus for action. Unlike the Stein of 1911, who thought that the American college was not the real field of battle, the Stein of 1926 engages directly with the British university in a way that reflects a desire, however nebulous, to transform it rather than either to destroy or ignore it.[37] The lecture is a performance that reflects her desire to signal and, indeed, to broadcast a position. Stein may critique academic thinking, but her performance, situated as it is in the university itself, is an engagement with it. The reception of her lecture in the universities themselves is therefore crucial in an understanding of its impact.

'Composition as Explanation' which was then entitled simply 'An Address', was delivered on 6 and 7 June 1926, and was responded to directly in the student papers and magazines for that week. At Cambridge, it was reviewed in *The Granta*, and at Oxford, *The Isis*, *The Oxford Magazine*, *The Oxford University Review*, and *The Cherwell*. The reviews are characterised markedly by admissions of a lack of understanding. In *The Granta*, this is expressed in the assertion that 'she merely states what are to her facts; and to make these facts more difficult she has couched them in her personal idiom, which is very hard to understand'; *The Isis* reviewer admits that he 'Frankly ... could scarcely understand a quarter of what she said'; *The Oxford University Review* compares the experience to that which he 'used to obtain as a child by pressing my knuckles hard against my eyes'; and *The Cherwell* states the view that, 'the matter of the discourse was unintelligible to the ears of an ordinary mortal man'.[38] The drama of this unintelligibility is a significant aspect of the lecture's performance, in that it articulates an understanding that this text offers a challenge to established ways of thinking. Rather than causing the reviewers to dismiss the lecture, it encourages them to change something in their mode of engagement to grasp what it means. There is also a strong sense in these reviews that the very unintelligibility in itself is thrilling and moving. In these ways, it seems that the lecture offers a direct challenge to the individual minds in the room.

There is also a tendency to react to the lecture by overtly claiming a position on it. The most timid is *The Granta*, which describes Stein as 'an enigmatic figure', and presents the equivocal phrase, 'What her value may be is unguessable'.[39] Others – in fact, the bulk of the reviews – respond with passionate advocacy couched in belligerent terms. *The Isis* enters the fray and takes her side against the 'sheep' who have 'come there because they thought it would be correct and fashionable', and dismisses Stein's hecklers as 'two stupid young men' whose arguments are 'prepubescent'.[40] *The Oxford Magazine* takes her side on the imaginary battleground against the same hecklers' 'ignorance and bad manners', and it also recognises and defends her against the broader public opposition to her represented by 'Messrs. Clive Bell and Wyndham Lewis' who have presented her as 'a freak and a humbug'.[41] *The Oxford University Review* defends her from 'the ranks of the highbrows', who 'were at first inclined to laugh at her' and attacks the hecklers in a prolonged rhetorical diatribe.[42] In a longer review the following week, *The Oxford Magazine* thinks that she is 'as important as she is neglected'.[43] The language of battle, struggle and conflict is deployed throughout many of the reviews: in *The Isis*, 'battled', and 'defeated', and *The Oxford University Review* describes an 'advance into the enemy's territory'. The event appears to have engendered the feeling that there is a battle over ideas, forms and meanings around which positions must be established. This is not simply to say that Stein is a controversial figure: what she awakens in the audience is the recognition that art, theory and ideology need to be struggled over, and that forms, modes of expression and meanings are being put under pressure in a way that is still new and unresolved.

The lecture also functions as an event which engenders in the audience a profound communion with the present moment. This is acknowledged in various ways in the reviews. JBF in *The Isis* admits that although he could not understand much of what she was saying,

> I could understand the motive that made her say it, and throughout her lecture I kept on thinking that, if only I could be allowed to read instead of listen, I could catch at least a little of that amazing driving force.[44]

The language here suggests an engagement with the present in its movement, both in the desire to arrest time ('if only', the repeated use of the modal 'I could', and the frustrated desire to 'catch') and in the exhilarating force of its forward movement ('the motive that made her say it'; 'I kept on thinking'; 'amazing driving force'). *The Oxford University Review* declares: 'the striving for the continuous present held us all the afternoon'. Like JBF in *The Isis*, this reviewer reflects an intense forward motion ('striving') and a simultaneous contradictory experience of being arrested in direct contact with the present ('held us'). [45]

These common aspects expressed in the student magazines – a lack of 'understanding' of Stein's lecture and yet the desire to defend her, the language of struggle and conflict, the intense feeling of the present, even the fear and anxiety it engenders – indicate the feeling that something profoundly meaningful and convincing has happened, but that this is something which cannot be named or understood in ready-made terms. This provides a significant insight into the performative possibility of Stein's text. Just as she seems to intend, the lecture begins to achieve its transformative function – it encourages its 'academic' audience to change the way they *think*. Indeed, what the reviews show is that this audience appreciate her intervention seriously as a direct challenge to normative paradigms in general and to the frameworks that regulate the validity of works of art and the legitimacy of art practices in particular.

The Challenge to Stein's Authorship

In the short period after the lecture, a series of publications, diverse yet forming a distinct network, contest both the value of Stein's work and the legitimacy of her authorship. These developing positions chart the outline of 'modernism' as a period and a movement and simultaneously delineate 'Gertrude Stein', and they come to prominence in a conversation that escalated sharply after the Hogarth Press publication of *Composition as Explanation*. The debate over her status as author and over what kind of literature her practice and her authorship might generate became the location for a set of complex and often contradictory ideological struggles, made more ambiguous because of their entanglement with a concurrent set of fears and uncertainties about the nature and form of literary culture. These fears and uncertainties in turn already refract anxieties about mass democracy: in the question of who has the right to write, the figure of the author is shadowed by the figure of the democratic subject.

The debate begins to take shape after Mina Loy's letters, a serious defence against those who 'write Gertrude Stein with their minds shut' that anticipates the argument that is brewing.[46] It gains momentum after the publication of Wyndham Lewis's highly critical representation of Stein's authorship in *The Art of Being Ruled* in October 1926 and *The New Criterion*'s anonymous and generally favourable review of *Composition as Explanation* in January 1927.[47] Around the same time, the first edition of Lewis's journal *The Enemy* prints Book 1 of what will become his monograph *Time and Western Man*, in which he unequivocally presents Stein as the element that should be excised from the contemporary scene.[48] Shortly after this, T. S. Eliot offers a damning review, in accord with Lewis, of *Composition as Explanation* in *The Nation and Athenaeum*.[49] In the same year, three monographs appear in close succession: John Rodker's *The Future of Futurism* (which Eliot reviews alongside *Composition as Explanation* in *The Nation and Athenaeum*), Lewis's *Time and Western Man* itself, and Laura Riding and Robert Graves's *A Survey of Modernist Poetry*.[50] These monographs all evoke the figure of Stein as they seek to conceptualise the period they call either '"revolution"' (Lewis), 'Futurism' (Rodker) or 'modernism' (Riding and Graves).[51] In 1928, Eliot writes an article in *The Dial* that rejects the notion of an early-twentieth-century revolutionary movement hypothesised in Lewis's monograph and posits the arrival of the genius Ezra Pound, in opposition to the invalid practice of Stein, as the only meaningful event of this time.[52] These texts represent vectors in a conversation about the recent past and long-term future of literature, and they all include Stein as a significant component of the recent literature under discussion.

The practices of the 1900s and 1910s, as we have seen, are not simply a number of theories or a series of texts; they are also a range of social practices and actions which intervene in and challenge the cultural field itself. Stein's work and the activity surrounding it are examples of those artistic and social practices. The centrality of the group, the commitment to a collective project, and the radically critical engagement with the institutions which provide a context for the production and reception of art and literature, are all significant aspects of that praxis. This conversation in the 1920s shows us how a series of new positions emerge which attempt to secure the outcome of those interventions and consolidate the challenges they offer. All these writers take a position outside the 'movement' as if standing ahead of it and looking back across a fixed temporal domain. The monographs in particular propose competing theories about the nature and significance of the artistic changes of the early twentieth century as a totality, identifying the phenomenon as a revolution in cultural and artistic practice. Adopting the apparent standpoint of literary history, these texts move toward a theoretical account of these practices as a whole – toward a unified concept.

In doing so, the consolidations also begin to see this movement as a completed event, effectively consigning it to literary history, and in that process they consider Stein as exemplary of the movement which has ended or must end. These revisions make their claims to legitimacy by reconstituting the products of a group culture, that is, of a range of collective projects to transform the cultural field, as a series of masterworks by individual creative geniuses. In these representations, the movement ended in or around 1927, leaving a series of isolated figures unbound either to each other or to any collective ideas about culture, art, the role of the artist or the nature of the engagement with the artwork. And this sets the terms upon which the figure of Gertrude Stein can be isolated as the example of the literary history which must be finished. Indeed, in many ways, the 'Stein' they debate is constituted in these critical terminations: these representations wrangle over a Stein who is a cypher for the illegitimate, the liminal and the heretical. In short, Stein becomes modernism's abject.

The Death of Modernism

The critical enterprise of cultural intervention turns in this period to revisions of recent literary history which attempt to identify and end the story of a movement and look back at it as a phenomenon in the past. In consolidating those changes the writers feel have been wrought by the practices of the early twentieth century, they mark the period off, constructing a finished narrative and, in doing so, pronouncing the death of modernism. The end of this period is achieved in the overt discrediting or historicising of the work of the group and in a turn to the figure of the individual author genius, which displaces or replaces the collective work that comprised the new works of art and the concomitant innovations on the field of production. This dialectical move that is at once identification and elimination is perhaps most marked and overt in the *Survey of Modernist Poetry*. For most of the book, Riding and Graves argue for a 'modernism' that has the conceptual irrelevance of the author as its basis, but in the final chapter they use the figure of Stein to radically review and ultimately renounce this position entirely:

> It is now possible to reach a position where the modernist movement itself can be looked at with historical (as opposed to contemporary) sympathy as a stage in poetry that is to pass in turn, or may have already passed . . . As nothing can remain contemporary for very long, we were obliged to assume this position if our criticism was to stand before rather than behind its subject (129).

The statement 'nothing can remain contemporary for very long' parodies the modernist emphasis on the new and presents it as a dead end. In suggesting that it is over because it is no longer contemporary, Riding and Graves turn modernism against itself. The categorisation of the contemporary, which they argue is the founding principle of modernism, immediately sends it into the past. Their contention is that the poetry it demands is far too concerned with the question of what poetry is or should be at the moment it was written. The poem, therefore, can only ever be the expression of a theory about what 'the *art* of poetry' is at that instant. As they say later in the chapter 'creation and critical judgement being made one act, a work has no future history with readers; it is ended when it is ended' (131–132). Thus, the modernist poem is about itself, doing the work of criticism because its function is to express its own value and meaning in its contemporary moment in the history of poetry. At this late point in the monograph, they question the reliance of modernist poetry on the 'objective' measures of the historical value of the poem which they have supported through most of the text. The production and reception of modernist poetry, they argue, are governed by an autogenic theoretical taxonomy which reduces the poem to the expression of its 'forced relation' to the 'historical period to which it accidentally belonged' (132). For Riding and Graves, the modernism predicated upon a premise of autonomy and the concomitant irrelevance of the writer's 'personality' has, by 1927, become impossible to sustain.

It is at this point that Stein is identified as the exemplar of these modernist theories in practice:

> Gertrude Stein is perhaps the only artisan of language who has succeeded in practising scientific barbarism literally. Her words are primitive in the sense that they are bare, immobile, mathematically placed, abstract: so

primitive indeed that the theorists of the new barbarism have repudiated her work as a romantic vulgar barbarism, expressing the personal crudeness of a mechanical age rather than a refined historical effort to restore a lost absolute to a community of co-ordinated poets (136).

Stein's work is the ultimate example of the intensely context-determined nature of modernist meaning-making – the meaning the poem derives from its position on the cultural scene, its relations to other cultural artefacts, and its expression of those relations – that Riding and Graves now seek to resist. Misread even by modernists, they argue, Stein presents modernism with a vision of itself from which it recoils in horror. Her method is the ultimate expression of modernism because it only means anything in the context of the modernist project. As they see it, this is the task of defining absolutely the contemporary moment as the set of historical relations, 'mathematically placed', which determine the act of writing in the present. The modernist work becomes a document which records that set of historical relations, and Stein's work is the purest example of that recording process. As Jean-Michel Rabaté puts it:

> Graves and Riding, apparently intent on presenting modernism in its broadest sense, in fact attempt to bury it, to close off modernism as an active movement. In order to achieve this cunning sleight of hand, they have to identify the termination of modernism with what they see as its inception – namely, with the works of Gertrude Stein.[53]

The way Riding and Graves bind Stein to the death of modernism elaborates their dialectic by exemplifying how she can be figured at once as everything that modernism achieved and everything which means it has failed – a dialectic which imagines a modernism whose function is to resolve itself out of existence, leaving an 'embarrassed pause after an arduous and erudite stock-taking' (132). Stein's practice works out the end for modernism not because it ushers in an undesirable future for poetry, but because it has achieved the function of purifying poetry in order that it can be reactivated or re-originated. Graves and Riding's descriptions of Stein's work – 'she used language automatically to record pure ultimate obviousness' that she has succeeded in 'purging it completely of its false experiences' and that 'these words have no history' – contend that Stein takes modernism to its logical conclusion by emptying language of meaning (139). For them, Stein's work performs an absolute expression of modernism which clears history away by achieving such an excessive emphasis on time that it becomes a meaningless record of pure duration. And, particularly for Riding, who develops this theory further in her 1928 book *Contemporaries and Snobs*, poetry must begin again in the hands of the individual as opposed to the context of modernism, which for her is the context of collective meaning generated around abstract theoretical accounts of the function of art in modernity.[54] Thus, for Riding, Stein has opened literature up to full participation in the new work of meaning-making that can begin without reference to a regulatory or normative literary tradition. The work of literature's democratisation has been done, and Stein stands as its exemplar and its finalisation.

Wyndham Lewis's *Time and Western Man* reveals a similar preoccupation with the figure of the individual poet stifled by a literary system. Once again, the oppressiveness of the movement he delineates is exemplified by Stein's practice. Lewis ascribes a revolutionary quality to early-twentieth-century art, which he defines as 'a form of artistic expression that has attempted something definitely new; something that could not have come into existence in any age but this one'. Lewis, rather than attributing modernism's radical transformation of art, literature and cultural production to its group culture, as Riding and Graves do, however, separates the real innovations of the movement from the activity of the group and assigns the authentic revolutionary praxis to the individual. For Lewis, 'Art of [the revolutionary] type is confined to a very small number of workers', and he wishes 'to mark this off distinctly from the much greater mass of work which . . . is in no way revolutionary'. Lewis's description of the contemporary art scene provides an image of the proliferation of groups and the fluorescence of minority cultures: 'The first thing that would be noticed by anyone entering the art world for the first time would be that it was discriminated into "movements" rather than into individuals' (24). Although Lewis wishes to have a modernism whose real value arises from the work of a few talented originals, rather than denying the group character of the revolution, he, like Riding, designates this character explicitly as its original defining feature. In Lewis's argument, the collective form must come to an end because

> The effect of that form of organisation, to start with, is, inevitably, to advertise the inferior artist at the expense of the better . . . Or else 'the group' is more simply an organisation of nothing but inferior artists directed, sometimes by means of propaganda, against the *idea* of individual talent altogether (25).

This formulation reflects the desire for a new consensus around the figure of the individual set in opposition to group practice.

In order to reconfigure the genuine revolution as the work of a few individuals, in Lewis's narrative the group must be reconfigured as the sect, and for these purposes he isolates Stein as exemplary of the power of this undesirable form, calling her 'one of the most eminent writers of . . . our time-society' (47). Indeed, he uses her to denounce the idea of cultural influence and exchange as such, implying that her status as exemplar in itself reflects the slavish lack of originality in the scene. This negative portrayal of artistic exchange is particularly marked in his representation of parallels between her work and that of Joyce. Describing her practice as so 'contagious' that 'Mr Joyce even has caught it' (50), he attributes what he calls Joyce's 'vices of style' to 'his unorganized susceptibility to influences' (73), in particular the influence of Stein's writing. Lewis's analysis of these 'vices' compares the final paragraph of *Ulysses* to an excerpt from Stein's 'Saints in Seven' in order to 'show a good material for a predatory time-philosophy bearing down upon it and claiming his pen as its natural servant' (108). In a reversal of the argument in Wilson's 1923 review, the comparison of Stein and Joyce provides Lewis with evidence that her influence has stifled and corrupted Joyce's work, and this serves to reveal the fate of genius under the sway of the group. The metaphor of predator and prey presents the genius as the victim of collective ideas. In both of these monographs, *A Survey of Modernist Poetry* and *Time and Western Man*, 'modernism' or the 'revolutionary' phase is indeed defined as a movement predicated on group activity and mutual influence, but only in order to underscore a new endorsement of authorship defined by personal originality and individual talent. The person of Stein is constructed as the avatar for the illegitimate, invalid aspects of the movement, namely its esoteric quality and its series of experimental collective cultural interventions. Rolled up, as it were, into the body of Stein, the characteristics that trouble the desire for legitimacy are displaced onto the aberrant person of Stein.

The Primitive Body of Stein

The indication that Stein is primitive or barbaric forms the basic material from which many of the other abject configurations emerge. It begins in earnest with Lewis, who uses the trope in the section of *Time and Western Man* first printed in *The Enemy*: Stein is 'working in the strictest conformity with all the other "time"-doctrinaires, who have gathered in such disciplined numbers, so fanatically disciplined, as though to the beating of a ritualistic drum' (49). This is picked up in Rodker's characterisation in *The Future of Futurism* of her work as an extreme form of the 'primitive and savage' force of Futurism. Riding and Graves, in defence of Stein, develop a notion of the 'barbaric' into a conceptualisation of the modernism Stein exemplifies. The trope of the primitive is developed through the conversation about Stein and it comes to have a number of resonances all of which function to remove her from the cultural scene of 1927: it rewrites her work as cult, not culture, displaces it from its contemporary context as pre- or post-historic, presents her as a barbaric totem rather than a writer, and, perhaps most potently, figures her as a primordial form of the human rather than as a fully achieved self.

The concepts of primitivism and barbarism are also strongly associated with popular culture, and this is one of the key anxieties expressed about the direction of art in this conversation. Stein and the practices she exemplifies are represented as being too close to mass culture, and this fear, and its connection with the trope of the primitive, are exemplified in Lewis's description of her work as 'the monstrous, desperate, soggy *lengths* of primitive mass-life' (82). For Lewis, the identification of Stein with popular culture is very explicit: 'there is all the craft of the Charlie Chaplin appeal, all those little dissimulated threads run cunningly to the great big silly heart of the innocent public, in the mannerism of Miss Stein and Miss Loos' (57).[55] Lewis provides the comparison in order to imply the fraudulence of Stein's art, emphasised in his references to 'craft', to dissimulation, to cunning and Stein's 'mannerism'. Lewis alludes to *Three Lives* as 'the simplicity, the illiterateness, of the mass-average of the Melancthas and Annas' and describes Stein's work as 'undoubtedly intended as an epic contribution to the present mass-democracy'. The cheap tawdriness of consumerism is also ascribed to Stein's work, described as 'jumbled, cheap, slangy and thick to suit' (60).

The conception that Stein – and therefore the position she exemplifies – is bound up with mass culture is revealed more subtly and perhaps less consciously in *A Survey of Modernist Poetry*. Stein's work is 'divinely inspired in ordinariness', 'so grossly, so humanly, so all-inclusively ordinary', and an example of 'mass-automatism' (139). Although not explicitly referencing it, the juxtaposition of the ordinary and the mass and the notion of inclusiveness allude to popular culture's majority appeal and the global reach of its representations of the human condition. For Riding and Graves, Stein's pure expression of modernism as ordinary, inclusive and human is tinged, despite their ostensibly supportive stance towards her work, with disgust and fear. The adverb 'grossly' intimates this disgust, but it is also conveyed in the repetition of phrases such as 'mass humanity', 'mass-ordinariness', and 'mass-automatism', which they use to define the 'barbaric absolute' that modernism, in their conception, appears to seek. The accumulation of these references has the effect of reinforcing the horror of the mass tide overwhelming the 'talent of the artist to see things "as no one else sees them"' (138). There are parallels with Lewis's portrayal of the modernism embodied in Stein's work as too close to modernity: for Riding and Graves, too, the problem with modernism is that it no longer enables the artist to be defined by difference from the time in which s/he stands, the 'creative originality which is supposed to reveal the eccentricity latent in obviousness to this mass humanity equipped only to see the obvious' (138). Thus, modernism is undifferentiated from the unprocessed modernity which makes up the mass culture they want it to stand beyond.

These 1927 examples suggest that the practice and the position embodied for them in Stein is problematic because it cannot be differentiated from mass culture. Alongside the apprehension that the literature of the early twentieth century is too close to the modernity of mass culture runs another related current in these critiques: the association of Stein's forms with racial otherness. The experience of racial difference in modernity for these writers is fused with the exotic and the 'savage' and becomes a significant trope in the othering of Stein. Perhaps the strangest example of this is Lewis's characterisation, 'Gertrude Stein's prose-song is a cold, black, suet-pudding', which imbues the reassuring food of an Empire childhood with a sinister difference imparted by blackness (59). Rodker also figures Stein in these terms, in his definition of her writings as 'mantrams' and by suggesting that her repetitions have a 'hypnotic value' (38). Significantly, the mutual influence of these currents of conceptualisation are overtly displayed in Rodker's quotation from Lewis's opinions on Stein. Rodker's citation of Lewis's view that Stein 'lyricises her utterances on the same principle as that of Hebrew poetry', shows how far the depiction of Stein as racially other is the product of this kind of conversation (35, n.1).

The otherness connoted in these references is also manifested in images of physical difference. References to the sick, grotesque or ill-formed body proliferate in particular in Lewis's account. Stein is imagined as an obese or disabled child 'bloated, acromegalic, squinting and spectacled' (47), suggesting an incompleteness, a sick self only marginally human. Her work is often envisaged as an obese body, as 'slab after slab of this heavy, insensitive, common prose-song churns and lumbers by' (59) which is 'all fat, without nerve', implying ill-health and weakness. She is also associated with 'contemporary inverted-sex fashions' (52), again portrayed as mental and physical sickness. Riding also figures Stein as vast and formless in her 'gross automatism' and 'large-scale process'.[56] Stein is presented as an unformed, indeterminate, unbounded subject which resists the definition required of the isolated genius. Stein is suspect because she cannot be identified – unlike the genius, isolated both from modernity and in literary history.

All the texts use Stein as the central trope in their identification of the culture of the group, movement or artistic revolution as threats to individual greatness. These revisions achieve a number of things. They mean that these writers can dismiss the movements they identify as characterised by slavish faddishness. This in turn means they can deny the validity of mutual meaning-making and so assert the necessity for judgements of value predicated on the author's individuality. Central to all the figurings of Stein as abject, therefore, is the concept of authorial identity.

Eliot in the Periodicals

These histories and their attendant positioning of Stein embody a definition of and a conversation about a movement, a wrangling over its genealogy and its legacy, which treats it as a finished thing. This conversation was also being had, alongside and in direct response to the 1927 monographs, in the magazines which still formed an important part of the immediate cultural production of that 'movement'. These, too, speaking from the still-living body of the movement presented in the guides as a corpse, reveal an anxiety over the future of literature bound into their representations of Stein.

By 1927, however, it appears that Eliot in particular feels compelled to distance the art he values as far from Stein as possible. In his (now notorious) review, published in *The Nation and Athenaeum* in January 1927, Stein and the practices she exemplifies are represented as being too close to the modernity of mass culture, evident in his wondering 'whether the omens are not with Miss Stein and the author of "I'm Gona Charleston Back to Charleston" rather than with Mr Cummings or Mr D.H. Lawrence' (595). Eliot's binary aligns Stein with popular culture and distinguishes her from other poets who, in this formulation, provide a civilised alternative to mass culture rather than being entangled with it. Eliot's condemnation of Stein's authorship as an outcrop of a debased mass culture that will, he argues, 'make trouble for us' is of a piece with his critiques of democracy in *The Criterion* (595).

Eliot's essay 'The Idea of a Literary Review', which launched its iteration as *The New Criterion* in 1926, offers a series of authors as exemplary of what he describes as the 'modern tendency . . . which we may call classicism' (quoted in Harding, 353). As Jason Harding remarks, Eliot's list presents 'A disparate set of texts' in which 'the "modern tendency" they most obviously supported was a marked distaste for liberal democracy'.[57] The consistency of this view is clear in Eliot's earlier 'Commentary' in the April 1924 edition of *The Criterion*, in which he argues that 'Democracy appears whenever the governors of the people lose the conviction of their right to govern'.[58] The essay offers a critique of 'the modern democracy of culture', characterised as 'that meanness of spirit, that egotism of motive, that incapacity for surrender or allegiance to something outside oneself, which is a frequent symptom of the soul of man under democracy' exemplified in the 'aversion for the work of art' and a 'preference for the derivative, the marginal' (235). What Eliot's pronouncements here show is the relationship he assumes between the extensions in democratic rights and the development of a degenerate mass culture without standards. In associating Stein's work with popular music, Eliot aligns her with the burgeoning mass culture that Lewis also condemns. Stein, of course, also sees her work on those terms, but for her the expansion of mass cultural participation in is a form of democratisation separate from representative democracy, a scene that has a life of its own outside formal democratic processes, that can include her own innovations and which she welcomes and courts.

As suffrage extends further in Britain, Eliot's critique deepens. The Representation of the People (Equal Franchise) Act, which widened suffrage to include all women over 21, was introduced in March 1928 and given royal assent that July, and Eliot's essay 'The Literature of Fascism', published in the December 1928 *Criterion* clearly expresses his dismay. Decrying this as a moment at which 'democratic government has been watered down to nothing' he warns of the dangers of a situation in which 'suffrage is considered as a right instead of as a privilege and a duty and a responsibility'.[59] Here Eliot makes an argument against rights and for privilege, arguing that a broad franchise amounts to a 'pretended democracy' in which, rather than being presided over by a visible ruling class, the population will inevitably be controlled by an 'invisible oligarchy' (287). He makes it clear, therefore, that it is the mass democracy that confers rights along with citizenship, rather than democracy as such, that he objects to. For Eliot 'A real democracy is always a restricted democracy, and can only flourish with some limitation by hereditary rights and responsibilities' (288). The insistence on limitation by heredity reflects Eliot's faith in the British class system but it also indicates a belief in the genetic inheritance of superior qualities espoused in an article on Stein and Pound earlier in the same year.

Eliot's 1928 article in *The Dial* reflects a desire to draw a line under the debate and end the discussion of modernism by ending the discussion of Stein. He rejects the notion of a revolutionary movement, sets up the individual in its place, and explicitly selects Ezra Pound as the valid exemplar in contrast to Stein, suggesting that 'We can now see that there was no movement, no revolution, and there is no formula. The only revolution was that Ezra Pound was born with a fine ear for verse'.[60] Eliot's isolation of Pound and Stein enables him simultaneously to dissolve the category of the 'revolutionary' period that Lewis constructs and to isolate Stein as an individual pursuing her own esoteric aims. Thus, in erasing the scene within which this writing made its meaning, Eliot brings the single authors forward into sharp relief. In order to dismiss Stein as he dismisses the revolution, Eliot says of Lewis's book 'Mr Lewis is a little hasty, and might lead the inexperienced reader to believe that Pound's rhythms spring from the same source as those of Miss Stein. And this is wholly untrue: they have nothing in common' (6). In a development of the previous representation of Stein's 'rhythms' as springing from the same source as jazz, Pound is presented as a fount of poetic genius founded on a genetic trait that he has been 'born with', in direct contrast to Stein. The gesture of deliberately distinguishing Stein from Pound is clearly designed to draw a line between the acceptable and the unacceptable that places Stein beyond the pale. In one movement, this representation grounds authorship in biology, in the originary and unique, as an ontological property rather than a discourse mode or cultural designation, refuses Stein's place in a creative community, and denies not just the validity but the existence of communal meaning-making. It is also significant that this distinction is presented as a definitive one, yet one which can only be understood by the expert. The view that the 'inexperienced reader' would be excused for drawing the conclusion, prompted by Lewis's argument, that Stein and Pound share an aesthetic suggests that, to the untrained eye, they have qualities in common.[61]

Eliot's concern for the reader is also highly significant because it grants him the position of the expert whose special knowledge confers the authority to determine not just the value of a writer's work, but the definition of what a writer is. To this end, the question of whether or not Pound's and Stein's works share overt characteristics, how far their work has value, is not Eliot's main concern. Rather, he is anxious to point out that they do not 'spring from the same source'. The most important distinction for Eliot is that of origin, and his metaphor here proposes an ontological difference, not between Pound's and Stein's work, which may, to the inexperienced reader, seem to have something in common, but between the very bases of their practice. This is not therefore so much a defence of Pound's fine ear for verse or his devotion to poetry, as an argument that what Pound writes, and what he has devoted himself to, is 'the art of verse', and that what Stein is doing is something other than that (4). For Eliot, Stein is not a writer. It is this use of Stein as a trope for what writing either is not, should not be or can no longer be that is the characteristic activity of all these disavowals of the revolutionary experimental practices of the previous decades. Indeed, the isolation of individual figures means that the expert can determine, not just which writing has value and which writing does not, but who is an author and who is not.

All the texts use Stein as the central trope in their identification of the culture of the group, movement or artistic revolution as threats to individual greatness. These revisions achieve a number of things. They mean that these writers can dismiss the movements they identify as characterised by slavish faddishness. This in turn means they can deny the validity of mutual meaning-making and so assert the necessity for judgements of value predicated on the author's individuality. The critiques of Stein coalesce around the question of the author's sincerity, connected to the resurgence in all these commentaries of the figure of the coherent genius. On Eliot's terms, this is the, 'isolated' 'devoted', figure of the hermetic artist; for Lewis it is 'the individual talent', stifled by group identity; and for Riding, the emphasis is on the 'personal authority' of the 'Genius' excessively compromised by the professionalisation of poetry. The question of Stein's sincerity, therefore, is the question of authorship that these writers struggle with in their reframings, and this is expressed in the intimations that she is not a full, coherent or stable 'person'.

The desire to reinstate or insist upon the unity of the creative genius comes out of an anxiety about the relative status of the artist, the work and its audience, which was in itself created by the early problematizing of existing paradigms. This resurgence represents an urge to stabilise these relations in order to re-establish a firm set of criteria with which to judge the value and meaning of the work. Significantly, then, these constructions of Stein's difference serve to map a landscape of anxieties about this history. The complex of tropes around Stein is generated in anxieties over the incomplete, split or contradictory self they use her to embody: Stein is a locus for the anxieties about the loss of the coherent author figure. In order to isolate the author from the context into which many of these writers feel it has dissolved, Stein becomes the icon for what the author is not or should not be. The identification of Stein as a cypher for group culture of modernism is claimed as the ground upon which she can be dismissed. This reinforces once again the emphasis on the value of the authenticity of the individual genius set up in opposition to the cultural interchange figured the context in which the fraudulent artist can flourish.

The Modernist Author Figure

The attempts to fix historical parameters and to isolate individual practitioners and works, I would argue, has much to do with the urge to construct a legitimate movement which must define itself against the illegitimate forms which have been mocked, trivialised or demonised in the public sphere. The fact that the 1920s' reframings of the early period use the same figures to dismiss Stein reveals a significant point about the ways in which the narratives attempt to construct a more acceptable form. The early mockeries in the popular press attempt to delegitimise the new art by using these tropes. The portrayals of Stein in the 1920s, in appropriating these same tropes in their disparagement of her, in one clean stroke distance them from that condemnation and the practices which drew it. Stein's dismissal in these 1920s' texts is, in essence, a necessary action in order to construct a legitimate form against which such accusations cannot be brought. Because they are the same as the mockeries and outrage of the popular reception of the 1910s, these claims against Stein's legitimacy perform the same kind of activity: just as the early parodies, as Leonard Diepeveen argues in the introduction to his recent anthology *Mock Modernism*, 'fenced things off by precluding serious, nuanced discussion', so the memoirs fence Stein off from the serious contemplation of literary history.[62]

Foucault, writing in 1969 from the other side of literary history's reconstruction of the author, captures in his definition the delimiting function this figure provides in the late 1920s' revisions of modernism:

> the author is not an indefinite source of significations that fill a work; the author does not precede the works; he is a certain functional principle by which, in our culture, one limits, excludes, and chooses; in short, by which one impedes the free circulation, the free manipulation, the free composition, decomposition, and recomposition of fiction.[63]

The 'free circulation', manipulation, composition and so on, which Foucault claims the author function impedes, could well be a description of the network movement which is displaced by the late 1920s' narratives by the author figure. The early-twentieth-century activities had complicated the concept of the author because its works were, overtly, not 'made' in isolation. Indeed, these practices challenged the paradigm that takes authorship for granted. Stein is the locus of this fear about the uncertainty of authorship in the 1920s, and this uncertainty reflects the fear at the heart of these reconfigurations, in which 'the author is therefore the ideological figure by which one marks the manner in which we fear the proliferation of meaning'.

The banishment of Stein from the future is a way of marking a difference between the fraudulent and the authentic poet and between the empty persona and the genius author, but it is also a way of dismissing the multiple group culture in order to establish a canon of legitimised authors producing individual masterworks.

In these revisions, modernism seeks a future for itself by reasserting the author function. The individual works, however, have thus far only made sense in relation to the context of other works and the multiple cultural fields generated by the provisional institutions – magazines, groups, international networks, its own bodies of theory and scholarship, anthologies, collections – it throws up. Its texts have produced meaning through a process of reciprocity which means that the attempt to identify an author function that stabilises the identity of the author and conceives the work as a sincere expression of the individual is a highly contradictory move. The urge for the author to be a whole discrete thing is a mask to put over the riven and always incomplete subject, itself represented in early-twentieth-century works and in the network meanings of the cultural production of the period. Stein becomes the figure of the split, fragmented, unbounded subject in order that this can be excised and replaced with the whole self of the authorial genius.

Notes

1. See Dydo, *Gertrude Stein*, 94, n.21.
2. See Leick, 24.
3. For example, see Aaron Jaffe, *Modernism and the Culture of Celebrity* (Cambridge: Cambridge University Press, 2005). Crowninshield, an important supporter of the Armory Show, promoted modernist writing throughout his editorship of *Vanity Fair*. See Hammill and Leick (n.5 below).
4. Paul K. Arthors, 'Cheating the Nature: A Literary Challenge to Opal Whiteley, Patience Worth and Gertrude Stein', *Vanity Fair*, October 1920, 11. All references are from this page. These are references to the childhood diary of child prodigy and nature writer Opal Whiteley and the novels of Patience Worth, a seventeenth-century author whom, it was claimed, was channelled in spiritualist sessions through the pen of Pearl Curran. Both of these contemporary publications were received as literary fakes.
5. 'Their circulations, advertising revenues, content, and readership all located them in a middle space between the author-centred production model of the avant-garde magazines and the market-driven arena of the daily papers and mass-circulation weeklies'. See Faye Hammill and Karen Leick, 'Modernism and the Quality Magazines', in *The Oxford Critical and Cultural History of Modernist Magazines: Volume II: North America 1894–1960*, ed. Peter Brooker and Andrew Thacker (Oxford: Oxford University Press, 2012), 176–196 (176).
6. See my discussion below.
7. These included the 1920 Bodley Head reprint of *Three Lives*, the Four Seas publication of *Geography and Plays*, and two publications of abridged versions

of *The Making of Americans* by Maurice Darantiere and Albert and Charles Boni respectively.
8. Stein funded the printing costs herself. See Donald Gallup, *The Flowers of Friendship: Letters Written to Gertrude Stein* (New York: Octagon Books, 1979), 143.
9. *Little Review*, Vol. 8, No. 2 (Spring 1922), 29–32 and 5–6; *Chicago Tribune* (Paris Edition), 5 March 1923, 2. See Edward M. Burns, 'Gertrude Stein as a Book Reviewer', *Turtle Point Press Magazine* (Fall 2014), http://www.turtlepointpress.com/traveltainted/gertrude-stein-book-reviewer for an overview of Stein's work as a reviewer.
10. 'Recent Publications' column of the Paris edition of the *Chicago Tribune* on 27 November 1923, 4.
11. See Burns, 'Gertrude Stein as a Book Reviewer'.
12. Alfred Kreymborg, *Troubadour: An American Autobiography* (New York: Sagamore Press, [1925] 1957), 169, 292.
13. Gertrude Stein, 'Troubadour, an Autobiography', *Ex Libris*, Vol. 2, No. 9 (June 1925), 278. The American Library in Paris was founded in 1920, born out of the Library War Service started by the American Library Association in 1917 to provide books for American troops. The Library's journal began publication in 1923. Stein joined the American Library in 1922. See Susan Otis Thompson, 'The American Library in Paris: An International Development in the American Library Movement', *The Library Quarterly: Information, Community, Policy*, Vol. 34, No. 2 (April 1964), 179–190, and https://americanlibraryinparis.org/history.
14. John Lane published a reprint of *Three Lives* in 1920.
15. Ulla Dydo, *A Stein Reader* (Evanston, IL: Northwestern University Press, 1993), 376.
16. Sherwood Anderson, 'The Work of Gertrude Stein', in Gertrude Stein, *Geography and Plays* (Boston, MA: Four Seas Company, 1922), 6, 5.
17. Lewis, *Modernism, Nationalism, and the Novel*, 7.
18. Sherwood Anderson, 'Four American Impressions: Gertrude Stein, Paul Rosenfeld, Ring Lardner, Sinclair Lewis', *The New Republic*, Vol. 32, No. 410 (11 October 1922), 171–173 (171). Subsequent references are to this page.
19. Michael McGerr, *A Fierce Discontent: The Rise and Fall of the Progressive Movement in America* (New York: Free Press, 2003), 244.
20. The urgency of identifications with the national, increasingly significant in the nineteenth century, becomes even more acute after the displacements of the First World War: 'The stateless people were as convinced as the minorities that loss of national rights was identical with loss of human rights, that the former inevitably entailed the latter. The more they were excluded from right in any form, the more they tended to look for a reintegration into a national, into their own national community'. Hannah Arendt, *The Origins of Totalitarianism* (New York: Meridian, 1962), 292.
21. Emeline Jouve, '"Geography and Plays": Spaces in Gertrude Stein's Early Plays (1913–1919)', *South Atlantic Review*, Vol. 76, No. 4 (Fall 2011), 101–116 (109).
22. See Wineapple on Stein's interests at Johns Hopkins at the turn of the century:

'she was drawn to the overlapping fields of neurology and psychology and evidently planned to continue her experimental work in that direction' (*Sister Brother*, 126). Stein's psychology experiments attended to the activities of the brain under particular conditions. See Gertrude Stein, and Leon Solomons, 'Normal Motor Automatism', *Harvard Psychological Review*, Vol. 3, No. 5 (September 1896), 495–512.

23. Gertrude Stein, 'The Psychology of Nations, or What Are You Looking At', *Geography and Plays* (Boston, MA: Four Seas Company, 1922), 416–419 (416).
24. 'Point VIII: All French territory should be freed and the invaded portions restored, and the wrong done to France by Prussia in 1871 in the matter of Alsace-Lorraine, which has unsettled the peace of the world for nearly fifty years, should be righted in order that peace may once more be made secure in the interest of all'. Woodrow Wilson, *Address of the President of the United States Delivered at a Joint Session of the Two Houses of Congress, January 8, 1918*. (Washington, DC: U.S. Government Printing Office, 1918).
25. Although the slogan initially referred to the conflict with Mexico, voters assumed it referred to the war in Europe. See John Milton Cooper, *Woodrow Wilson: A Biography* (New York: Random House, 2009), 322.
26. See Chapter 4 below for a full discussion of this text.
27. President Woodrow Wilson, *Joint Session of Congress to Seek a Declaration of War against Germany on April 2, 1917*. Sixty-Fifth Congress, 1 Session, Senate Document No. 5.
28. Quoted in Adam Tooze, *The Deluge: The Great War and the Remaking of Global Order 1916–1931* (London: Penguin Books, 2014), 348. Tooze points out that Wilson was not as internationalist as this suggests, but that Harding's propaganda to that effect was very successful.
29. Lyndsey Stonebridge, 'Refugee Style: Hannah Arendt and the Perplexities of Rights', *Textual Practice*, Vol. 25, No. 1 (2011), 71–85 (71).
30. Edmund Wilson, 'A Guide to Gertrude Stein: The Evolution of a Master of Fiction into a Painter of Cubist Still-Life in Prose', *Vanity Fair* (September 1923), 60, 80 (cont.) (60).
31. T. S. Eliot, 'Book Reviews: *Ulysses*, Order, and Myth', *The Dial*, Vol. 75, No. 5 (November 1923), 480–484 (480); Edmund Wilson, '*Ulysses*', *The New Republic*, 5 July 1922. Note that, taken as a whole, Wilson's review was not as gushing as this statement suggests.
32. Gertrude Stein, 'Two Women', in *Contact Collection of Contemporary Writers*, ed. Robert McAlmon (Paris: Contact Editions, 1925), 303–325; Stein, 'Mildred's Thoughts', in *American Caravan: A Yearbook of American Literature*, ed. Alfred Kreymborg, Lewis Mumford and Paul Rosenfeld (New York: Macaulay Company, 1927), 653–675. *American Caravan* was widely read in America because of its selection by the Literary Guild book club. See Leick, 114. Hemingway also facilitated the publication of 'Ireland' in the Berlin journal *Der Querschnitt* (March 1925). See Erika Esau, 'The Magazine of Enduring Value: *Der Querschnitt* (1921–1936) and the World of Illustrated Magazines', in Brooker, Peter, et al., eds., *The Oxford Critical and Cultural History of Modernist Magazines*, Vol. III, 868–887.

33. This American press might be thought of as somewhere between the small press and the larger publishing houses. Through the late 1920s it published around thirty titles, an esoteric range including Blaise Cendrars's *The African Saga*, crime and mystery novels (Dorothy L Sayers, Maurice Dekobra), works on art and architecture (Le Courbusier, Paul T. Frankl) and other titles representing a range of interests, such as *The Diary of a Communist Undergraduate* by Nikolai Ognev. Many of the publications are translations from European writers into English for the American market. Sources: https://books.bibliopolis.com; https://open library.org/publishers/Payson_&_Clarke.
34. Dydo, *Gertrude Stein*, 106–107.
35. Gertrude Stein, 'The Fifteenth of November', in *The New Criterion*, Vol. 4, No. 1 (January 1926), 71–75 (71).
36. Gertrude Stein, 'Composition as Explanation', in *Gertrude Stein: Selections*, ed. Joan Retallack (Berkeley: University of California Press, 2008), 215–225 (217).
37. See Stein's notebook entry, 'Eastern colleges too dam anxious to be safe. They needn't be so afraid it ain't so easy to be hurt as they seem to think least at least not by getting hit hard on the head. They needn't be so scared of any of us got any chance of real stuff in us just because we are made different ... They needn't be so afraid of their damn culture, it'd take more than a man like me to hurt it', quoted in Ulla Dydo, *A Stein Reader*, (Evanston, Ill.: Northwestern University Press, 1993), 1.
38. CUMC, 'She Cam, She Saw, She Conquered', *The Granta May Week Double Number*, 12 June 1926, 440; JBF, 'Miss Gertrude Stein', *The Isis*, 9 June 1926, 8; 'It Confuses, It Shows . . . It Likes It as It Seems', *The Oxford University Review*, 10 June 1926, 332; 'Miss Stein', *The Cherwell*, 12 June 1926, 248.
39. *Granta*, 440.
40. *Isis*, 8.
41. *Oxford Magazine*, 564.
42. *Oxford University Review*, 332.
43. Gilbert Armitage, 'A Word on Gertrude Stein', *The Oxford Magazine*, 17 June 1926, 584.
44. *Isis*, 8.
45. *Oxford Magazine*, 10 June 1926, 564; *Oxford University Review*, 332.
46. Mina Loy, 'Gertrude Stein', *The Transatlantic Review*, Vol. 2, No. 4 (October 1924), 427–430 (427).
47. Anonymous, '*Composition as Explanation* by Gertrude Stein' *The New Criterion*, Vol. 5, No. 1 (January 1927), 162.
48. Wyndham Lewis, 'The Revolutionary Simpleton', in *The Enemy*, Vol. 1 (January 1927); reprint (London: Frank Cass and Company Limited 1968), 25–192.
49. Eliot, 1927, Reviews section, 595. This particular review has been endlessly quoted in discussions of Stein's relations with Eliot and 'establishment' modernism, in particular by the twentieth- and twenty-first-century arguments I am dealing with: see Quartermain, 42; Perloff, 45; Spahr, 18.
50. John Rodker, *The Future of Futurism* (London: Kegan Paul, Trench, Trubner & Co., 1926). All references are to this edition. Wyndham Lewis, *Time and Western Man* (London: Chatto and Windus, 1927): reprinted as *Time and Western Man*,

ed. Paul Edwards (Santa Rosa, CA: Black Sparrow Press, 1993). All references are to this reprint. Laura Riding and Robert Graves, *A Survey of Modernist Poetry* (London: Heinemann, 1927): reprinted in *A Survey of Modernist Poetry and a Pamphlet Against Anthologies*, ed. Charles Mundye and Patrick McGuinness (Manchester: Carcanet, 2002). All references are to this reprint.

51. These terms are used throughout the texts. See, for example, Lewis, 60; Rodker, 2; Riding and Graves, 75.
52. T. S. Eliot, 'Isolated Superiority', in *The Dial*, Vol. 84, No. 1 (January 1928), 4–7.
53. Jean-Michel Rabaté, *The Ghosts of Modernity* (Gainesville: Florida University Press, 1996), 189–190.
54. Laura Riding, *Contemporaries and Snobs* (Garden City, NY: Doubleday Doran & Company, 1928).
55. Charlie Chaplin's 1925 *The Gold Rush* is the fifth-highest-grossing silent film in cinema history and Anita Loos's 1926 *Gentlemen Prefer Blondes* was a bestseller.
56. Riding, *Contemporaries and Snobs*, 81.
57. Jason Harding, 'The Idea of a Literary Review: T. S. Eliot and The Criterion', in *The Oxford Critical and Cultural History of Modernist Magazines: Volume I: Britain and Ireland 1880–1955*, ed. Peter Brooker and Andrew Thacker (Oxford: Oxford University Press, 2013), 353.
58. T. S. Eliot, 'A Commentary', *The Criterion*, Vol. 2, No. 7 (April 1924), 231–235 (233).
59. T. S. Eliot, 'The Literature of Fascism', *The Criterion*, Vol. 8, No. 31 (December 1928), 280–290 (287).
60. Eliot, 'Isolated Superiority', 5.
61. Indeed, the *Survey* originated as a proposed collaboration between Eliot, Graves and Riding initially entitled 'Untraditional Elements in Poetry'.
62. Leonard Diepeveen, *Mock Modernism: An Anthology of Parodies, Travesties, Frauds, 1910–1935* (Toronto: University of Toronto Press, 2014), 163.
63. Michel Foucault, 'What Is an Author?', in *Essential Works of Foucault 1954–1984, Vol. 2, Aesthetics, Method and Epistemology*, ed. James D. Faubion, trans. Robert Hurley and others (New York: The New Press, 1998), 205–222 (221–222).

CHAPTER 4

Useful Knowledge and the Mind of Mass Democracy

Democracy and Intelligence

As we have seen, after the first flush of positive reviews of *Geography and Plays* and the serialisation of *The Making of Americans* in *The Transatlantic Review*, a series of publications, largely in the context of modernist literary culture in Britain, contested the value of Stein's authorship in a public wrangle that explicitly debated the legitimacy of her participation. In this chapter, I will explore in more detail the recurrent trope of intellectual disability used to present her work as engendering a future of Western cultural degeneration, and the contrasting claims that her writing reflects a new democratic sensibility, situating these ideas in their context of the broader public discourse on the future of intelligence in democracy represented by the pamphlet series *To-day and To-morrow*. I will also argue that *Useful Knowledge*, the 1928 publication that repackaged a collection of pieces written between 1919 and 1925, is Stein's attempt to frame both her work and her authorship as exemplary of the successfully democratised, future-oriented mind of America in a direct response to the arguments that contest the validity of her literary practice.

In the texts debating Stein's legitimacy, her work is portrayed as either expressive of identifiable mental 'defects', as a degenerate strain of human thought that cannot or should not be reproduced, or as a manifestation of the new type of intelligence emerging with modern democracy. The discussions of Stein use her work to make predictions about the future of the collective intellect in mass democracy. These representations of her authorship are cast in the same terms as the broader discussion of the ethics of democratic participation across Anglo-American inter-war literary culture, reflecting a growing concern with the regulation of the minds that have the right to participate in new contexts of full suffrage. The debate over the merit of Stein's work in the mid-to-late 1920s takes place in the context of broader discussions of the ethical ramifications of full democratic participation. As we have seen in Chapter 3, it is a pacy, responsive conversation in which the writers involved wrangle over the value of Stein's work and the legitimacy of her author status in a shifting network of fragile positions and allegiances that reveal fundamental and interconnected anxieties about authorship and democracy.

The emphasis on the modern mind in general, and on the issue of intelligence in mass democratic participation in particular, is there from the outset in Mina Loy's October 1924 *Transatlantic Review* defence of Stein's work as a democratising force that represents the 'ideal' intent of 'modernism' to free the mind of the constraints of tradition and 'track intellection back to the embryo' (429). Wyndham Lewis's *The Art of Being Ruled* sustains this emphasis on the relationship of modernist literary methods and the collective intellect with a critique of Stein's work as exemplary of a degenerate 'literary system' that elevates the mental processes of the 'moron' and the 'demented'.[1] John Rodker's more circumspect *To-day and To-morrow* essay, *The Future of Futurism*, marks Stein's work as a dead end in the range of possible futures for the human mind, while Eliot's review in *The Nation and Athenaeum* asserts more forcefully the danger that Stein's work poses for the 'thought and sensibility of the future' (595). Lewis's second monograph, *Time and Western Man*, augments the critique in *The Art of Being Ruled* with a discussion of *Composition as Explanation* and figures Stein's work more vehemently as a 'monotonous, imbecile' form that should be excised from literary culture (1927, 56). Laura Riding and Robert Graves's *A Survey of Modernist Poetry* engages directly with Eliot's critique and asserts Stein's status as the ultimate modernist author for the collective mind of 'mass humanity' (1927, 279). In their taking stock, and as her work comes more clearly into their purview, Stein becomes the locus for a debate about what kind of practice the human mind of the future (both immediate and long-term) should want.

To-day and To-morrow and the Future of the Human Mind

The pamphlet series *To-day and To-morrow*, a sequence of speculative non-fiction essays published in Britain and the US that aimed to 'combine the popularization of expert knowledge with futurology', is the context for Rodker's essay *The Future of Futurism* and an important background for this debate.[2] Questions about the future of the human mind formed a significant strand of discussion in the series from its inception, in essays on the role of education in democratic participation and in engagements with eugenicist arguments about the development of the national 'race'. Predictions about the future presaged by advances in scientific knowledge were more often than not set explicitly in the context of the development of Western society and the democratic nation-state. The series performed a dual role in the transatlantic discourse on the future of democracy. On the one hand, the essays processed and disseminated knowledge for and brought debates to an increasingly educated public in an era of mass information, forming opinion and providing access to ideas: The *To-day and To-morrow* series represented the 'high-brow' end of a spectrum of popular publications that aimed to inform and educate a rapidly democratising readership on advances in knowledge across a range of disciplines.[3] On the other hand, the essays almost invariably dealt, either directly or indirectly, with questions about the nature and role of the democratic subject. The series offered position-papers presenting often controversial critical analyses of developments in knowledge and their potential future applications. Its reception and discussion in the press 'suggest[s] that the books aroused a good deal of interest in the educated classes' and points to the role of the series in generating ideas and influencing the direction of the wider discourse (Bowler, 139). As Elise Schraner points out, contributors 'often wrote in response to previously published content' and the debate in the wake of many of the essays continued into British and American daily and weekly papers and periodicals, reflecting the role of the series in encouraging 'a continuous dialectic among contemporaries'.[4] Thus, *To-day and To-morrow*'s relatively small middle-class audience was enlarged and extended in the filtering of the ideas through these more broadcast conduits, and the series worked to develop ideas and generate debates in the context of the extension of advances in knowledge to a broader public. This dual concern, to both reach the expanding demos and engage with the questions raised by increasing democratisation, is echoed in the Stein debate, which, like so many of the issues the series engaged, began outside *To-day and To-morrow*, looped through it, and generated further discussion and other positions beyond it. In the arguments around Stein, the question of who should write what is freighted with questions about who should participate in a democratic future and which forces might be forming it.

The *To-day and To-morrow* publications were clearly of interest in the inter-war literary culture that formed the context for the Stein debate: beyond Rodker's contribution, the writers involved in the dispute were very much engaged with the series and the issues it explored. *To-day and To-morrow* pamphlets were regularly reviewed in *The Criterion* and *The Dial*, and, in his joint review of Stein's *Composition as Explanation* and Rodker's *To-day and To-morrow* essay for *The Nation and Athenaeum*, T. S. Eliot is clearly familiar with the series and expects his audience to be.[5] Wyndham Lewis engages directly with Bertrand Russell's essay from the series in *The Art of Being Ruled*, Robert Graves contributed two pieces in 1927 and 1928, and Stein herself submitted twice (unsuccessfully) to the editorial board. Indeed, in the draft of her letter offering the alternative texts, she describes them as 'express[ing] the future of composition as I see it', revealing her knowledge of the remit of the series as speculation about future developments in science, politics, society and culture and reflecting its role as a significant location for cutting-edge ideas.[6] Like the essays in the *To-day and To-morrow* series, the contributions to the Stein debate were attempts to both predict and direct a future for literature. Significantly, they all also address or reference the readership identified by publications like *To-day and To-morrow* that aim to provide popular accounts of contemporary advances in knowledge. In the concern for the dissemination of knowledge of 'advances' in literature, Stein is singled out as exemplary of a literary future either to be embraced or resisted.

From the outset, the question of the mind of the future that appears in the considerations of Stein's authorial validity is very much present in the public discourse represented by *To-day and To-morrow*, where the ethics of the future of 'mental defectives' in democratic society is a significant theme. The series began in 1923 with what Saunders and Hurwitz describe as a 'classic modern debate about the ethics of scientific developments': J. B. S. Haldane's *Daedalus, or Science and the Future*, and Bertrand Russell's *Icarus, or the Future of Science*, followed by F. C. S. Schiller's eugenicist contribution, *Tantalus, or the Future of Man*.[7] Within the broader exploration of the implications of genetics research, this discussion confronts the ethical questions raised about the future of intelligence by the development of a body of knowledge that could enable the control of intellectual ability in the early identification of intellectual disability and in the possibility of gene manipulation that might breed a more intelligent race. Haldane's predictions of ectogenesis as a method of 'selective breeding to change character' (Haldane, 69), are greeted pessimistically in Russell's argument because, although it 'will be used, at first, to diminish imbecility, a most desirable object' it enables a dystopian future in which 'opposition to the government will be taken to prove imbecility, so that rebels of all kinds will be sterilized' (Russell, 49). The form of Russell's objection reveals the broad acceptance of the principles of selective breeding for the elimination of intellectual disability, and, in the many essays in the series that deal with the subject of eugenics or related methods, this point is consistently conceded.[8] Schiller's contribution to this discussion, expressing 'a pretty shrewd suspicion that certain types, say the feeble-minded, the sickly, the insane, are undesirable, and that no good can come of coddling and cultivating them', and a desire to correct the 'dysgenical working of civilized society' narrows the initial debate from a broad exploration of the possibilities for the range of advances in the sciences to a eugenicist argument for the elimination of these 'types' (Schiller, 64–65). His view of intellectual disability is, nonetheless, reflected across the series, whether or not the authors are wholeheartedly committed eugenicists, from the pseudo-science of F. G. Crookshank's racialised account of Down's syndrome *The Mongol in Our Midst* to the American geneticist H. S. Jennings's essay *Prometheus, or Biology and the Advancement of Man* (both 1925) on the relationship between genetic inheritance and acquired characteristics.

The Clinical Discourse of Intelligence

These debates intersected contiguous clinical and legal discourses that were having real-world effects on the lives of those considered to have mental 'deficiencies'. Throughout the 1900s, 1910s and 1920s, the place of people with intellectual disabilities, learning difficulties and mental illnesses in society was the subject of reports, legislation and clinical intervention across the US and Britain.[9] These debates intensified after extensions in suffrage in the 1920s, and, indeed, legislation tended to become increasingly drastic, replacing the nineteenth-century emphasis on attempts at the 'improvement' of those considered intellectually or morally unfit and reflecting a developing culture of regulation and control around concerns about the expansion of rights.[10] Sterilisation programmes were legalised in many American states in the 1910s, with increased powers introduced through the 1920s.[11] In Britain, compulsory detention and sterilisation programmes were recommended by the 1908 report of the British Royal Commission on the Care and Control of the Feeble-Minded. Although sterilisation never passed into British law, with the 1913 Mental Deficiency Act and the establishment of the Board of Control for Lunacy and Mental Deficiency emphasising segregation and institutionalisation in colonies, the issue was debated in legal and political contexts throughout the period.[12] Clinical expertise was drafted in to form the legislation, and the account considered most authoritative, A. F. Tredgold's *Mental Deficiency: Amentia*, first published in 1908 and running through eight editions until 1952, formed the basis for the definitions of 'types' of deficiency identified in the Act.

Tredgold's textbook, used in the training of nurses and doctors across the country, was at its inception motivated by the conviction that a lack of regulation of the 'feeble-minded' would produce a future of 'National Degeneracy'. In a 1909 lecture, 'The Feeble-Minded – a Social Danger', delivered at the Annual Meeting of the National Association for the Welfare of the Feeble-minded and published in *The Eugenics Review*, Tredgold asserts,

> National Degeneracy is no myth but a very serious reality. In the past, more nations have sunk to a position of utter insignificance or have been entirely blotted out of existence, as the result of the moral, intellectual, and physical degeneracy of their citizens, than of wars, famine, or any other conditions. To-day the contest is perhaps rather more one of intellect than of muscle, but competition between nations is still as keen as ever it was in the past, and it is impossible for any nation to progress or even to hold its own, which contains a preponderance of individuals who are deficient in moral, intellectual, and physical vigour. It would be well if we English were to ponder these facts.[13]

The idea of national degeneracy conceptualises the nation on entirely biological terms as the codification and circumscription of race and inscribes the project of nation as a project of successful breeding. The fact that Tredgold sets the control of the 'feeble-minded' in this context reveals the significance of this discourse of intellectual disability as a marker of the biopolitical character of nationhood in this period. The opening chapter of the 1923 edition of *Mental Deficiency: Amentia*, the edition that would have been current during the discussions in *To-day and To-morrow* that inform our understanding of the deployment of these tropes in the Stein debate, sets out the system of 'grades' used in the 1913 Act:

> All civilised nations are composed of men of varying grades of intellect. At the one extreme we have the genius of a Bacon, Newton, Kepler, Copernicus, Shakespeare, Goethe, Plato or Galileo. These are succeeded by individuals of lesser but still conspicuous ability, and these again merge into the ordinary average mass of mankind. Below this we have a section composed of persons of inferior intelligence whom we may term 'dullards'. The dullards are followed by the class designated 'feeble-minded'; the feeble-minded merge imperceptibly into the imbeciles, and these again are connected by insensible gradations with the idiots. The gross

idiot is characterised by a complete negation of intellect, and thus stands at the lowest extreme of mental development.[14]

By putting the categorisation of intellect into the context of the 'civilised nation', Tredgold draws the system of grades into an idea of the legitimate nation that works on the presupposition of the 'uncivilised' as an undifferentiated morass and so designates this stratification as such as a feature of civilisation. Moreover, in conceptualising the categories of 'mental development' as a schema that covers the whole nation, the system offers a regulatory framework that elides specificity to promulgate a logic of class and hierarchy that enables the construction of a 'clinical' objectivity in decisions about the worth of individual lives. Although both Tredgold's textbooks and the 1913 Act they so closely informed claim the care of people with intellectual disabilities as their aim, Tredgold's deployment of categories as a means of regulation and the emphasis on control rather than care in the establishment of a Board of Control reveal the biopolitics at the heart of the clinical and legislative approaches to intellectual disability and at the heart of ideas of nation.

The *To-day and To-morrow* pamphlets reflect this discourse, often dealing explicitly with clinical developments in the identification, categorisation and treatment of the 'feeble-minded', using intellectual disability to stand at the threshold of any ethical debate about the limits of the value of human life. H. S. Jennings, for example, invokes an assumption of shared values around a taxonomy of intellectual ability that markedly echoes Tredgold: 'all agree that it is better to be normal than deformed or feeble-minded. There is, indeed, a great series of grades, from the fool up to Shakespeare' in his explanation of developments in genetics in *Prometheus*.[15] Despite the essay's presentation of an explicitly enlightened view of the relationship between genes and acquired characteristics, Jennings uses feeble-mindedness as an example of an undesirable characteristic that genetics has an interest in as the result of 'defects' which produce 'worthless' offspring (36), asserting that 'there are a few social practices that recognizably and directly work toward racial degeneration; these should obviously be stopped. Such are the freedom and encouragement of reproduction among the feeble-minded, the criminal and the insane' (78). Jennings, echoing the many other essays that deal with this theme, suggests those categories to be written out of society, asserting these as the unequivocal limit in the question of which lives are valid.

In Part Three of *Homo Sacer*, Agamben includes as part of his definition of the twentieth century *homo sacer* a discussion of *Authorisation for the Annihilation of Life Unworthy to be Lived*, a 1920 pamphlet written by the Germans Karl Binding and Alfred Hoche, a lawyer and a medical ethicist, advocating euthanasia for the 'incurably lost' – those who feel, themselves, that their life is not worth living – and for 'incurable idiots' – whose life can be taken without consent (quoted in Agamben, 138). In his discussion, Agamben argues that 'The fundamental biopolitical structure of modernity – the decision on the value (or nonvalue) of life as such – therefore finds its first juridical articulation in a well-intentioned pamphlet in favour of euthanasia' (137). Although the US and British discussions of and legislation around intellectual disability most commonly debate sterilisation rather than euthanasia, the 'decision on the value' of life is evidently articulated in the resultant policies, whether they are the sterilisation programmes that proliferated in state after state in the US, or the British 'colonies' set up after the 1913 Act in which men and women were separated in order to prevent reproduction. Indeed, these policies profoundly embody the biopolitics of modern democracy because, in their intention to prevent the reproduction of a 'genetic' strain identified in a taxonomy of grades in order to forestall the racial degeneration of the nation, they aim at the elimination not of an individual but of a 'type', a whole stratum of society categorised as worthless. The 1920s arguments about the regulation and elimination of the 'feeble-minded' in *To-day and To-morrow*, which seep into the discourse on Stein's fitness for authorship, carry with them the biopolitical character of modern democracy.

The Trope of Intellectual Disability in the Stein Debate

Rodker's contribution to the Stein debate, *The Future of Futurism*, published in the series in 1926, engages with the broader discourse of desirable intellectual heredities, in its discussion of which authors represent a valid future for literary culture, in its treatment of the future of literature as the future of the human mind, and in the discourse of genetic inheritance that subtends his narrative of the diverging strains of literary evolution. Rodker's essay considers the future of 'futurism' conceived as a broad revolution, a 'violent effort' necessary to 'disengage' art and literature from the 'mush of traditional and effete forms' (92). Rodker's opening position is that futurism has created 'confusion in the popular mind' (6) and the essay works to support his conclusion that 'if it is at all vital it must become part of the tradition of posterity' (91–92). This reference to his audience and his concern for the effect on the 'popular mind' suggests his belief that the literature of the future will have a direct influence on the collective intellect. As he says, 'the present condition of man's mind and its possible mutations does interest us, and the possibility of new inventions to keep his mind spongy and promise wider horizons' (23). Rodker identifies several strands in the development of literature, all of which have the potential to flourish. He names a number of authors with diverse practices, and, despite some reservations, he accepts them all as potentially valid inheritances. Although he concedes that Stein's work 'may prove some sort of discipline by a mind debauched (?) by too much compressed literature' (37) and that because 'many people ask specially for "long books"' this 'may be an admission of the hypnotic value of repetition' (36), Rodker characterises Stein's texts as having no 'other motive than to grow and flower exactly as she wishes them to grow and flower', ascribing to her work, in this metaphor of growth and reproduction, the dead end of a fruitless clone unable to adapt or hybridise (38). His concluding evaluation of Stein's work in the field of possible futures for literature and human thought is also predicated on this characterisation in his exhortation to 'turn from the ungrateful method of Miss Stein, who means words to be words only, and to mean nothing but what she would have them mean', which implies a hardening or termination of meaning that offers nothing to other writers or to other minds (85). Rodker invokes Stein as a significant practitioner of contemporary literature and a writer 'about which everyone knows something', only to exclude her from its future (14).[16] Capable of producing nothing outside itself, Stein's authorship is not a productive strain in the evolution of literature.

As well as co-opting the language of the scientific and pseudo-scientific discourses of genetic inheritance represented in *To-day and To-morrow* to cast doubt on the future of Stein's work, Rodker's essay engages the terms established in Lewis's monograph *The Art of Being Ruled*, reflecting the function of the series in contributing directly to live debates. In a footnote glossing his dismissal of 'the mantrams of Miss Stein', Rodker quotes Lewis:

> Mr Wyndham Lewis says of her 'Miss Gertrude Stein is the best known exponent of a literary system that consists in a sort of gargantuan mental stutter. What she is exploiting in her method is the process of the demented.' (28, n.1).

The trope of the stutter and its collocation with the reference to mental deterioration are employed by Lewis to present Stein's work as unproductive and decadent, and Rodker uses it to reinforce his argument that Stein's authorship has no future. Lewis's satire on Stein's work is a key component of his critique of mass democracy. For him, Stein's exploitation of the 'process of the demented' is an 'illustration of the fascination felt for not only disease and deformity, but imbecility' (*The Art of Being Ruled*, 1926, 401) associated with 'the socialist religion of Demos' (400). In Lewis's argument, Stein's work is exemplary of the elevation of the mediocre, the sick and the defective afforded by democracy and reflected in the visual art with which she is associated: the 'goitrous torpid and squinting husks provided by Matisse in his sculpture' for example, are described as 'worthless except as tactful decorations for a mental home' (405).

Lewis's description of 'The highly intellectual and methodic gibber of Miss Gertrude Stein' reveals another important dimension of his critique, however: not only is Stein's writing replicating those elements of the demos that are 'worthless', it is also a fraudulent addition to the false narrative that mass democracy is radically egalitarian (405). Lewis's critique of the contemporary political situation argues that mass democracy desires 'Useful and docile citizens, not learned ones or people trained to think for themselves', a mush of mass-produced subjects, aspiring to the average, happily herded into a classificatory caste system of huge associations and sects, and living contentedly in equalised stupidity (416). Lewis satirises and disdains this, but in the end, he argues that these conditions enable the great intellects to rise up, separate themselves, and be free for the 'great and difficult tasks of intelligence of the first order' (433). In a typically perverse move, in the final chapter of *The Art of Being Ruled*, Lewis welcomes the situation he has used most of the book to condemn, arguing that a softened, docile, 'moronic' society can be ruled more easily by intellectuals who can detach themselves from the caste system and rise beyond it. Both in his critique and in this apparent equanimity, Lewis is concerned to assert the hierarchy of intellectual ability that the figure of the imbecile holds in place.

The trope of intellectual disability as a signifier of the worthlessness of Stein's corpus is comprehensively deployed in Lewis's 1927 *Time and Western Man*, an extension of the arguments he sets out in *The Art of Being Ruled* that develops further his critique of what he sees as an undisciplined, deindividuated, conformist contemporary culture that serves to create a docile populace and enable the covert control of mass democratic society by an invisible corporatist elite. Associating Stein's work with mass production and popular culture, as 'jumbled, cheap, slangy, and thick to suit', Lewis uses the trope of feeble-mindedness to further satirise what he sees as the fraudulent levelling of mass democratic politics (*Time and Western Man*, 1927, 78). By figuring her writing as imitating the 'moron' with its 'monotonous, imbecile, endlessly-repeated, lumbering words' (56) or as 'the dull stupor of complete imbecility', Lewis makes Stein the chief participant in a culture that defrauds the population of its liberty by appearing to elevate the 'lowest' forms of human life and so seeming to offer a profound equality (60). Lewis's conclusion 'My general objection, then, to the work of Miss Stein is that it is *dead*' aligns Stein with a vapid degeneracy that is the real effect of mass democracy and whose most representative figure is the 'imbecile' (56). In constructing the text as a heavy, pointless body ('lumbering'), as formless and degraded 'like a confused, stammering, rather "soft" (bloated, acromegalic, squinting and spectacled, one can figure it as) child', or as a poor specimen, as 'low-grade', deformed, abnormal or sick, Lewis loads the full weight of his vision of a degenerate culture onto Stein (47).

Lewis uses terms originating in the clinical textbooks and legislative language that seek to define and regulate intellectual ability in his figuring of Stein's work as a genetic aberration. His grim joke, 'The massive silence of the full idiot is, unfortunately, out of her reach, of course', reflects a knowledge of the contemporary taxonomy of 'grades' of 'mental deficiency', defined by Tredgold and in the Mental Deficiency Act, from the 'highest' grade of the feeble-minded through the imbecile to the 'lowest' grade, the idiot (60–61). This terminology, as we have seen, is also circulating in *To-day and To-morrow*, and, indeed, the work of Tredgold and other clinicians is directly cited in eugenicist arguments represented in the series.[17] Lewis's image of a degenerate mass democratic society also echoes F. C. S. Schiller's defence of eugenics, offered as a response to Bertrand Russell's scepticism in the preliminary *To-day and To-morrow* debate, which articulates a similar belief that 'the human race' will be subject to 'gradual decay as its arts and sciences slowly fossilize, or peter out, in an overwhelming flood of feeble-mindedness' (Schiller, 1924, 53). Although it presents a much simpler, straightforwardly eugenicist argument, there are a number of parallels here. In their emphasis on the effects of contemporary institutions on the nation's intelligence, in their concern for the development of social conditions that will preclude the generation of great minds in the future, and in their images of a social order overwhelmed by an 'imbecilic' mass-mind, both Lewis and Schiller position intellectual disability as the dysgenic element that democratic institutions allow to proliferate. In both these texts, contemporary democracies have created the conditions for degeneration the most dangerous aspect of which is what Schiller calls the 'world-wide dearth of ability' (48) which is the result of a population whose 'continued growth is mainly due to the unrestrained breeding of the casual labourers and the feeble-minded' (47).

Another illuminating comparison is with F. G. Crookshank's essay *The Mongol in Our Midst* (1925), which draws feeble-mindedness into a narrative of failed evolution, racial degeneration and dysgenic breeding, referencing the work of Tredgold and other experts to develop a troublingly racialised account of Down's syndrome. There is a striking correspondence in Lewis's conception of the modernism he wants to reject as a 'child-cult' (with Stein as the ultimate expression of that – the imbecile child) and Crookshank's insistence that 'the Mongolian type' are 'persons who in maturity still are a kind of children', that 'Mongolian imbeciles are unfinished children' (Lewis, *Time and Western Man*, 9).[18] This trope is productive for both writers in that it enables them to construct the story of a failed type that never achieves full development which can then be mapped on to conceptions of a 'primitive' contemporary species. Lewis uses the idea of a feeble-minded, primitive 'child-cult' to discredit the aesthetic forms he draws into an association with Stein's work, whereas for Crookshank this suggestion that the 'mongol' is a primitive form unable to develop and is 'in some respects pre-human, rather than human, in "type"' means that neither people with Down's nor the 'asiatics' he claims as their genetic stock are fully human (Crookshank, 1925, 27). Lewis and Crookshank also emphasise both the embeddedness of this aberrant, degenerate species and the difficulty one might have in identifying them. In Lewis's account, Stein is 'living comfortably at the heart of things' just like Crookshank's mongol 'in our midst', and this reflects the desire to identify and separate those who should not participate – as author or as human (Lewis, *Time and Western Man*, 111). The emphasis on the embeddedness of the degenerate species also constructs and sustains a horror of miscegenation, for example in Crookshank's assertion that one 'may easily observe within the compass of a day's ramble in London a range of Mongolian or semi-Mongolian types, among our native Cockneys' (Crookshank, 1925, 15). This is refracted in Lewis's text as fear of disease with the suggestions that Stein's style of writing has 'infected' other writers: 'This habit of speech, like a stuttering infection, is very contagious. Mr Joyce even has caught it' (Lewis, *Time and Western Man*, 50). The co-opting and recycling of scientific discourses characterises the representations of Stein's work, but, as we can see in Crookshank's example, it is really only one end of a continuum in which the boundaries of science and metaphor, empirical observation and fictional narrative, are already blurred.

In the context of these ideas, Rodker's taxonomy of literary inheritances for the future of the collective mind has a great deal more urgency. These fears and warnings about the effect of literature on the mind of the populace and the concomitant urge to identify the degenerative literary method and the contaminating effect of the fraudulent author spill over into the other texts on this side of the debate, including Eliot's unambiguous attack on Stein as the undesirable element in literary culture in *The Nation and Athenaeum*. Eliot reviews *Composition as Explanation*, alongside Rodker's *To-day and To-morrow* essay *The Future of Futurism*, as well as one other Hogarth Essay and one other pamphlet in the *To-day and To-morrow* series. It is important to note that Eliot is already familiar with the pamphlet series, calling it 'a precious document upon the present time', and, significantly, referring in passing to *The Mongol in Our Midst*. Eliot's comment, 'Mr Rodker is up-to-the-minute, if anyone is; we feel sure he knows all about hormones, W.H.R. Rivers, and the Mongol in our midst', presents Crookshank's essay as merely one in a series of modern, faddish theories about which judgement is to be reserved.[19] His juxtaposition of Crookshank alongside Rivers's important psychiatric work on shell shock reveals a low level of concern about Crookshank's racist, eugenicist views and pseudo-scientific conflations. This casual list also suggests these ideas are broadly in circulation – that everyone reading will understand these references. Stating directly that he 'entirely agree[s] with Mr. Rodker's remarks about Miss Stein', he presents a critique of Stein in which her work 'has a kinship with the saxophone' that associates her with the development and influence of American popular culture that presages the unchecked future of mass participation in Western civilisation.

Eliot's discussion of Rodker's views also engages emphatically with the discourse of the future of the human mind that forms the most striking and consistent aspect of this conversation. Eliot provides a precis of Rodker's argument as presenting two broad strands for the future of literature, both of which propose a reciprocity in the development of qualities of the mind and qualities of writing:

> Mr Rodker seems to think, in short, that the future of literature lies in two directions: in the line of Blake, Mallarmé, Roussel, and the development of all those qualities we have called mental agility, and in the other the line of ... Tchekhov and Dostoevsky ... the investigation of the subconscious.

In Eliot's representation, these two literary directions both reflect and develop the 'thought and sensibility' of the future, investing literature with a powerful dual function. Eliot's emphasis on the power of literary culture to influence the collective human mind means his critique of Stein's work can take the form of a dire warning for the future of humanity. His sceptical take on Rodker's ideas about the futures for the mind opened up by technological developments (what Rodker calls 'mechanization'), 'I am inclined to wonder . . . whether the thought and sensibility of the future may not become more simple and indeed more crude than that of the present, whether the mechanical complication of life does not bring about such simplification of sensibility, rather than the reverse; whether the omens are not with Miss Stein and the author of 'I'm Gona Charleston Back to Charleston', identifies Stein's practice with the technology of the future and the intellectual deterioration and cultural regression he thinks it will bring about. Eliot also associates this path for the mind with those 'rhythms' of popular culture represented by the ragtime hit, and his conclusion, that Stein's work 'is not good for one's mind' seals the parallels between Stein's work, mass culture and intellectual degeneration. Eliot's final remark 'If this is of the future, then the future is, as it very likely is, of the barbarians. But this is the future in which we ought not to be interested' echoes the discourse which reciprocally constructs mass culture, primitivity and the defective, underdeveloped species. This implies, as Rodker and Lewis do, that Stein's work is an illegitimate form of literary practice precisely because it represents mass participation and therefore the degeneration of culture and the decline of the collective intellect. Indeed, Eliot's characterisation of the mind of this future as 'more simple' and 'more crude' clearly has a 'kinship' with Schiller's eugenicist rhetoric which presages the 'gradual decay' as 'arts and sciences slowly fossilize, or peter out, in an overwhelming flood of feeble-mindedness'.

The Stein Debate and the Democratic Mind

On the other side of the spectrum of opinion on Stein are Mina Loy's assertion, made in her *Transatlantic Review* letters, that Stein is the literary exemplar of the way 'Modernism has democratised the subject matter and the belle matiere of art' (October 1924, 430), and Laura Riding's argument, in *A Survey of Modernist Poetry*, that Stein's work represents 'a human mean in language' (287).[20] Loy's representation of modernism's democracy imagines it as a broadening in participation in the practice and appreciation of art and literature in terms of not just who participates, but in the crucial details of when, why and how aesthetic engagement takes place. In presenting Stein as the literary exemplar of the aesthetic democratisation modernism has achieved, she makes the following claim:

> The pragmatic value of modernism lies in it's [sic] tremendous recognition of the compensation due to the spirit of democracy. Modernism is a prophet calling in the wilderness of stabilized culture that humanity is wasting its aesthetic time. For there is a considerable extension of time between the visits to the picture gallery, the museum, the library. It asks what is happening to your aesthetic consciousness during the long, long intervals? (October 1924, 429).

The modernism that Loy describes here celebrates democracy as offering the potential for the extension of aesthetic consciousness beyond the institutions of 'stabilized culture' and into life. Her attention to its 'pragmatic value' suggests a modernism that is made for vital, purposeful action, contrasted here with the empty and barren 'wilderness' of a stable – or static – culture. The radical dynamism of modernism is also expressed in the juxtaposition of the counter-image of the 'frame or glass case of tradition' with the revolutionary call of modernism for the unrestricted participation that democracy means it can promise. The 'frame or glass case' stands as a representation of the institutional structures and discourses which have hitherto regulated and authorised the relationship between the work and its audience and marked off the legitimate work and thus the legitimate artist (and author). The rigidity of this image is amplified because Loy sets it against modernism represented as a call to action: 'Modernism says Why not each one of us, scholar or bricklayer, pleasureably [sic] realise all that is impressing itself upon our unconscious, the thousand odds and ends that make up your sensery [sic] every day life' (430). This contrasts the stasis, restriction and delimiting of the physical object of the 'frame or glass case' with modernism's dynamic vocal exhortation. The sense of unregulated and limitless action is emphasised because the rhetorical 'Why not' is an invitation rather than an imperative, and because the call to 'realise all' the 'thousand odds and ends' evokes a continuous, infinitely capacious and interminable activity. This extends the metaphor of Bergsonian 'flux' Loy engages at the beginning of the first letter, where she remembers encountering Stein's work for the first time 'when Bergson was in the air' (September 1924, 305), and which she returns to here with reference to 'the flux of life' that a democratised art now opens to the valid aesthetic pleasure of all. Her references to the 'scholar or bricklayer' clearly align modernism with the democratisation of class, and her use of plural pronouns again insists on a collective participation unencumbered by considerations of class or criteria of aesthetic value. This, along with the final reference to 'every day life' calls for a participation in aesthetics that is not defined or regulated by any stricture.

Loy's claim that Stein 'has given us the Word, in and for itself' makes her exemplary of the democratisation of literature because she clears away the ossified stability of tradition and frees other minds (430). Stein's work is 'Like all modern art' in that it 'makes a demand for a creative audience, by providing a stimulus...which leaves us unlimited latitude for personal response' (429). In quite the reverse of Rodker's critique, Loy argues that the work necessitates a creative response and so is, inherently, intellectually productive. It is crucial to note that Stein's 'democratisation' prompts, therefore, a broadening of participation: Loy uses her to signify an end to the delimiting of participation, the extension of authorship that, for her, is the 'compensation' democracy offers to literature.

Riding also characterises Stein's writing as the exemplary expression of modernism and as a reflection of the mind of mass democracy, the embodiment of 'mass humanity' (Riding and Graves, 1927, 279). For Riding, however, 'modernism' is a far more problematic literary development than it is for Loy. Riding's account of modernism's self-annihilation is coupled with a rather paradoxical defence of Stein formed around what she views as modernism's compliance with the organisation of 'modern civilisation'. In her argument, the systematic form of modern society has forced poetry from the position of an 'all-embracing human activity' (260) to that of 'a technical branch of culture of the most limited kind' which is 'only one of the specialized, professionalized activities of [the poet's] period, like music, painting, radiology, aerostatics, the cinema, modern tennis or morbid psychology' (261). Riding's libertarian critique of modern civilisation and of the modernist poetry it generates represents it as a regulatory system whose primary function is the monitoring and refinement of its own structures and processes. Poetry, she argues, has become, like any 'organization', 'confined' to its 'proper departmental technique' and interested in ensuring its 'prestige' (263) is sustained through 'a greater internal discipline, morality and study of tactics' (262). For Riding, this emphasis on the regulation and discipline of poetry means it 'ceases to be civilized in the sense of being more and more cultured with loose sentiment'. Instead, its emphasis on the precise kind of poetry required for its time means 'it seems to know at last how it should be written and written at the very moment'. So, rather than growing and fluctuating organically with the flux of history, modernist poetry superintends history by continually 'beginning as at the beginning' in a 'carefully calculated, censored primitiveness' (263).

Riding's defence of Stein rests on this definition of modernist poetry, in her argument that Stein's work has taken this 'critical tyranny', what Riding calls 'classicism' or 'the new barbarism', to its logical conclusion. Picking up Eliot's description in *The Nation and Athenaeum* of Stein's work as 'of the barbarians', Riding argues that Stein has reduced language to its purest, most primitive form and thus her work, ironically, forms the ultimate expression of the 'scientific barbarism' of the literary culture from which Eliot excludes her. For Riding, the logical conclusion of the modernist desire for a strict and absolute grasp of the present is Stein's 'sterilization of words until they are exhausted of history and meaning' (287). In Riding's argument, this means that Stein's work is the poetry of modern civilisation because it grasps this absolute and so serves the 'mass humanity equipped only to seize the obvious' (279). It is 'so grossly, so humanly, all-inclusively ordinary' (280), so precisely everyday, that it represents 'a mathematical equation of ordinariness' (287). In this final chapter, Riding argues that Stein has written poetry out of its regulatory strictures and into a liberated space in which writing becomes the ordinary rhythm of humanity moving through time. Riding's anarchist politics mean that, for her, any form of regulation is fundamentally problematic, and she uses the figure of Stein here to imagine an unregulated mass human participation that has worked itself free of any organisational apparatus and so expresses only its own organic, primitive collective rhythms.[21]

In *A Survey of Modernist Poetry*, however, what turns out to be Riding's critique of modernism is also a critique of modern democracy. In that critique, Stein is the ultimate expression of both, and, as such, offers in her extreme exemplification a paradoxical and antinomial writing-out of the systems which regulate participation into an absolute liberation of the collective mind. For Loy, modernism resists regulation; for Riding, it is a component of the administrative system of modern civilisation. In both their arguments, however, Stein is an ultimate form of modernism that enables a mass aesthetic and the literary expression of a collective 'every day' or 'average' experience. These representations figure Stein's writing as the kind of thought necessary for and generated by mass participation, reflecting the large-scale processing of ideas and freeing the 'human mean' of the collective mind.

Riding's analysis is particularly interesting in relation to the regulatory taxonomies that structure the discourse of intellectual abilities and genetic types used to narrate Stein's invalidation. It is also pertinent to discussions of the ways in which the mass might be organised and controlled in the *To-day and To-morrow* essays arguing for changes in the education system. The question of the form of intelligence necessary in an era of full participation is also a significant strand of discussion in *To-day and To-morrow*, from Vernon Lee's 1925 *Proteus, or The Future of Intelligence*, which imagines a new democratic form of intelligence, to M. Alderton Pink's 1927 essay *Procrustes: Or The Future of English Education*, which argues vehemently against the view that 'the success of democracy depends upon the diffusion of culture among the masses' to the later M. Chaning-Pearce's *Chiron, or the Education of a Citizen of the World* (1931) which advocates the education of upper-class 'citizens of the world' to manage the global mass.[22] Vernon Lee's contribution defines a new conception of intelligence that she describes as 'particular, and perhaps rather modern'.[23] In her argument, this new intelligence is 'the living, changing mass of unprofessional thought, the averaged, habitual thought of the majority of us' that is 'for current use and pleasure' and whose 'varied exercise', 'nimbleness', and 'elasticity', reflect the variety and dynamism necessary for the fast pace of modern life (55–56). Lee sets this against the rigidity and authority of the intelligentsia in the figure of 'the Man of Letters' in a way that corresponds with Loy's counter-image of the glass case (5). Lee's notion of a modern intelligence is also fundamentally connected in her essay to 'civic liberty' and has parallels in Loy and Riding's conceptions of Stein's texts as manifestations of the free democratic mind (51). The question of Stein's authorship, then, is framed around questions of both mental capacity and democratic participation which are very much at the forefront of public debate.

Useful Knowledge, Democracy and the Human Mind

Recent scholarly examinations of *Useful Knowledge* tend to use it as evidence for the 'democratic' nature of Stein's work or as the expression of a fluid, playful relationship to her American nationality. Such scholarship focuses on the individual works to explore these ideas, mentioning the title of the collection, the additional 1928 framing material – 'Advertisement' and 'Introducing' – and the cultural and political context in which it was conceived and executed only briefly or not at all.[24] In the light of the publication scene I have set out here and the positions on Stein's authorship represented in it, however, *Useful Knowledge* takes on a new set of resonances. The title itself is taken from the cover page of a *carnet*, the French children's notebooks that Stein used for drafting her work. The series she was using at the time had the title *Connaissances Utiles* and depicted educational representations of objects of knowledge, from instructions on how to tie a bouquet to inventories of Greek Gods.[25] In a 1928 letter to Carl Van Vechten, Stein tells him, 'Payson and Clarke are bringing out a book of collected things, Useful Knowledge or Americana, all my or at least some of my American things collected'.[26] Stein's equivocation around the title – 'Useful Knowledge or Americana' – reflects the importance for her of producing a selection of works defined as American, reflecting the emphasis of Payson and Clarke's projected Two Rivers series on distinctively American publications of avant-garde works, but also bespeaking her discomfort with the consequences of 'the fact that England seems to be discovering me'.[27] Her ultimate decision to use the title *Useful Knowledge*, however, suggests that this conceptualisation is finally more significant for her, configuring the collection as a pertinent intervention at a moment when the usefulness of her practice and the place it might occupy in an era of mass democratic participation are being debated. Stein sustains her insistence on the American character of *Useful Knowledge* in the 'Advertisement', a newly composed addition to the collection that foregrounds its Americanness.[28] What I will argue here is that the framing of this collection offers at once a forceful engagement with the debate about Stein's authorship, an act of resistance to it, and a reconfiguration of Stein's status that attempts to rehabilitate her as a distinctly American author of the democratic mind of the future.

The use of this title picks up on the cultural scene of mass-produced knowledge that Stein's French notebook covers reference, pointing to the context of the surge in popular self-education titles in the inter-war period, and perhaps even looking back to the earlier iteration of this genre, for example the periodicals produced by the American Philosophical Society (subtitled *For Promoting Useful Knowledge*) and the Boston Society for the Diffusion of Useful Knowledge (published as *The Library of Useful Knowledge*).[29] I would argue that the title *Useful Knowledge* references publications that form part of a broadcast print culture that Stein saw as her territory. As I have shown, Stein's belief that her work should appeal to a wider audience is reflected in her repeated attempts to get her work in *Atlantic Monthly*, in the appearance of her texts in *Vanity Fair* and *Life*, in her avid reading of *The Literary Digest* and, indeed, in her submissions to *To-day and To-morrow* itself.[30] Thus, Stein's title identifies her work with a genre that seeks to democratise knowledge through the greater availability and accessibility of advances in a range of disciplines, a genre that burgeons with the gradual emergence of mass democracy and aims at a popular audience Stein also wished to claim.

Beyond its allusion to mass-produced self-education titles, the idea of useful knowledge does much useful work for Stein. It resonates strongly with Loy's claim that Stein's work has made 'the Word' accessible to everybody: knowledge in Stein's texts is democratised in that it is both freed and freely available, offering language in a liberated state because it is 'in and of itself'. Similarly, it chimes with Riding's emphasis on the quality of the 'human mean' in Stein's writing, which intimates a kind of knowledge that is reflective of and accessible to the majority. 'Useful knowledge' also suggests the pragmatic view of the mind that is apparent in Vernon Lee's conception of intelligence 'for current use and pleasure'. Knowledge that can be put to use is the form of knowledge required for action, for the dynamism and vitality Lee advocates. These writers are engaged in a discourse that is generating and circulating conceptions of democratic knowledge, and Stein's title draws her practice into this discourse and aligns her authorship with the democratic modernity it imagines. Just as significantly, Stein's title can also be read as resisting those critics who present her authorship as unproductive and use the discourse of mental deficiency to figure her work. The trope of 'useful knowledge' counters these charges by signifying a unity of mind and action in a productive, democratic form.

In constructing and framing *Useful Knowledge*, Stein also asserts a uniquely American attitude to knowledge as exemplary of the democratic spirit. The 'Advertisement', carefully placed before the other additional text, 'Introducing', in order to frame the collection, establishes its terms and directs responses to it, presenting the text as 'put together from every little that helps to be American'.[31] As has been pointed out, this conceptualises *Useful Knowledge* at the outset as an 'American' text, and the advertisement goes on to develop the theme of what it means to be American using a number of key signifiers which interact to construct a complex conception of American democracy.[32] First, the notion of American consumerism and mass production initially evoked in the title 'Advertisement'; second, the idea of 'romance' as representing the elevation of the individual; and, finally, what turns out to be the overarching trope of useful knowledge itself. The references to American mass production: 'in America the best material is used in the cheapest things because the cheapest things have to be made of the best material to make them worth while making it' insists on a levelling-up through a shift in values. Because this formula means that the 'cheapest things', those available to everyone, are now the things that have the most worth, value becomes associated not with what is scarce, rare or exclusive, but with the commonplace and the readily available – perhaps, even, the 'every day' or the 'human mean'. This revaluation is transposed onto the concept of romance at the end of the paragraph: 'Romance is everything and the very best material should make the cheapest thing is making into living the romance of human being'. This has romance as the idealisation of everyday life, the elevation of the individual on a mass scale, achieved by the insistence on the worth of the things available to everybody and offering a simple and idealised notion of American democracy which literally romanticises the valuing of 'every little thing'. The central short paragraph in this text draws the concept of useful knowledge into the equation: 'This is the American something that makes romance everything. And romance is Useful Knowledge'. Thus, the reformulation of values also applies to knowledge: in America, the knowledge that can be put to use in ordinary life is the knowledge that is valued, not the rarefied knowledge available only to a few. This understanding of the knowledge and the thinking that best serves this conceptual democracy comes close, once again, to that discourse of democracy and knowledge apparent in Loy, Riding and Lee.

The other text deployed in this 1928 reframing, 'Introducing', presents a significant intervention into the contemporary discourse that marks Stein's inappropriateness as an author in terms of the figure of the 'mental defective'. The 1920s texts that debate Stein's validity objectify her work and her authorship as the body of the demos, whether as the subject of regulation and control or as a liberated collective mass. Stein becomes, in these debates, a subject constructed either in the discourses of the pseudo-sciences that cluster around evolutionary biology or as the mass-average recipient of democratic rights. The quasi-regulatory objectification her authorship is subjected to in this period therefore fundamentally challenges her author status, and this is particularly significant for Stein in the context of the 'clinical' tenor of the authorial gaze apparent in much of the work she has produced up to this point. As we have seen, the processes of recording and documenting in her work as a student at Johns Hopkins have had a profound and complex influence on the studies of character and type in *Three Lives* and *The Making of Americans*. We have seen the ways in which the agency of the author is bound up with the activity of experimentation that emerges as the literary reformulation of her clinical experience. Moreover, Daylanne English suggests that Stein considered that her 'own rarer strain marks her a genius'; that 'Stein, along with the heroines of *Three Lives*, may fail to conform to racial, sexual or cultural norms of early twentieth-century America; but, unlike them, she, along with the characters in Q.E.D., is not selected against as a result' (English, 2005, 114). For Stein, whose professions of her own 'genius', were multiple and (however complex or ludic) profoundly felt, the construction of an image of her authorship as a degenerate intellectual strain must have been acutely galling. I would argue that *Useful Knowledge* also reflects a defensiveness around this and a concern to reassert the authoritative standpoint of the expert observer and the scholar of epistemological method.

The framing text 'Introducing' therefore claims at the outset the standpoint of observation and knowledge gathering, resisting the regulatory gaze that constructs Stein as degenerate by reasserting her own position as experimental agent rather than subject-in-discourse. The attention to method and its refinement as in 'he certainly was quite completely then understanding his doing that thing' (3), the emphasis on the utility of knowledge in the gradual assimilation of knowing and doing, and the focus on the task of interpretation in, for example, 'what was the way that something could come to have the meaning that thing had in being existing', all put the protagonist in an authoritative relationship with the objects of knowledge (2). 'Introducing' therefore reflects the position that Stein wants to reaffirm: the 'Marie Curie of the laboratory' described in the poem that Mina Loy writes as a preface to her 1924 defence; the experimenter not the subject of experiment, the free democratic subject, not the subject of regulation and control.

Continuing the theme of useful knowledge as a counter to the trope of the 'feeblemindedness' that will overwhelm the literature and the society of the mass democratic future, this text also develops Stein's inverse image of the productive mind with a meditation on the activity of acquiring, communicating and using knowledge. In doing so, 'Introducing' has Stein's work as representative of the useful mind of a democratic future, the mind that learns from the popular dissemination of knowledge that levels 'grades' and rejects 'intelligence' as a fixed quality in favour of a belief in self-improvement. Indeed, 'Introducing' is about learning as a continuous process of self-development.

'Introducing' is therefore also about knowledge, but, rather than attending to the objects of knowledge, it emphasises the communicative operations of the mind, namely, 'understanding', 'explaining', 'asking', 'listening', and attends instead to the process of coming to know: that is, to the process of learning. It opens with 'One was a completely young one and this one was very clearly understanding this thing'. This central, youthful figure is the focus throughout. Following the protagonist's experiences and actions, 'Introducing' moves through a series of repetitive and subtly differentiated operations, reflecting the complex and active movements in knowledge acquisition. Stein uses repeated gerunds to trace the recursive, habituated functions of the mind, and adverbs to shift these iterations and sustain a sense of active forward movement through the repetitive operations. The modification moves from 'clearly understanding' to 'certainly very clearly then understanding' to 'completely clearly understanding', reflecting a deepening of the mind's grasp as both a quantitative and a qualitative succession (1). The text also suggests that learning is not a process that occurs simply within the brain, but rather one that engages the communicative functions in external exchanges. Thus, it moves from the emphasis on 'understanding' through 'explaining' to focus on 'asking' and 'listening', with the new terms augmenting rather than replacing the previous terms in a manner that reflects an overlapping and concurrence of mental functions. The repetitive formal features, then, are reiterations with very necessary differences which map the operations of recurrent brain functions involved in learning, tracking the constantly modifying, ever incomplete, necessarily communicative vitality of the learning mind.

Another important term is initiated in the third paragraph with the framing of the protagonist as 'This one . . . who was doing something'. The move from 'understanding' to 'doing' occurs early in the text, and from this point the references to 'doing' weave in and out more and more finely in the fabric of the piece. At first, blocks of alternating repetition dominate, with 'explaining' and 'understanding' in separate sentences or larger units from 'doing'. The references begin to alternate in increasingly integrated forms, however, until their consolidation in the final paragraph: 'he was doing something and he was completely steadily doing that thing and he was completely clearly understanding his doing that thing' (3–4). What happens in the text is a gradual and purposeful amalgamation of knowledge and action, of 'understanding', and 'doing', that reiterates the theme of 'useful knowledge' as knowledge that is productive, generated by activity and prompting activity.

Finally, 'Introducing' sustains the trope of youthfulness that appears at the outset in a way that indicates it is fundamental to the approach to knowledge that enables action. In the context of a text framed, in the 'Advertisement', as being 'about Americans' and 'put together' out of the 'Useful Knowledge' that 'helps to be American', the attribute of being young seems to situate its protagonist as exemplary of the American mind in particular, reflecting Stein's characterisation of America in *The Making of Americans* as 'the new people made out of the old' (3). In the opening paragraph, the knowledge at stake is, in fact, the protagonist's knowledge of his youthfulness: he 'was completely a young one', he was 'clearly understanding that this one was a young one' and 'clearly explaining this thing', this being young, 'to every one' (1). The references to his youth are interspersed through the next three paragraphs with the references to his 'doing something' that represent the other objects of the useful knowledge he is gaining and disseminating, indicating a connection between his youth and his ability to use knowledge actively. This resurgent trope also occurs in the final sentence of the piece, indicating its significance in constructing the quality of mind that Stein wants to present in the expression of both her Americanness and her authorship. Stein is, no doubt, herself the 'young one' who introduces her texts, but this is fused with her Americanness in the assertion in the previous framing text, 'Advertisement', that *Useful Knowledge* is a collection 'put together from every little that helps to be American'. In that sense, America's status as a 'young' nation is paralleled in Stein's feeling that her mind is young, the mind of the modern world.

The American Ideal

In part, this representation of the dynamism and fluidity of the learning mind counters the stasis attributed to the 'mental defective' used to figure Stein's work, among some modernists working in Britain, as degenerate. It presents Stein's work as proceeding from a complex flux of intellectual engagement opposed to those representations of the mind of the 'imbecile'. It is also, as we have seen, an insistence on the productivity of learning and the propagation of ability as the protagonist acquires, generates and disseminates the knowledge of how to do things. This attention to the processes of acquiring useful knowledge also insists on its communicative, collaborative nature. Stein has already established the particularly American ideal of useful knowledge in 'Advertisement'. In 'Introducing', knowledge is dependent on the active interaction of individuals: the 'one' who is learning relies on other participants in the process, both in the practice of 'explaining' that is always coupled with, and so crucial to, 'understanding', and in the practice of asking questions that deepens the quality of his knowledge. This parallels the emphasis on the usefulness of American collectivity in 'Advertisement'. Stein's positing of the useful, productive, collaborative yet individualised mind of the American draws into its scope her radically simple idea of democracy, in the 'many', 'different' who are successful, powerful and happy 'altogether', with a positive ideal of mass consumer culture in the 'romance' of the 'cheapest thing' and the secure assumption that Americans will 'own the earth' as they ever have. This offers a reverse image of the Stein proposed in the critical futurology of Rodker, Lewis and Eliot as the embodiment of the dysgenic effect of mass democracy on the collective intellect, engaging positively with the democratisation of knowledge, the burgeoning scene of popular publication and the potentially levelling effects of mass production and full participation.

The construction, in this reframing, of a radically simple ideal of Stein's authorship as representative of an American democracy that champions the dissemination of useful knowledge and enables full participation has a number of problematic features, however, that reflect the complexity of the position ascribed to her authorship. In perhaps the most influential critical examination of *Useful Knowledge*, Barbara Will's *Gertrude Stein, Modernism and the Problem of 'Genius'*, Will examines two pieces from the collection as evidence for her overarching contention that Stein's conception of genius is 'dialogic' and inclusive, arguing that these texts are 'Stein's effort to rewrite the American national myth as an ideal relationship between the individual unit . . . and the collective "whole"' and represent an 'enlightened American collectivity' (Will, 2000, 14). Rather than representing either a positive new model for her own genius or Stein's coming-to-terms with her American identity, however, being American in *Useful Knowledge* is, I would argue, the solution to Stein's problem of how to reassert the position of author for herself in the face of fundamental challenges to the value and authenticity of her work.

The claim that to be American is to be fundamentally democratic is initially suggested by the relationship between States and individuals evoked in the 'Advertisement' with the observation 'When there are many Americans and there are there is a great deal of pleasure in knowing that not only they differ from one another but that Iowa and California are very pleasant and different from one another'. The nature of the political federation of the States is directly paralleled with the identity and status of individuals, making the political makeup of the US a model of democratic agency that originates, constitutes and patterns American identity as ontologically democratic. Coupled with the declaration that Americans 'own the earth just as pleasantly as ever' the 'Advertisement' affirms a nationalism predicated on an essentialist birthright of possession and self-determination.

The selection and arrangement of texts in the collection work to assert the profound identification of Americanness and democracy and to affirm Stein's own claim to this identity. The collection falls roughly into sections that reference various aspects of 'America' as a broad theme. It opens with 'Farragut or A Husband's Recompense', a two-part piece named for the civil war admiral and so suggesting a meditation on the historic origins of modern American democracy. The following text 'Wherein the South Differs from the North' ostensibly continues the civil war theme but also begins a series of four pieces indicating a focus on America as a geographical or geopolitical entity with an emphasis on comparison and difference that foregrounds geographical definitions as patterns of locational and linguistic relationality. After two texts, 'Among Negroes' and 'Business in Baltimore', dealing with American culture, the selections turn to recent history, with 'Scenes from the Door' and 'Three Leagues' obliquely indicating Stein's position on American involvement in the First World War and in the League of Nations. The following six pieces narrow to representations of individual Americans, offering 'portraits' of Stein's American friends and acquaintances, and culminating with the portrait of Woodrow Wilson that sets up the final tranche of texts dealing more explicitly, though in very abstract forms, with an idealised politics of American democracy. The result of Stein's selections and combinations is, I would argue, the promotion of a simplistic nationalism that affirms the nation as the appropriate vehicle for democracy, presented in the most notional sense as a proposition far removed from any of the violent realities of democracy as it is lived in the inter-war nation state. Moreover, the democracy Stein idealises is not simply actualised within the nation, it is embodied in the Americans Stein includes, beginning with herself, running through the bourgeois Baltimore Steins but not through the 'negroes' of 'Among Negroes', through the individuals in her portraits and to the synthesised diversity of the 'prominent men' in 'An Instant Answer or A Hundred Prominent Men'.

The initial piece in the collection, 'Farragut or A Husband's Recompense', refers to David Glasgow Farragut, the Unionist civil war admiral who won several decisive naval battles and was famous for his obstinacy. Ostensibly, the position of this piece signifies the originating force of the civil war in American history and serves as a preface to 'Wherein the South Differs from the North', but the text is undoubtedly about Stein herself rather than presenting an engagement with the civil war or Farragut's place in it. It opens with a breathless scene of tense 'anticipation' that, as the text unfolds, is clearly a representation of the aftermath of a disagreement between Stein and Toklas, perhaps about Toklas feeling 'Neglected'(5), but certainly documented more or less straightforwardly in snatches throughout, for example, 'I can't remember the detail. The first that I can remember is asking do you mean to deny you heard me' (9–10), and 'I said go home if you like./ I said I was an authority./ I said I could be angry./ I said nothing' (15) . The text is 'A Husband's Recompense' in that it is Stein's apology to Toklas and an exploration of the reasons for her behaviour, and Stein is 'Farragut' either because she identifies with him or because Toklas makes this comparison. At points in the text, Stein is accused of and admits to the 'stubborn' and 'severe' character of the civil war admiral (and the early reference to 'Caesar drinking' evidently has a similar function of identifying Stein with a domineering male military figure).

The origins of Stein's obstinacy are traced to 'the year 1877' and her journey from the US to Europe aged three, the 'resolution' and 'quicker travelling' of the family's year-long residence in Vienna and Paris (5).[33] The young Stein's experiences around this displacement are presented as formative and the basis of the temperament that leads to the comparison with Farragut and requires her to make recompense for her intractability. The text dwells on the moment of crossing over: 'Crossing./ What was crossing./ The boat./Where was it going./ It wasn't going it was coming./ When did it come./ It came on time' using an interrogatory mode that represents a child's relentless questioning and suggests a point of transition freighted with anxiety. This, followed by 'I was naughty' and the insistence 'I was there./ When./ When I was there./ I was there all the time./ When I was there./ I was there when I was there' locates Stein's stubbornness and naughtiness at this point of high agitation (8). In short, Stein's intransigence is traced back to her childhood feeling of belonging and her desire to stay put. The exploration of these motives does make this initial text a story of origins, but of the origins of Stein's character rather than of American democracy. The placing of this text, however, reactivates the conflation of Stein and Farragut and the originating story of her early, foundational and perhaps traumatic memory of leaving the US as a story of Stein's

American identity. 'Farragut' is placed at the head of the collection in order to re-originate Stein as a fundamentally American author.

The other representative Americans in the collection seem to be selected to give an image of democratic inclusivity. Stein includes subjects from a plurality of social groups, in the form of the wealthy art collector Emily Chadbourne, the self-educated working-class writer Sherwood Anderson, the low-ranking infantry soldier 'Emmett Addis the Doughboy' and the academic and American President Woodrow Wilson, as well as the pianist Allen Tanner and writer and photographer Carl Van Vechten, friends whose homosexuality was an open secret in Stein's circle. These selections are shadowed, however, by the more troubled inclusion of 'Among Negroes', in which the subjects, the African American performers Josephine Baker, Maud de Forrest and Ida Lewelyn, are identified in the title not by their names but by Stein's designation of their race.[34] This is striking in the context of the celebrity status of Josephine Baker and the Paris show 'La Revue Négre', at its height in 1925 when the piece was written: at this point, Baker was definitely a 'name'. It is also significant that this text is not included in the section of 'portraits', but is, rather, between the 'geographical' texts with their abstracted linguistic landscapes of American cities and states and 'Business in Baltimore', which explores the culture of the Baltimore Steins as the essence of comfortable wealthy bourgeois America. Detached from the 'portraits' of individual Americans and situated with texts that deal in places, positions and milieus, 'Among Negroes' has its subjects as part of the landscape of Americanness rather than as participants in it.[35] The inclusion of this piece suggests that to be American is to be 'Among Negroes', but not to be a 'negro'. Thus, 'negroes' form part of the fabric of the experience of being American, but they are not, themselves, citizens of the democratic American nation.

Alongside the selective inclusion of representative Americans, the image of America Stein puts together here presents a distinctly nationalist version of democracy. These ideas are exemplified in the swathe of texts on patriotism and war, from 'Scenes from the Door' to 'Three Leagues', subjects that the collection returns to with the portrait of Woodrow Wilson and the critique of pacifism 'Or More (or War)'. 'Three Leagues' and 'Woodrow Wilson', in particular, reflect the profundity of Stein's nationalism and its complex association with a mythic vision of American democracy. As we have seen, the three short poems that make up 'Three Leagues', satirise President Wilson's campaign for the League of Nations and condemn what Stein saw as his paternalistic liberal internationalism.[36] 'Woodrow Wilson' reflects a similar scepticism about Wilson's rarefied distance from the average American and about his commitment to America as a national project. The text offers a series of images of Wilson as standing above or beyond ordinary life and outside the lived experience of being American. From the outset, Wilson is 'heartily immersed in the very necessary process of illusion and reason and teaching and surveying'(104), suggesting a cloistered, academic distance from real life, a view that is also intimated in Stein's much earlier representation of Wilson as the philosophy professor Philip Redfern in her 1904 novel *Fernhurst* and in the references in this text to 'Wooded Princeton' (112) and 'School men' (107).[37] This scholarly distance comes to characterise the language around Wilson in the portrait, with its proliferation of grand abstractions and generalisations: 'All language is evil'; 'All songs are not songs'; 'In youth we nurse' (104); 'realisation was personality' (105). This is augmented with repeated references to the seriousness associated with a staid and patrician rationalism: 'I accuse myself of earnestness of appreciation of reason and of learning' (104); 'Can you be more solemn than serious more earnest than flagrant' (107); 'Everyone is earnest in earnest' (111); 'When a baby sings and the baby is a boy, he sings seriously and at length. He understands frowning and order and he means to avoid comedy' (112). The oppositional relationship this text sets up between the ordinary American and the intellectual elite extends in interesting and important ways that shed light on the nature of Stein's nationalism, the form of democracy *Useful Knowledge* projects, and the authorial identity she uses it to project.

This is the 'democracy' her work engages, and it is set in opposition to Woodrow Wilson and 'Wooded Princeton', to Wilson's 'earnestness', that is, to the sincere and intense conviction of 'School men'. In other words, it is opposed to Wilson's perceived scholasticism, and that of the other legislators of the new world order. The nationalism expressed in *Useful Knowledge*, however, is ordinary, it is everyday, and it is a form of nationalism that emerges as the nation-state that is the site of democracy in the inter-war period consolidates, inextricably connected to the democratising possibilities of the mass production, dissemination and consumption of 'useful knowledge'. Stein's commitment to democracy is an isolationist American nationalism resistant to the expansion of collective rights to those not considered essentially American, revealing the difficulty in cleanly marking off the forms of nationalism that develop out of this period from those that emerge in the 1930s.

In the debate among modernists working in Britain, Stein's authorship is placed at the interface between democracy and biopolitical regulation. At this point, that is the line she must tread in order to legitimise her author status, resisting those discourses that have her as the subject of clinical or regulatory observation and embracing the vision of her work as democratic in a form that enables authorial agency – or 'genius'. Lewis, Eliot and Rodker want to decide on the exception for literary culture, revealed in their co-opting of the discourse that constructs the exception of the 'feeble-minded'. Stein, however, includes herself by also excluding the limit-figure of the mental defective. By insisting on the dynamic, productive mental processes of both her work and her Americanness to affirm her inclusion, she asserts the exception on the same terms as the narrative that excludes her. She accepts the status of the citizen as an essentially biological status, and she founds her authorship, her right to write, on this status.

Notes

1. Wyndham Lewis, *The Art of Being Ruled* (Santa Rosa, CA: Black Sparrow Press, [1926] 1989), 346.
2. Max Saunders and Brian Hurwitz, 'The *To-day and To-morrow* Series and the Popularization of Science: An Introduction', *Interdisciplinary Science Reviews*, Vol. 34, No. 1 (2009), 3–8, (3). The series was instigated by C. K. Ogden as part of his project to enable a broader audience to engage with issues in science and culture (see Saunders and Hurwitz, 3–4).
3. The booklets in the *To-day and To-morrow* series, priced at 2/6, reached a smaller audience than the cheaper ranges, those which cost 6d or 1/-, and its status as an 'innovative' contribution to this publication scene meant it did not achieve

anything like the huge popularity of Wells's *Outline of History*. See Peter J. Bowler, *Science for All: The Popularization of Science in Early Twentieth-Century Britain* (Chicago: University of Chicago Press, 2009), 139. It is, nevertheless, part of a phenomenon of the 'sheer number of educational book series' published in the inter-war period (Bowler, 10).

4. Elise Schraner, 'The To-day and To-morrow Series', *Interdisciplinary Science Reviews*, Vol. 34, No. 1 (2009), 107–115 (107). A very broad range of reviews is quoted in the 'Volumes Ready' advertising sections of these pamphlets, including national papers such as the *Daily Telegraph* and the *Observer*, local papers like the *Manchester Guardian* and the *Yorkshire Post* and specialist publications such as the *British Medical Journal* and the *Law Times*.

5. See my discussion of T. S. Eliot's review below.

6. Graves's essays are *Lars Porsena, or the Future of Swearing and Improper Language* (1927) and *Mrs Fisher, or the Future of Humour* (1928). Stein initially proposed *Lucy Church Amiably* for consideration in March 1928 and, when this was rejected, offered 'Patriarchal Poetry' or 'Phenomena of Nature'. The draft letter is in the Beinecke collection at YCAL MSS 76 Box 113 f. 2317.

7. Both the popular reach of these first three contributions and their presentation as an interconnected debate is reflected in the judgement in the conservative London newspaper the *Morning Post*, that 'They are all (*Daedalus, Icarus* and *Tantalus*) brilliantly clever, and they supplement one another'. This quotation is used to recommend and advertise Schiller's piece in the 'Volumes Ready' section of F. C. S. Schiller, *Tantalus, or the Future of Man*, third impression (London: Kegan Paul, Trench, Trubner & Co., 1931).

8. Note that Haldane is not advocating eugenics, which manipulates reproduction by controlling behaviour, but 'ectogenesis' (his own term), which imagines a more direct intervention in the development of genetic material in artificial conditions (i.e. 'test-tube' babies).

9. The texts that use these tropes in the Stein debate appear in the British context, so my discussion here concentrates mainly on British clinical and legislative discourses. For a detailed discussion of the history of legislation in the US, see Allison C. Carey, *On the Margins of Citizenship: Intellectual Disability and Civil Rights in Twentieth-Century America* (Philadelphia, PA: Temple University Press, 2009).

10. For a discussion of this shift in emphasis in England, see Mark Jackson, 'Institutional Provision for the Feeble-Minded in Edwardian England: Sandlebridge and the Scientific Morality of Permanent Care', in *From Idiocy to Mental Deficiency: Historical Perspectives on People with Learning Disabilities*, ed. David Wright and Anne Digby (London: Routledge, 1996).

11. See Luke Kersten, 'New Hampshire Enacted Voluntary Sexual Sterilization Laws. It Was Later Reenacted as Compulsory in 1929', retrieved 14 March 2022, from http://eugenicsarchive.ca/discover/timeline/532335f2132156674b00023: 'Up until 1928, the 1917 legislation had resulted in only 39 sterilizations (Kaelber, 2011). However, with amendments of 1929, that number rose significantly. For example, 80 in 1932 alone; culminating in a total 679 sterilizations. The significance of the New Hampshire legislation was that kept in step with legal

developments in the United States. The consent based approach of the 1917 legislation reflects the legal tentativeness of sterilization laws at the time. However, after 1927, the Supreme Court, in *Buck vs. Bell*, upheld the constitutionality of sterilization legislation. The result was a stronger, compulsory based approach in the reenacted 1929 version.'

12. For discussions of the history of this legislation and its implementation in what Mathew Thomson terms 'an era of "adjustment to democracy"' (207), see Mathew Thomson, 'Family, Community and State: The Micro-Politics of Mental Deficiency' in *From Idiocy to Mental Deficiency: Historical Perspectives on People with Learning Disabilities*, ed. David Wright and Anne Digby (London: Routledge, 1996), 207–230.
13. A. F. Tredgold, 'II. The Feeble-Minded – a Social Danger', *The Eugenics Review* Vol. 1, No. 2 (1909), 97–104 (100).
14. A. F. Tredgold, *Mental Deficiency: Amentia* (New York: William Wood and Co., 1923), 2. This passage is unchanged from the 1914 edition, suggesting it forms a persistent feature of Tredgold's attitude.
15. H. S. Jennings, *Prometheus: Or, Biology and the Advancement of Man* (London: Kegan Paul, Trench, Trubner & Co., 1925), 10.
16. It is interesting to note, however, that Rodker's own small press published an edition of *Three Lives* in 1927. This reveals the instability of these writer's positions on Stein and, indeed, on conceptions of authorship.
17. See my discussion of Crookshank below. Crookshank's essay *The Mongol in Our Midst* references Tredgold, *Mental Deficiency* (1923), Shuttleworth and Potts, *Mentally Deficient Children* (1923), W. H. B. Stoddart, *Mind and Its Disorders* (1919), Kohler, *The Mentality of Apes* (1924) and C. B. Davenport, *Proceedings, American Association for the Study of the Feeble-Minded* (1924). See Crookshank, 1925, 119–128.
18. F. G. Crookshank, *The Mongol in Our Midst: A Study of Man and His Three Faces*, second edition (London: Kegan Paul, Trench, Trubner & Co., 1925), 85. Note that the essay was published in three editions – 1923, 1925 and 1931.
19. T. S. Eliot, 'Charleston, Hey! Hey!', *The Nation and Athenaeum*, 29 January 1927, Reviews section, 595. All references are to this page.
20. Riding had more or less sole authorship of this chapter.
21. In 1928, Riding published *Anarchism Is Not Enough* (London: Jonathan Cape, 1928), a manifesto against all forms of systematic thinking.
22. M. Alderton Pink, *Procrustes: Or The Future of English Education* (London: Kegan Paul, Trench, Trubner & Co., 1927), 10; M. Chaning-Pearce, *Chiron, or the Education of a Citizen of the World* (London: Kegan Paul, Trench, Trubner & Co., 1931), 5.
23. Vernon Lee, *Proteus, or The Future of Intelligence* (London: Kegan Paul, Trench, Trubner & Co., 1925), 2–3.
24. In *Gertrude Stein, Modernism and the Problem of 'Genius'*, Barbara Will includes some reference to the general context for the collection but no specific details (120). Ulla Dydo discusses 'Woodrow Wilson' and 'Or More (or War)' (*Gertrude Stein*, 135, 91) and 'Business in Baltimore' (*A Stein Reader*, 478) with little or (in the latter case) no discussion of their inclusion in the collection. Linda

Voris's 'Interpreting Cézanne: Immanence in Gertrude Stein's First Landscape Play, "Lend a Hand or Four Religions"' discusses an individual text without referring to the framing material. Karen Leick's *Gertrude Stein and the Making of an American Celebrity* puts *Useful Knowledge* into the context of print culture but does not examine the collection itself (69). Examples that discuss texts from the collection as exemplary of Stein's relationship to America include Elliott L. Vanskike, '"Seeing Everything as Flat": Landscape in Gertrude Stein's *Useful Knowledge* and *The Geographical History of America*' and Michael Moon, '"Wherein the South Differs from the North": Naming Persons, Naming Places, and the Need for Visionary Geographies'. See also Will, 'Stein and Zionism', which includes a discussion of Stein's text, 'The Difference between the Inhabitants of France and Inhabitants of the United States of America'.

25. Ulla Dydo refers to Stein's appropriation of details from these notebooks for *A Novel of Thank You* (1926) in *Gertrude Stein* (257). My examples of front covers are taken from the Beinecke Digital Collections Site.
26. Edward Burns, *The Letters of Gertrude Stein and Carl Van Vechten, 1913–1946* (New York: Columbia University Press, 2013), 161.
27. Letter from Stein to Van Vechten dated 22 February 1925 (Burns, 110).
28. In a letter of February 1928, Brewer thanks Stein for the 'grand blurb' she has sent him. See Gallup, *Flowers of Friendship*, 216.
29. For a discussion of *The Library of Useful Knowledge*, see Margaret Blanchard: 'began publication in 1831 and is generally considered the first book series appealing to a mass market. Published by the Boston Society for the Diffusion of Knowledge, the self-help series echoed a similar series begun four years before in England' (348). The British version ran from 1826 to 1848, whereas the American Society was active until 1947. Iterations of this title proliferated in the nineteenth century, with publications such as the *American Pocket Library of Useful Knowledge* (1841) and the *American Family Library of Useful Knowledge* (1856).
30. *Life* published pieces in 1917 and 1919. See Leick, 59–62. Stein submitted to *Atlantic Monthly* on a number of occasions, and the journal did eventually publish extracts from *The Autobiography of Alice B. Toklas* in 1933. See Bryce Conrad, 'Gertrude Stein in the American Marketplace'. *Vanity Fair* also published other modernist writing and features about modernists, but, as I have discussed in Chapter 3, Stein formed a long correspondence relationship with the editor Frank Crowninshield that reveals her commitment to popular publication. See Beinecke Rare Book and Manuscript Library Digital Collections,: Stein, Gertrude. [Letters : Frank Crowninshield to Gertrude Stein and Gertrude Stein to Frank Crowninshield], https://brbl-dl.library.yale.edu/vufind/Record/3582252. Stein's attachment to *The Literary Digest* is suggested by her reference to 'My literary digest' in 'Woodrow Wilson', one of the texts published in *Useful Knowledge*, and by its presence in the papers at Yale.
31. Gertrude Stein, *Useful Knowledge* (New York: Payson and Clarke, 1928), frontispiece: no page numbers.
32. See Will, *Gertrude Stein*, 121.
33. Incidentally, this date removes any doubt that the text is not about David Glasgow Farragut, who died in 1870.

34. Note that Emmett Addis is also identified in terms of his rank.
35. This attitude is also reflected in the reference to the visit that is the subject of 'Among Negroes' in *The Autobiography of Alice B. Toklas*: 'Carl Van Vechten sent us quantities of negroes beside there were the negroes of our neighbour Mrs. Regan who had brought Josephine Baker to Paris. Carl sent us Paul Robeson. Paul Robeson interested Gertrude Stein. He knew american values and american life as only one in it but not of it could know them' (237).
36. See my discussions in the Introduction and in Chapter 3.
37. Wilson was President of Princeton from 1902 to 1910.

Coda: Stein's Democratic Authorship in *The Autobiography of Alice B. Toklas*

The exclusionary discourse generated as modernists debated the legitimacy of Stein's authorship had its effects, as Figure 1 shows. The waning of Stein's 1920s publication surge, however, prompted in turn two divergent events: the establishment of her private press, Plain Editions, which attracted almost no readers, and the composition and publication of *The Autobiography of Alice B. Toklas*, which became a bestseller. The subject of the *Autobiography* is, of course, Gertrude Stein's authorship, and in this text her desire to control conceptions of her authorial identity is both more overt and, ultimately, more successfully achieved than in her earlier attempts. The essential characteristics delineated in the collation and structuring of the texts in *Useful Knowledge* are reiterated and insisted upon in the *Autobiography*. Stein offers an idealised vision of her authorship that is asserted in the presentation of the Rue de Fleurus as a democratic space aligned with mass culture forms, the identification of Alice B. Toklas as the ideal average audience of mass democracy, and the location of democratic liberation in an Americanness that frees Gertrude Stein the American citizen from biological constraints. These features are subtended, however, by the differentiation of racialised unAmerican others constrained by biology, and by an obfuscation of strategies of exclusion.

The scene of Stein's authorship, 27 Rue de Fleurus, is presented in an early passage that conveys both open spaciousness and unassuming homeliness, qualities that immediately signify the artless and simple liberality of a democratic ideal:

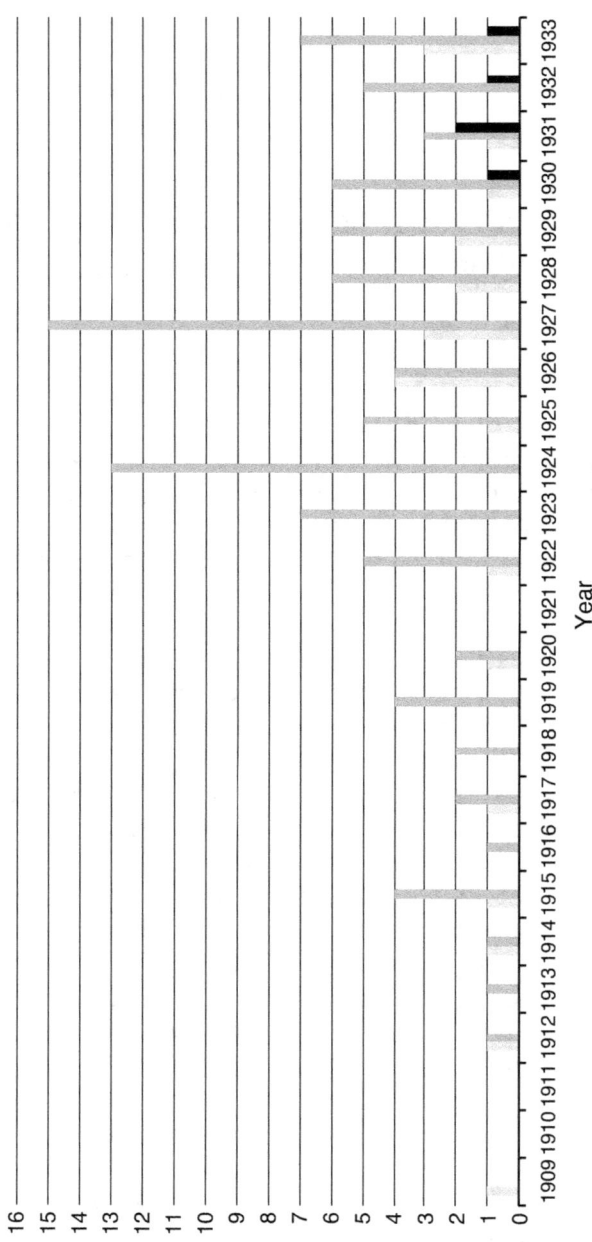

Figure 1 Gertrude Stein: publications 1909–1933
Source: *Gertrude Stein: A Bibliography*, compiled by Robert A. Wilson (New York: The Phoenix Bookshop, 1974).

> The home at 27 rue de Fleurus consisted then as it does now of a tiny pavilion of two stories with four small rooms, a kitchen and bath, and a very large atelier adjoining. Now the atelier is attached to the pavilion by a tiny hall passage added in 1914 but at that time the atelier had its own entrance, one rang the bell of the pavilion or knocked at the door of the atelier, and a great many people did both, but more knocked at the atelier. I was privileged to do both. I had been invited to dine on Saturday evening which was the evening when everybody came, and indeed everybody did come.[1]

The atelier, juxtaposed with the cosy and rather humble 'tiny pavilion' with 'small rooms', is 'very large', suggesting by contrast a free open space. Both of these descriptions, however, contribute to an implication of egalitarian liberty. Stein's home in the pavilion is modest, connoting a simple, ordinary life, and the space given over to those who, it seems, come and go as they please, is generous, asserting both her classlessness and the pre-eminence of the social and the collective. The language used to describe the architecture of Stein's world – 'pavilion' and 'atelier' – also intimates fluidity and ephemerality, an impression augmented by the spatial arrangement in which one freely passes from one place to another, at first through the two entrances and later via the 'tiny passage'. The availability of these spaces reflected in the sounds of bell and knock and the remark 'a great many did both' heightens the sense of latitude indicated by the provisional, mobile architectonics of 'pavilion' and 'atelier', both of which denote indeterminate and temporary spaces. As Toklas's narrative progresses, we return repeatedly to the scenes of the atelier in which it is populated with an array of guests from all walks of life. The kaleidoscopic effect of these recursive scenarios – foregrounded by Alice's characterisation 'it was like a kaleidoscope slowly turning' (98) – amplifies a sense of the absolute openness of the world created in and by Stein's authorial presence. The inclusivity of Stein's world is accentuated in Alice's first account in the abundance and variety of visitors, and, more significantly, in the emphasis on randomness:

> The room was soon very very full and who were they all. Groups of hungarian painters and writers, it happened that some hungarian had once

been brought and the word had spread from him throughout all Hungary, any village where there was a young man who had ambitions heard of 27 rue de Fleurus and then he lived but to get there and a great many did get there. They were always there, all sizes and shapes, all degrees of wealth and poverty, some very charming, some simply rough and every now and then a very beautiful young peasant . . . (17–18).

The foregrounding of the contribution of chance – 'it happened that some hungarian had once been brought' – to the composition of guests in the narrative of Alice's first encounter signals a resistance to criteria and thus indicates a practice of total acceptance without formulae or formality. The lack of any criterion for entry is attached to the presence of Hungarians of all kinds ('all sizes and shapes') from all classes ('all degrees of wealth and poverty'), suggesting that to embrace chance is to reject choice, and that this position in itself produces egalitarianism. This opening exemplar serves to assert an ethic of inclusivity that is repeatedly reproduced throughout the depictions of Stein's salon.

The function of Toklas in the construction of Stein's participatory world in the *Autobiography* is crucial. Alice, with her naïvely knowing voice and her personal history of inconsequentiality, is ordinary. Her initial response to the avant-garde artworks in Stein's collection, 'Now I was confused and I looked and I looked and I was confused', is marked in the following sentence, 'Gertrude Stein and her brother were so accustomed to this state of mind in a guest that they paid no attention to it', as representative of the usual response of the average viewer (15). Alice is also, significantly, both a wife and a worker, taking care of Stein's domestic needs and typing her manuscripts. Thus, she represents the private and public worlds of the average family while sustaining the feminisation of popular culture exemplified in Wyndham Lewis's caricatures.[2] Rather than distancing her authorship from the popular culture that accompanies mass democracy, Stein emphasises the spectacular mass-media tropes of physical and visual positioning, figuring and performance in its presentation of the avant-garde scene through the eyes of Toklas, a spectator in the movie theatre of modernism.[3] Presented in the text as an eternal ingénue, her wondering appreciation of the scene and her lack of direct engagement with it provide a subject position that grasps Stein's 'epoch' in terms of its exterior shows. Toklas's passive position and the continual references to her ordinariness posit her as a stand-in not for the 'highbrow' avant-garde cognoscenti, but for the average spectator of mass culture. Indeed, the oft-quoted assertion in the opening chapter that a bell rings when Toklas meets a genius indicates that the modern genius can be identified by anyone at a single glance. In the narrator's reiteration of this at the end of the chapter: 'I have only known three first-class geniuses and in each case on sight within me something rang', the emphasis on sight points to the 'image-based' currency of popular culture (9).[4] This conflates the identification of genius, a concept associated with the elaborated codes of high culture, with the superficial immediacy of the mass-media spectacle. It is also, however, a conscious figuring which continues rather than negating a relationship to the earlier moment of the avant-garde group with its collective authorial self-fashioning. Importantly, Alice, in representing the average citizen, exemplifies the *Autobiography*'s insistence that the ordinary American is the audience for the avant-garde.

The theatrical, cinematic nature of both the world that the *Autobiography* represents and of the *Autobiography* itself is further foregrounded in a conversation between Stein and Matisse:

> Matisse laughed and said, yes I know Mademoiselle Gertrude, the world is a theatre for you, but there are theatres and theatres, and when you listen so carefully to me and so attentively and do not hear a word I say then I do say that you are very wicked (19–20).

In a text that signals its function in composing both Toklas's and Stein's personae and the history of their modernist scene, it is highly significant that Stein includes this comment. At first glance, this is not a positive representation of Stein, portraying her as both superficial and wilfully solipsistic. Matisse is critical of Stein's world-as-theatre on ethical grounds. For Matisse, Stein's insincere performance of attention is morally wrong – it is 'wicked' – suggesting that sincerity has a positive moral value. The fact that this barbed remark is included suggests that it, in fact, signals an important aspect of Stein's authorship. The staginess of Toklas's impressions and the representation of Stein as a character in the drama of modernism suggests the world is indeed 'a theatre' for Stein. The description of Stein's atelier in Chapter 2, from the perspective of Toklas's entry onto the scene, presents the furniture and objects in the room as props which, as in a drama, suggest a fictional world of meaning which will unfold in the action on stage – or screen.[5] In the lines 'in the middle of the room was a big renaissance table, on it a lovely inkstand, and at one end of it note-books neatly arranged' (13), the objects in the world of the atelier stage Stein's authorial presence and highlight the act of writing. This kind of dramatisation is also used to create an impression of the group and Stein's centrality in it as Toklas introduces us to the other avant-garde 'characters', each time positioning them in relation to Stein. In keeping with the text's cinematic coding, Picasso is portrayed as a sound effect, closely allied to Stein in the representation of 'the high Spanish whinnying laugh of Picasso and the gay contralto outbreak of Gertrude Stein' (18). Stein's intimacy with Matisse is also signified in the observation 'Miss Stein and he seemed to be full of hidden meanings' (19), which evokes a noirish chiaroscuro of exaggerated facial expressions and stage whispers.[6] Toklas's blank, gauche persona, performing the role of passive observer, replicates the position of the movie theatre audience.

The inclusion of Matisse's remark also serves to make this dramatisation explicit. Just as Stein stages the modernist scene and her authorial position in it, so she includes this comment in the first 'Paris' chapter in order to foreground her own use of cinematic theatricality as a narrative technique. The dialogue between Matisse and Stein performs Stein's recognition of the *Autobiography* as illusion. The phrase 'there are theatres and there are theatres' in the context of Stein's staging – the text itself, the kaleidoscopic theatre of modernism it portrays, and the broader spectacle of mass culture – takes on a complex significance. Stein overdetermines the notion of theatricality, through the repetition of the word here, in the representation of the atelier as a fluid stage across which actors pass – 'people came and went, in and out' (18) – in the emphasis on her own authorial persona, and in the function of Toklas as movie audience.

This is, then, a cinematic staging of a world of inclusion and participation that blurs the distinction between the real and the constructed, the authentic and the staged, and which has other significant functions in the presentation of Stein's authorship. As well as asserting the mass audience of twentieth-century mass democracy as the appropriate audience for the avant-garde in general and Stein's work in particular, the *Autobiography* also points to her authorial self-composition as an aspect of the Americanness that enables her to escape apparently biological designations. Stein's American identity is asserted as an effect of the simple act of repetition – 'American' is repeated 181 times – and it is also made explicit in the second chapter:

> I did not realise then how completely and entirely american was Gertrude Stein. Later I often teased her, calling her a general, a civil war general of either or both sides. She had a series of photographs of the civil war, rather wonderful photographs and she and Picasso used to pore over them (20).

Alice's early expression of this identity also reflects the association of Stein with civil war generals in *Useful Knowledge* in a reiteration that more overtly determines her Americanness as a fundamental quality. Stein's identification with the civil war general as an exemplification of her Americanness figures this identity as masculine and ethnically Northern European, and thus it is also bound up with her rejection of other potential identities: her gender and her Jewishness.[7] Her resistance to her other – and othering – potential identifications is also intimated at particular moments in the *Autobiography*. In an example of her 'explosive temper', Alice narrates Stein's anger at the arrival of Albert C. Barnes, the chemist, businessman and art collector. Stein 'did not like the stranger's looks' and asks, 'Who is that . . . He looks like a Jew' (15). Given that a large section of Stein's American milieu, including Alice, are American Jewish, the inclusion of this casual anti-Semitism is highly significant. The apparent triviality of the slur, which is not, of course, aimed at someone Jewish – as Stein's friend Alfy answers, 'he's worse than that' – insists on Stein's ordinary Americanness because it suggests Jewishness is not a specific concern of hers, merely a background prejudice upon which she draws occasionally for rhetorical purposes. This seemingly inconsequential example is the only reference to Jewishness in the entirety of the text, and thus effaces her own Jewishness much more effectively than an outright rejection would. In a similar way, her rejection of gender is intimated in a minor incident that underplays its significance in order to more successfully erase it. Recounting a conversation with Marion Walker, a fellow medical student in Stein's university days, Alice notes that 'they were as fond of each other and disagreed as violently about the cause of women as they did then'. This is not simply a recapitulation of Stein's arguments with progressive reformism, as indicated in the clarification that follows: 'Not, as Gertrude Stein explained to Marion Walker, that she at all minds the cause of women or any other cause but it does not happen to be her business' (92). In her insistence that the cause of women is not her business, Stein exempts herself from the question of gender as she effaces the issues of Jewish identity and anti-Semitism, and, in these withdrawals, she claims, once again, an American identity that means she can make herself up. Thus, the theatricality of the *Autobiography* achieves a significant function: it foregrounds Stein's fabrication of her own identity and reflects her belief in the liberation from biological and ethnic designations that American identity bestows on the individual.

Stein's liberated self-construction, however, is not extended to those she considers outside its possibility. In identifying her own freedom, she insists on the insurmountable biological constraints she imagines in others. Though intimated in her pronouncement 'He looks like a Jew', her politics of racialisation are most overt in her representation of African Americans. Alice's report, 'Carl Van Vechten sent us quantities of negroes beside there were the negroes of our neighbour Mrs. Regan who had brought Josephine Baker to Paris' (256), echoes the narrative stance of Stein's *Useful Knowledge* piece 'Among Negroes' to reiterate the insistence on the determining function of race for African Americans and to position them as objects. Here, 'sent us' is suggestive of the shipping of exotic curios, 'quantities' indicates an undifferentiated mass, and 'the negroes of our neighbour' compounds the objectification by evoking a relationship defined by possession. Returning to her conception in 'Among Negroes' that African Americans are not American, Stein's view of Paul Robeson – 'He knew american values and american life as only one in it but not of it could know them' (257) –

distinguishes African Americans from those who are made by being American: they experience life in America but do not belong there. While this might be read as an accurate interpretation of the history of oppression and exclusion that characterises the place of African Americans in American cultural, political and social life, Stein indicates that what she means is very much other than that. After explaining why she is more 'interested' in Paul Robeson than she is in the other 'negroes' – an opinion that serves to deepen the objectification – Alice reports Stein's conclusion: 'negroes were not suffering from persecution, they were suffering from nothingness'. Alice elaborates: 'She always contends that the african is not primitive, he has a very ancient but a very narrow culture and there it remains. Consequently nothing does or can happen' (257). The 'nothingness' of the African American – here, 'the african' – is therefore a result not of their subjugation and erasure but of the determining racial characteristics that mean that as a race they cannot develop. In Stein's judgement, African Americans can mean nothing in the modern world exemplified by the America Stein credits with having 'created the twentieth century' (87).

The function of racialisation as a strategy of exclusion is also clear in the indication that the 'negroes' could only be admitted to the atelier, the space of democratic participation, a site authored by Stein and the site of her authorship, because they are 'sent' by Van Vechten or belong to Mrs Regan. This stipulation gestures to the complex concealment of the exclusionary mechanism that, in fact, governs entry to the salon, and this is strikingly exemplified in Alice's explanation of the 'formula' for entry into Stein's salon in the Rue de Fleurus:

> She usually opened the door to the knock and the usual formula was, de la part de qui venez-vous, who is your introducer. The idea was that anybody could come but for form's sake and in Paris you have to have a formula, everybody was supposed to be able to mention the name of somebody who had told them about it. It was a mere form, really everybody could come in and as at that time these pictures had no value and there was no social privilege attached to knowing any one there, only those came who really were interested. So as I say anybody could come in, however, there was the formula (17).

The diminution of 'formula' to 'mere form' suggests the formula has no meaning, an effect augmented because it is continually denied by the concurrent variations on 'anybody could come in'. The apparent lack of social, cultural or economic value ascribed to the salon supports the claim that this is a space delineated by a formula that in itself means nothing. The repetition of 'formula' and 'form', however, asserts the significance of the formula that authorises entry even as it is repudiated, an oscillation that is insisted upon in the final sentence 'So as I say anybody could come in, however, there was the formula'. These balanced phrases create a paradox which holds the narrative at the door in way that defers entry and heightens attention to the boundary. The presentation of the salon as a participatory space embodies Stein's claim for the role of her authorship in the democratisation of the cultural sphere, and the fugitive presence of the formula that holds us at the perimeter marks the practices of inclusion and exclusion that do indeed characterise the democracies of the early twentieth century.

Notes

1. Gertrude Stein, *The Autobiography of Alice B. Toklas* (London: Penguin Books, [1933] 1966), 10–11.
2. For a discussion of Toklas, typing and women's labour, see Natalia Cecire, 'Ways of Not Reading Gertrude Stein', *ELH: English Literary History*, Vol. 82, No. 1 (2015), 281–312. While typing, as Cecire points out, is women's work, the labour that Toklas undertakes in typing Stein's work is differentiated from her domestic labour and is meaningful in the public rather than the private sphere. Note that Cecire also writes helpfully about the disparagement of the woman reader.
3. For Aaron Jaffe, the prestige of modernist authorship is grounded upon its distinctiveness from popular culture, in that 'Unlike movie stardom, the matrix of associations supporting their reputations is not intrinsically image-based, but predicated instead on a distinctive textual mark of authorship, a sanction for distinguishing a high literary product from the inflating signs of consumption.' See Aaron Jaffe, *Modernism and the Culture of Celebrity* (Cambridge: Cambridge University Press, 2005), 1.
4. See note 3 above.
5. For a discussion of the staginess of 1930s film as talkies replaced silent movies, see, for example, David Bordwell, *On the History of Film Style* (Cambridge, MA: Harvard University Press, 1997).

6. See Mark Bould, *Film Noir: From Berlin to Sin City* (London: Wallflower Press, 2005) for an overview of the origins of noir in 1920s Berlin and early 1930s Hollywood.
7. For a detailed discussion of Stein's masculine identity, see Chris Coffman, *Gertrude Stein's Transmasculinity* (Edinburgh: Edinburgh University Press, 2018).

BIBLIOGRAPHY

Agamben, Giorgio, *Homo Sacer: Sovereign Power and Bare Life* (Stanford, CA: Stanford University Press, 1998).

Agamben, Giorgio, *State of Exception* (Chicago: University of Chicago Press, 2005).

Agran, Edward G., *'Too Good a Town': William Allen White, Community, and the Rhetoric of Middle America* (Fayetteville: University of Arkansas Press, 1998).

Anderson, Sherwood, 'Four American Impressions: Gertrude Stein, Paul Rosenfeld, Ring Lardner, Sinclair Lewis', *The New Republic*, Vol. 32, No. 410 (11 October 1922), 171–173.

Anderson, Sherwood, 'The Work of Gertrude Stein', in Gertrude Stein, *Geography and Plays* (Boston, MA: Four Seas Company, 1922).

Anonymous, 'Miss Tarbell's History of Standard Oil', *McClure's Magazine*, Vol. 19, No. 6 (November 1902), 588–592.

Anonymous, Review of *Three Lives*, *Washington Herald*, 12 December 1909 in Curnutt, 9.

Anonymous, Review of *Three Lives*, *Boston Globe*, 18 December 1909, 9.

Anonymous, Review of *Three Lives*, *New York Sun*, 25 December 1909, 5.

Anonymous, Review of *Three Lives*, *Pittsburgh Daily Post*, 17 January 1910, 7.

Anonymous, Review of *Three Lives*, *The Nation*, 20 January 1910 in Wagner-Martin, 371.

Anonymous, Review of *Three Lives*, *Chicago Record Herald*, 22 January 1910 in Curnutt, 12.

Anonymous, Review of *Three Lives*, *Kansas City Star*, 30 January 1910, 24.

Anonymous, Review of *Three Lives*, *Pittsburgh Post-Gazette*, 30 January 1910, 29.

Anonymous, Review of *Three Lives*, *Vancouver Province*, 8 February 1910, 16.

Anonymous, Review of *Three Lives*, *Brooklyn Daily Eagle*, 2 March 1910, 10.

Anonymous, 'The American Section: The National Art, An Interview with the Chairman of the Domestic Committee, Wm J. Glackens', *Arts and Decoration*, Vol. 3, No. 5 (6 March 1913), 159–164.

Anonymous, 'Gertrude Stein', *New York City Call*, 7 June 1914 in Diepeveen, 122–124.

Anonymous, 'Time to Show a Message', *Omaha World Herald*, 7 June 1914 in Diepeveen, 125–127.
Anonymous, "What Is Lunch?" *Chicago Tribune*, 12 June 1914 in Diepeveen, 129.
Anonymous, 'Gertrude Stein as Literary Cubist', *Philadelphia North American*, 13 June 1914, in Diepeveen, 130–131.
Anonymous, 'Gertrude Stein, Plagiary', *New York Evening Sun*, 13 June 1914 in Curnutt, 16–17.
Anonymous, 'And She Triumphed on the Tragic Turnip Field!' *Cleveland Leader*, 21 June 1914 in Curnutt, 159–160.
Anonymous, 'It Confuses, It Shows . . . It Likes It as It Seems', *Oxford University Review*, 10 June 1926, 332.
Anonymous, 'Miss Stein', *Cherwell*, 12 June 1926, 248.
Anonymous, '*Composition as Explanation* by Gertrude Stein' *The New Criterion*, Vol. 5, No. 1 (January 1927), 162.
Antliff, Allan, *Anarchist Modernism: Art, Politics, and the First American Avant-Garde* (Chicago: University of Chicago Press, 2001).
Ardis, Ann, 'Staging the Public Sphere: Magazine Dialogism and the Prosthetics of Authorship at the Turn of the Twentieth Century', in *Transatlantic Print Culture, 1880–1940: Emerging Media, Emerging Modernisms* (London: Palgrave Macmillan, 2008), 30–47.
Arendt, Hannah, *The Origins of Totalitarianism* (New York: Meridian, 1962).
Armitage, Gilbert, 'A Word on Gertrude Stein', *Oxford Magazine*, 17 June 1926, 584.
Arthors, Paul K., 'Cheating the Nature: A Literary Challenge to Opal Whiteley, Patience Worth and Gertrude Stein', *Vanity Fair*, October 1920.
Bailey, Fred Arthur, 'Thomas Nelson Page and the Patrician Cult of the Old South', *International Social Science Review*, Vol. 72, Nos 3/4 (1997), 110–121.
Baker, Ray Stannard, 'Admiral Sampson. A Character Sketch', *McClure's Magazine*, Vol. 13, No. 5 (September 1899), 388–397.
Baker, Ray Stannard, 'J. Pierpont Morgan', *McClure's Magazine*, Vol. 17, No. 6 (October 1901), 507–518.
Baker, Ray Stannard, *Following the Color Line: An Account of Negro Citizenship in the American Democracy* (New York: Doubleday Page, 1908).
Benstock, Shari, *Women of the Left Bank: Paris, 1900–1940* (Austin: University of Texas Press, 1986).
Bernstein, Charles, 'Ulla Dydo, 1925–2017', *Jacket 2*, 1 January 2018.
Blackmer, Corinne E., 'African Masks and the Arts of Passing in Gertrude Stein's "Melanctha" and Nella Larsen's "Passing"', *Journal of the History of Sexuality*, Vol. 4, No. 2, Special Issue, Part 1: Lesbian and Gay Histories (October 1993), 230–263.
Blackshaw, Gemma, *Facing the Modern, 9 October 2013–12 January 2014* (London: National Gallery, 2013).
Blake, Casey Nelson, Kimberly Orcutt and Marilyn S. Kushner, eds, *The Armory Show at 100: Modernism and Revolution* (New York: New York Historical Society, 2013).
Bluemner, Oscar, 'Audiator et Altera Pars: Some Plain Sense on the Modern Art Movement', *Camera Work*, Special Number (June 1913), 25–37.
Bordwell, David, *On the History of Film Style* (Cambridge, MA: Harvard University Press, 1997).

Bould, Mark, *Film Noir: from Berlin to Sin City* (London: Wallflower Press, 2005).
Bowers, Jane Palatini, 'Experiment in Time and Process of Discovery: Picasso Paints Gertrude Stein; Gertrude Stein Makes Sentences', in *Harvard Library Bulletin*, Vol. 5, No. 2 (1994), 5-30.
Bowler, Peter J., *Science for All: The Popularization of Science in Early Twentieth-Century Britain* (Chicago: University of Chicago Press, 2009).
Brown, Milton W., *The Story of the Armory Show* (New York: Joseph H. Hirshhorn Foundation, 1963).
Brunkhorst, Hauke, 'The Crisis of Legitimization in the World Society', in *The Twilight of Constitutionalism?*, ed. Petra Dobner and Martin Loughlin (Oxford: Oxford University Press, 2010).
Buckman, David Lear, *Old Steamboat Days on the Hudson River* (New York: Grafton, 1907).
Bürger, Peter, Michael Shaw and Jochen Schulte-Sasse, *Theory of the Avant-Garde* (Minneapolis: University of Minnesota Press, 1984).
Burke, Jill, *Changing Patrons: Social Identity and the Visual Arts in Renaissance Florence* (Philadelphia: Penn State University Press, 2004).
Burns, Edward M., *The Letters of Gertrude Stein and Carl Van Vechten, 1913-1946* (New York: Columbia University Press, 2013).
Burns, Edward M., 'Gertrude Stein as a Book Reviewer', *Turtle Point Press Magazine*, Fall 2014.
Burton, Richard, 'Posing', *Minneapolis (Minnesota) Bellman*, 17 October 1914 in Curnutt, 163-164.
Butterfield, Roger, 'Henry Ford, the Wayside Inn, and the Problem of "History Is Bunk"', *Proceedings of the Massachusetts Historical Society*. Vol. 77 (1965), 53-66.
Cardinal, Jody, 'Gertrude Stein and College Education for Women: Early Activism and Its Modernist Legacy', in *Modernist Women Writers and American Social Engagement*, ed. Jody Cardinal, Deirdre E. Egan-Ryan and Julia Lisella (Lanham, MD: Rowman & Littlefield, 2019), 91-114.
Carey, Allison C., *On the Margins of Citizenship: Intellectual Disability and Civil Rights in Twentieth-Century America* (Philadelphia, PA: Temple University Press, 2009).
Casanova, Pascale, *The World Republic of Letters* (Cambridge, MA: Harvard University Press, 2004).
Casanova, Pascale, 'Literature as a World', *New Left Review*, Vol. 31 (January/February 2005), 71-90.
Cecire, Natalia, 'Ways of Not Reading Gertrude Stein', *ELH*, Vol. 82, No. 1 (Spring 2015), 281-312.
Chaning-Pearce, M., *Chiron, or the Education of a Citizen of the World* (London: Kegan Paul, Trench, Trubner & Co., 1931).
Chessman, Harriet Scott, *The Public Is Invited to Dance: Representation, the Body, and Dialogue in Gertrude Stein* (Stanford, CA: Stanford University Press, 1989).
Chessman, Harriet and Catharine Stimpson, *Gertrude Stein: Writings 1903-1932* (New York: Library of America, 1998).
Chessman, Harriet and Catharine Stimpson, *Gertrude Stein: Writings 1932-1946* (New York: Library of America, 1998).

Clark, T. J., *Farewell to an Idea: Episodes from a History of Modernism* (New Haven, CT: Yale University Press, 1999).

Coffman, Chris, *Gertrude Stein's Transmasculinity* (Edinburgh: Edinburgh University Press, 2018).

Cohen, Milton A., '"To stand on the rock of the word 'we'": Appeals, Snares and Impact of Modernist Groups before World War I', in *Modernist Group Dynamics: The Politics and Poetics of Friendship*, ed. Fabio A Durão and Dominic Williams (Newcastle upon Tyne: Cambridge Scholars, 2009), 1–24.

Conrad, Bryce, 'Gertrude Stein in the American Marketplace', *Journal of Modern Literature*, Vol. 19, No. 2 (1995), 215–233.

Cooper, John Milton, *Woodrow Wilson: A Biography* (New York: Random House, 2009).

Crookshank, F. G., *The Mongol in Our Midst: A Study of Man and His Three Faces*, 2nd edition (London: Kegan Paul, Trench, Trubner & Co., 1925).

CUMC, 'She Cam, She Saw, She Conquered', *Granta May Week Double Number*, 12 June 1926, 440.

Curnutt, Kirk, *The Critical Response to Gertrude Stein* (Westport, CT: Greenwood Press, 2000).

Davies. Arthur B., 'Explanatory Statement: The Aim of The Association of American Painters and Sculptors', *Arts and Decoration*, Vol. 3, No. 5 (6 March 1913), 149.

DeKoven, Marianne, *A Different Language: Gertrude Stein's Experimental Writing* (Madison: University of Wisconsin Press, 1983).

Diepeveen, Leonard, *Mock Modernism: An Anthology of Parodies, Travesties, Frauds, 1910–1935* (Toronto: University of Toronto Press, 2014).

Dodge, Mabel, 'Speculations, or Post-Impressionism in Prose', *Camera Work*, Special Number (June 1913), 6–9.

Dodge, Mabel, 'Speculations, or Post-Impressionism in Prose', *Arts and Decoration*, Vol. 3, No. 5 (6 March 1913), 172–174.

Dubnick, Randa, *The Structure of Obscurity: Gertrude Stein, Language, and Cubism* (Urbana and Chicago: University of Illinois Press, 1984).

Durão, Fabio A. and Dominic Williams, eds, *Modernist Group Dynamics: The Politics and Poetics of Friendship* (Newcastle upon Tyne: Cambridge Scholars, 2009).

Dydo, Ulla, *A Stein Reader* (Evanston, IL: Northwestern University Press, 1993).

Dydo, Ulla, *Gertrude Stein: the Language That Rises 1923–1934* (Evanston, IL: Northwestern University Press, 2003).

Eliot, T. S., 'Book Reviews: *Ulysses*, Order, and Myth', *The Dial*, Vol. 75, No. 5 (November 1923), 480–484.

Eliot, T. S., 'A Commentary', *The Criterion*, Vol. 2, No. 7 (April 1924), 231–235.

Eliot, T. S., 'Charleston, Hey! Hey!', *The Nation and Athenaeum*, 29 January 1927, Reviews section, 595.

Eliot, T. S., 'Isolated Superiority', *The Dial*, Vol. 84, No. 1 (January 1928), 4–7.

Eliot, T. S., 'The Literature of Fascism', *The Criterion*, Vol. 8, No. 31 (December 1928), 280–290.

English, Daylanne K., *Unnatural Selections: Eugenics in American Modernism and the Harlem Renaissance*. (Chapel Hill: University of North Carolina Press, 2005).

Esau, Erika, 'The Magazine of Enduring Value: *Der Querschnitt* (1921–1936) and the World of Illustrated Magazines', in *The Oxford Critical and Cultural History of Modernist Magazines*, ed. Peter Brooker et al., Vol. III, 868–887.

Everett, Patricia R., *A History of Having a Great Many Times Not Continued to Be Friends: The Correspondence between Mabel Dodge and Gertrude Stein, 1911–1934* (Albuquerque: University of New Mexico Press, 1996).

Fishbein, Leslie, 'The Paterson Pageant (1913): The Birth of Docudrama as a Weapon in the Class Struggle', *New York History*, Vol. 72, No. 2 (April 1991), 197–233.

Flanner, Janet, 'A Frame for Some Portraits', in *'Two' and Other Early Portraits: Volume One of the Yale Edition of the Unpublished Writings of Gertrude Stein* (New Haven, CT: Yale University Press, 1951), ix–xvii.

Flynt, Josiah and Francis Walton, *The Powers that Prey* (New York: McClure, Phillips, 1900).

Foucault, Michel, 'What Is an Author?', in *Essential Works of Foucault 1954–1984, Vol. 2, Aesthetics, Method and Epistemology*, ed. James D. Faubion, trans. Robert Hurley et al. (New York: New Press, 1998), 205–222.

Foucault, Michel, 'Society Must Be Defended', Lecture at the Collège de France, 17 March 1976, in *Biopolitics: A Reader*, ed. Timothy Campbell and Adam Sitze (Durham, NC and London: Duke University Press, 2013).

Franssen, Gaston and Rick Honing, eds, *Celebrity Authorship and Afterlives in English and American Literature* (London: Palgrave Macmillan, 2016).

Gallup, Donald, *The Flowers of Friendship: Letters Written to Gertrude Stein* (New York: Octagon Books, 1979).

Gilbert, Sandra M. and Susan Gubar, *No Man's Land: The Place of the Woman Writer in the Twentieth Century* (New Haven, CT: Yale University Press, 1989).

Gladden, Washington, *The New Idolatry and Other Discussions* (New York: McClure, Phillips & Company, 1905).

Goodspeed-Chadwick, Julie, 'Reconfiguring Identities in the Word and in the World: Naming Marginalized Subjects and Articulating Marginal Narratives in Early Canonical Works by Gertrude Stein', *South Central Review*, Vol. 31, No. 2 (2014), 9–27.

Goody, Alex, *Modernist Articulations* (London: Palgrave Macmillan).

Gregg, Frederick James, 'The Attitude of the Americans', *Arts and Decoration*, Vol. 3, No. 5 (6 March 1913), 165–167.

G.V.S., 'Tender Buttons', *Pittsburgh Sun*, 17 July 1914, in Diepeveen, 131.

Hains, T. Jenkins, 'Beneath the "Bulldog's" Bilge', *McClure's Magazine*, Vol. 25, No. 4 (August 1905), 348–354.

Haldane, J. B. S., *Daedalus, or Science and the Future* (London: Kegan Paul, Trench, Trubner & Co., 1924).

Hammill, Faye and Karen Leick, 'Modernism and the Quality Magazines', in *The Oxford Critical and Cultural History of Modernist Magazines: Volume II: North America 1894–1960*, ed. Peter Brooker and Andrew Thacker (Oxford: Oxford University Press, 2012), 176–196.

Hapgood, Hutchins, 'Authority in Art', *New York Globe*, 28 January 1912, 10.

Hapgood, Hutchins, 'A New Form of Literature', *Camera Work*, No. 40 (1 November 1912), 42–45.

Hapgood, Hutchins, 'Art and Unrest', *New York Globe*, reprinted in *Camera Work*, Nos 42–43 (4 June 1913), 43–44.

Hapgood, Hutchins, 'The Picture Show', *New York Globe*, reprinted in *Camera Work*, Nos 42–43 (4 June 1913), 45–46.

Harding, Jason, 'The Idea of a Literary Review: T. S. Eliot and The Criterion', in *The Oxford Critical and Cultural History of Modernist Magazines: Volume I: Britain and Ireland 1880–1955*, ed. Peter Brooker and Andrew Thacker (Oxford: Oxford University Press, 2013).

Hartley, Marsden and Alfred Stieglitz, *My Dear Stieglitz: Letters of Marsden Hartley and Alfred Stieglitz 1912–1915*, ed. J. T. Voorhies (Chapel Hill: University of South Carolina Press, 2002).

Haselstein, Ulla, 'A New Kind of Realism: Flaubert's *Trois Contes* and Stein's *Three Lives*' *Comparative Literature*, Vol. 61, No. 4 (Fall 2009), 388–399.

Horton, Byron Barnes, *Horton Family Year Book* (New York: Grafton, 1908).

JBF, 'Miss Gertrude Stein', *Isis*, 9 June 1926, 8.

Jackson, Mark, 'Institutional Provision for the Feeble-Minded in Edwardian England: Sandlebridge and the Scientific Morality of Permanent Care', in *From Idiocy to Mental Deficiency: Historical Perspectives on People with Learning Disabilities*, ed. David Wright and Anne Digby (London: Routledge, 1996).

Jaffe, Aaron, *Modernism and the Culture of Celebrity* (Cambridge: Cambridge University Press, 2005).

James, William, 'Herbert Spencer', *Atlantic Monthly*, Vol. 94 (July 1904), 99–108.

James, William, *The Letters of William James*, Vol. 2, ed. Henry James (Boston, MA: Atlantic Monthly Press, 1920).

Jennings, H. S., *Prometheus: Or, Biology and the Advancement of Man* (London: Kegan Paul, Trench, Trubner & Co., 1925).

Johnson, Edward Austin, *Light Ahead for the Negro* (New York: Grafton, 1904)

Jouve, Emeline, '"Geography and Plays": Spaces in Gertrude Stein's Early Plays (1913–1919)', *South Atlantic Review*, Vol. 76, No. 4 (Fall 2011), 101–116.

Jung, Yeonsik, 'Why Is Melanctha Black?: Gertrude Stein, Physiognomy, and the Jewish Question', *Canadian Review of American Studies*, Vol. 49, No. 2 (Summer 2019), 139–159.

Katz, Leon, 'The First Making of The Making of Americans: A Study Based on Gertrude Stein's Notebooks and Early Version of Her Novel (1902–1908)', PhD dissertation, Columbia University, 1963.

Kersten, Luke, 'New Hampshire Enacted Voluntary Sexual Sterilization Laws. It Was Later Reenacted as Compulsory in 1929', retrieved 14 March 2022, from http://eugenicsarchive.ca/discover/timeline/532335f2132156674b00023

Kramer, Jacob, *The New Freedom and the Radicals* (Philadelphia, PA: Temple University Press, 2015).

Kreymborg, Alfred, 'Gertrude Stein – Hoax and Hoaxtress: A Study of the Woman Whose "Tender Buttons" Has Furnished New York with a New Kind of Amusement', *New York Morning Telegraph*, 7 March 1915.

Kreymborg, Alfred, *Troubadour: An American Autobiography* (New York: Sagamore Press, [1925] 1957).

Lee, Vernon, *Proteus, or The Future of Intelligence* (London: Kegan Paul, Trench, Trubner & Co., 1925).

Leick, Karen, *Gertrude Stein and the Making of an American Celebrity* (New York: Routledge, 2009).

Levenson, Michael, *Modernism* (New Haven, CT: Yale University Press, 2011).

Levine, Stephen L., '"Forces which cannot be ignored": Theodore Roosevelt's Reaction to European Modernism', *Revue Française d'Études Américaines*, Vol. 2, No. 116 (2008), 5–19.

Lewis, Pericles, *Modernism, Nationalism, and the Novel* (Cambridge: Cambridge University Press, 2000).

Lewis, Wyndham, 'The Revolutionary Simpleton', in *The Enemy*, Vol. 1 (January 1927); reprint (London: Frank Cass and Company Limited 1968), 25–192.

Lewis, Wyndham, *Blasting & Bombardiering* (London: Eyre & Spottiswoode, 1937).

Lewis, Wyndham, *Time and Western Man* (London: Chatto and Windus, 1927): reprinted as *Time and Western Man*, ed. Paul Edwards (Santa Rosa, CA: Black Sparrow Press, 1993).

Lewis, Wyndham, *The Art of Being Ruled* (Santa Rosa, CA: Black Sparrow Press, [1926] 1989).

Life magazine, Vol. 16, No. 1585 (13 March 1913).

Life magazine, Vol. 74, No. 1925 (18 September 1919).

London, Jack, 'The Unexpected', *McClure's Magazine*, Vol. 27, No. 4 (August 1906), 368–382.

Loy, Mina, 'Gertrude Stein', *The Transatlantic Review*, Vol. 2, No. 3 (September 1924), 305–309.

Loy, Mina, 'Gertrude Stein', *The Transatlantic Review*, Vol. 2, No. 4 (October 1924), 427–430.

Loy, Mina, 'Feminist Manifesto', *The Lost Lunar Baedeker*, ed. Roger Conover (New York: Noonday, 1996).

Lundén, Rolf, 'Translating Back: Re-embodying Gertrude Stein's "A Man"', *English Studies*, Vol. 101, No. 2 (2020), 174–196.

Marovitz, Sanford E., 'Melville among the Realists: W. D. Howells and the Writing of "Billy Budd"', *American Literary Realism*, Vol. 34, No. 1 (Fall 2001).

Marquis, Don, 'Gertrude Stein's Hints for the Table', *New York Sun*, 14 August 1914.

Marquis, Don, 'Gertrude Stein on the War', *New York Evening Sun*, 2 October 1914.

Marquis, Don, 'To G.S. and E.P.', *New York Sun*, 3 October 1914.

Marquis, Don, 'Gertrude Stein Is Stein, Gertrude: That is All Ye now on Earth, and All Ye Need to Know', *New York Evening Sun*, 14 October 1914.

Mazower, Mark, *Dark Continent: Europe's Twentieth Century* (London: Penguin Books, 1999).

McCann, Sean, *A Pinnacle of Feeling: American Literature and Presidential Government* (Princeton, NJ: Princeton University Press, 2008).

McGerr, Michael, *A Fierce Discontent: The Rise and Fall of the Progressive Movement in America* (New York: Free Press, 2003).

Mencken, H. L., 'A Cubist Treatise', *Baltimore Sun*, 6 June 1914 in Curnutt, 14–15.

Miller, Andrew John, *Modernism and the Crisis of Sovereignty* (New York: Routledge, 2008).

Miller, Michael B., *The Bon Marche: Bourgeois Culture and the Department Store, 1869–1920* (Princeton, NJ: Princeton University Press, 1981).

Mitchell, P., 'The Spencer–Weismann Controversy', *Nature*, Vol. 49 (February 1894), 373–374.

Mitrano, G. F., *Gertrude Stein: Woman without Qualities* (Aldershot, Hants: Ashgate, 2005).

Mix, Deborah, 'Gertrude Stein's Currency', in *Modernist Star Maps*, ed. Aaron Jaffe and Jonathan Goldman (Farnham, Surrey: Ashgate, 2010), 93–104.

Moody, William Vaughn, Robert Morss Lovett and Percy H Boynton, *A First View of English and American Literature* (New York: Scribner's, 1905).

Moon, Michael, '"Wherein the South Differs from the North", Naming Persons, Naming Places, and the Need for Visionary Spaces', *Southern Spaces*, 16 May 2008. https://doi.org/10.18737/M74P46.

Moyn, Samuel, *Human Rights and the Uses of History* (New York and London: Verso, [2014] 2017).

Münsterberg, Hugo, *The Americans* (Boston, MA: McClure, Phillips & Company, 1904).

Norris, Henry McCoy, *Ancestry and Descendants of Lieutenant Jonathan and Tamesin (Barker) Norris of Maine* (New York: Grafton, 1906).

North, Michael, *The Dialect of Modernism: Race, Language, and Twentieth-Century Literature* (Oxford: Oxford University Press, 1994).

Ogden, Rollo, 'Governor Odell of New York. A Man of Business in Politics', *McClure's Magazine*, Vol. 17, No. 3 (July 1901) 283–287.

Page, Thomas Nelson, 'Slavery and the Old Relation between the Southern Whites and Blacks', *McClure's Magazine*, Vol. 22, No. 5 (March 1904), 548–554.

Perloff, Marjorie, *The Poetics of Indeterminacy: Rimbaud to Cage* (Evanston, IL: Northwestern University Press, 1999).

Pink, M. Alderton, *Procrustes: Or The Future of English Education* (London: Kegan Paul, Trench, Trubner & Co., 1927).

Potter, Rachel, *Modernism and Democracy: Literary Culture 1900–1930* (Oxford: Oxford University Press, 2006).

Potter, Rachel and Lyndsey Stonebridge, 'Writing and Rights', *Critical Quarterly*, Vol. 56, No. 4 (December 2014), 1–16.

Quartermain, Peter, *Disjunctive Poetics: From Gertrude Stein and Louis Zukofsky to Susan Howe* (Cambridge: Cambridge University Press, 1992).

Quartermain, Peter, *Stubborn Poetries: Poetic Facticity and the Avant-Garde* (Tuscaloosa: University of Alabama Press, 2013).

Quinn, John, 'Modern Art from a Layman's Point of View', *Arts and Decoration*, Vol. 3, No. 5 (6 March 1913), 156–158.

Rabaté, Jean-Michel, *The Ghosts of Modernity* (Gainesville: Florida University Press, 1996), 189–190.

Rainey, Lawrence, *Institutions of Modernism: Literary Elites and Public Culture* (New Haven, CT: Yale University Press, 1998).

Riding, Laura, *Anarchism Is Not Enough* (London: Jonathan Cape, 1928).

Riding, Laura, *Contemporaries and Snobs* (Garden City, NY: Doubleday Doran & Company, 1928).

Riding, Laura and Robert Graves, *A Survey of Modernist Poetry* (London: Heinemann, 1927): reprinted in *A Survey of Modernist Poetry and A Pamphlet Against Anthologies*, ed. Charles Mundye and Patrick McGuinness (Manchester: Carcanet, 2002).

Rodker, John, *The Future of Futurism* (London: Kegan Paul, Trench, Trubner & Co., 1926).

Rogers, Robert Emons, 'New Outbreaks of Futurism: "Tender Buttons," Curious Experiment of Gertrude Stein in Literary Anarchy', *Boston Evening Transcript*, 11 July 1914, in Curnutt, 18–21.

Roosevelt, Theodore, 'A Layman's Views of an Art Exhibition', *The Outlook*, No. 103 (29 March 1913), 718–720.

Roosevelt, Theodore, 'The Man with the Muck-Rake', in *The Works of Theodore Roosevelt: American Problems*, National Edition, Vol. 16 (New York: Charles Scribner's Sons, 1926), 415–424.

Rowland, Henry C., 'Oil and Water', *McClure's*, Vol. 25, No. 6 (October 1905), 649–660.

Ruddick, Lisa Cole, *Reading Gertrude Stein: Body, Text, Gnosis* (Ithaca, NY: Cornell University Press, 1990).

Russell, Bertrand, *Icarus, or the Future of Science* (London: Kegan Paul, Trench, Trubner & Co., 1924).

Sanderson, Rena, 'Gender and Modernity in Transnational Perspective: Hugo Münsterberg and the American Woman', *Prospects: An Annual of American Cultural Studies*, Vol. 23 (1998), 285–313.

Saunders, Max and Brian Hurwitz, 'The *To-day and To-morrow* Series and the Popularization of Science: An Introduction', *Interdisciplinary Science Reviews*, Vol. 34, No. 1 (2009), 3–8.

Schiller, F. C. S., *Tantalus, or the Future of Man* (London: Kegan Paul, Trench, Trubner & Co., 1924).

Schocket, Eric, *Vanishing Moments: Class and American Literature* (Ann Arbor: University of Michigan Press, 2006).

Schoenbach, Lisi, *Pragmatic Modernism* (Oxford: Oxford University Press, 2012).

Schraner, Elise, 'The To-day and To-morrow Series', *Interdisciplinary Science Reviews*, Vol. 34, No. 1 (2009), 107–115.

Schurz, Carl, 'Can the South Solve the Negro Problem?', *McClure's Magazine*, Vol. 22, No. 3 (January 1904), 259–275.

Scott, Bonnie Kime, *The Gender of Modernism: A Critical Anthology* (Bloomington: Indiana University Press, 1990).

Scully, Richard and Marian Quartly, 'Using Cartoons as Historical Evidence', in *Drawing the Line: Using Cartoons as Historical Evidence*, ed. Richard Scully and Marian Quartly (Clayton, Victoria: Monash University Press, 2009).

Sedgwick, Ellery, *The Atlantic Monthly 1857–1909: Yankee Humanism at High Tide and Ebb* (Amherst: University of Massachusetts Press, 1994).

Sloane, David E. E., ed., *American Humor Magazines and Comic Periodicals* (Westport, CT: Greenwood Press, 1987).

Spahr, Juliana, *Everybody's Autonomy: Connective Reading and Collective Identity* (Tuscaloosa: University of Alabama Press, 2001).
Stein, Gertrude , 'Matisse', *Camera Work*, Special Edition (August 1912), 2.
Stein, Gertrude, 'Picasso', *Camera Work*, Special Edition (August 1912), 4.
Stein, Gertrude, *Geography and Plays* (Boston, MA: Four Seas Company, 1922).
Stein, Gertrude, 'The Psychology of Nations, or What Are You Looking At', in *Geography and Plays* (Boston, MA: Four Seas Company, 1922), 416–419.
Stein, Gertrude, 'Troubadour, an Autobiography', *Ex Libris*, Vol. 2, No. 9 (June 1925), 278.
Stein, Gertrude, 'Two Women' in *Contact Collection of Contemporary Writers*, ed. Robert McAlmon (Paris: Contact Editions, 1925), 303–325.
Stein, Gertrude, 'The Fifteenth of November', in *The New Criterion*, Vol. 4, No. 1 (January 1926), 71–75.
Stein, Gertrude, *Composition as Explanation* (London: Hogarth Press, 1926).
Stein, Gertrude, 'Mildred's Thoughts', in *American Caravan: A Yearbook of American Literature*, ed. Alfred Kreymborg, Lewis Mumford and Paul Rosenfeld (New York: Macaulay Company, 1927), 653–675.
Stein, Gertrude, *Useful Knowledge* (New York: Payson and Clarke, 1928).
Stein, Gertrude, *Selected Writings*, ed. Carl Van Vechten (New York: Random House, 1946), 465–468.
Stein, Gertrude, *Two: Gertrude Stein and Her Brother and Other Early Portraits* (New Haven, CT: Yale University Press, 1951).
Stein, Gertrude, *The Autobiography of Alice B. Toklas* (London: Penguin Books, [1933] 1966).
Stein, Gertrude, *The Making of Americans* (Funks Grove, IL: Dalkey Archive Press, 1995).
Stein, Gertrude, *Three Lives* (Bedford Cultural Editions), ed. Linda Wagner-Martin (New York: Bedford, 1999).
Stein, Gertrude, *Matisse Picasso and Gertrude Stein with Two Shorter Stories* (New York: Dover Publications, 2000).
Stein, Gertrude, *Three Lives*, ed. Andrew Moore (New York: Mondial, 2007).
Stein, Gertrude, *Gertrude Stein: Selections*, ed. Joan Retallack (Berkeley: University of California Press, 2008).
Stein, Gertrude, 'Composition as Explanation', in *Gertrude Stein: Selections*, ed. Joan Retallack (Berkeley: University of California Press, 2008), 215–225.
Stein, Gertrude, *Tender Buttons*, ed. Seth Perlow (San Francisco: City Lights Books, 2014).
Stein, Gertrude, *Tender Buttons*, ed. Leonard Diepeveen (Peterborough, ON: Broadview, 2018).
Stein, Gertrude and Leon Solomons, 'Normal Motor Automatism', *Harvard Psychological Review*, Vol. 3, No. 5 (September 1896), 495–512.
Stieglitz, Alfred, 'Advertisement', *Camera Work*, No. 13 (July 1912), 1.
Stimpson, Catharine, 'Gertrude Stein: Humanism and Its Freaks', *Boundary*, Vol. 2, Nos 12/13 (1984), 301–19.
Stimpson, Catharine, 'The Mind, the Body, and Gertrude Stein', *Critical Inquiry*, Vol. 3, No. 3 (1977), 489–50.

Stimpson, Catharine, 'The Somagrams of Gertrude Stein', *Poetics Today*, Vol. 6, Nos 1/2 (1985), 67-80.

Stonebridge, Lyndsey, 'Refugee Style: Hannah Arendt and the Perplexities of Rights', *Textual Practice*, Vol. 25, No. 1 (2011), 71-85.

Stonebridge, Lyndsey, *Writing and Righting: Literature in the Age of Human Rights* (Oxford: Oxford University Press, 2020).

Strate, Lance, *Media Ecology: An Approach to Understanding the Human Condition* (New York: Peter Lang Publishing, 2017).

Tarbell, Ida M., *The History of the Standard Oil Company*, 2 vols (New York: McClure, Phillips, 1904).

Tarbell, Ida M., 'John D. Rockefeller. A Character Study', *McClure's Magazine*, Vol. 25, No. 3 (July 1905), 227-249.

Taylor, Frederick Winslow, *Shop Management* (New York: Harper and Brothers, [1903] 1911).

Thacker, Robert, '"It's through myself that I knew and felt her": S. S. McClure's "My Autobiography" and the Development of Willa Cather's Autobiographical Realism', *American Literary Realism*, Vol. 33, No. 2 (2001), 123-42.

Thompson, Aidan, 'Language and Democracy: Meaning Making as Existing in the Work of Gertrude Stein', *Arizona Quarterly: A Journal of American Literature, Culture, and Theory*, Vol. 69, No. 3 (Autumn 2013), 129-155.

Thompson, Susan Otis, 'The American Library in Paris: An International Development in the American Library Movement', *The Library Quarterly: Information, Community, Policy*, Vol. 34, No. 2 (April 1964).

Thomson, Mathew, 'Family, Community and State: The Micro-Politics of Mental Deficiency', in *From Idiocy to Mental Deficiency: Historical Perspectives on People with Learning Disabilities*, ed. David Wright and Anne Digby (London: Routledge, 1996), 207-230.

Tooze, Adam, *The Deluge: The Great War and the Remaking of Global Order 1916-1931* (London: Penguin Books, 2014).

Tredgold, A. F., 'II. The Feeble-Minded – a Social Danger', *The Eugenics Review*, Vol. 1, No. 2 (1909), 97-104.

Tredgold, A. F., *Mental Deficiency: Amentia* (New York: William Wood and Co., 1923).

Vanskike, Elliott L., '"Seeing Everything as Flat": Landscape in Gertrude Stein's *Useful Knowledge* and *The Geographical History of America*', *Texas Studies in Literature and Language*, Vol. 35, No. 2 (1993), 151-167.

Voris, Linda, 'Interpreting Cézanne: Immanence in Gertrude Stein's First Landscape Play, "Lend a Hand or Four Religions"', *Modernism/modernity*, Vol. 19, No. 1 (January 2012), 73-93.

Wagner-Martin, Linda, *Favored Strangers: Gertrude Stein and Her Family* (New Brunswick, NJ: Rutgers University Press, 1997).

Waldman, Louis A. and Brenda Preyer, 'The Rise of the Patronage Portrait in Late Renaissance Florence: An Enigmatic Portrait of Giovanni Di Paolo Rucellai and Its Role in Family Commemoration', *Mitteilungen des Kunsthistorischen Institutes in Florenz*, Vol. 54 (2010), 133-154.

Walker, Alice M., *Historic Hadley: A Story of the Making of a Famous Massachusetts Town* (New York: Grafton, 1906)

Walker, Jayne L, *The Making of a Modernist: Gertrude Stein from 'Three Lives' to 'Tender Buttons'* (Amherst: University of Massachusetts Press, 1984).

Wheeler, Charles, Interview with Henry Ford, *Chicago Tribune*, 25 May 1916, 10.

White, William Allen, 'Hanna. A Character Sketch', *McClure's Magazine*, Vol. 16, No. 1 (November 1900), 56–64.

White, William Allen, 'Croker. An Analysis of the Man and an Explanation of His Power', *McClure's Magazine*, Vol. 16, No. 4 (February 1901), 317–326.

Will, Barbara, *Gertrude Stein, Modernism, and the Problem of 'Genius'* (Edinburgh: Edinburgh University Press, 2000).

Will, Barbara, 'Gertrude Stein and Zionism', *MFS Modern Fiction Studies*, Vol. 51 No. 2 (2005), 437–455.

Will, Barbara, *Unlikely Collaboration: Gertrude Stein, Bernard Faÿ, and the Vichy Dilemma* (New York: Columbia University Press, 2011).

Williams, Raymond, 'When Was Modernism?' *New Left Review*, Vol. 1, No. 175 (May/June 1989), 48–52.

Wilson, Edmund, '*Ulysses*', *The New Republic*, 5 July 1922.

Wilson, Edmund, 'A Guide to Gertrude Stein: The Evolution of a Master of Fiction into a Painter of Cubist Still-Life in Prose', *Vanity Fair*, September 1923, 60, 80.

Wilson, Robert A., comp., *Gertrude Stein: A Bibliography* (New York: The Phoenix Bookshop, 1974).

Wilson, Woodrow, *Joint Session of Congress to Seek a Declaration of War against Germany on April 2, 1917*, Sixty-Fifth Congress, 1 Session, Senate Document No. 5.

Wilson, Woodrow, *Address of the President of the United States Delivered at a Joint Session of the Two Houses of Congress, January 8, 1918* (Washington, DC: U.S. Government Printing Office).

Wilson, Woodrow and William Bayard Hale, *The New Freedom; A Call for the Emancipation of the Generous Energies of a People* (New York: Doubleday, 1913).

Wineapple, Brenda, *Sister Brother: Gertrude and Leo Stein* (London: Bloomsbury, 1996).

Zilczer, Judith, 'John Quinn and Modern Art Collectors in America, 1913–1924', *American Art Journal*, Vol. 14, No. 1 (1982), 57–71.

INDEX

References to notes are indicated by n.

291 (gallery), 113-14

'A League' (Stein), 20-2, 23-4, 26-8
academy, 164-8
'Ada' (Stein), 151
Addams, Jane, 6, 69
Addis, Emmett, 220
African Americans *see* race
Agamben, Giorgio
  Homo Sacer: Sovereign Power and Bare Life, 11-13, 197
  State of Exception, 11-12
Alsace-Lorraine, 153
America *see* United States of America
American Association of Painters and Sculptors, 105, 108-9
American Civil War, 218-20
American Library (Paris), 145, 185n13
American Magazine, The, 52
American Revolutionary War, 23, 108
Americanness, 8, 113, 147-50, 151
  and *The Autobiography of Alice B. Toklas*, 227, 233-5
  and *Geography and Plays*, 156-7
  and *Useful Knowledge*, 209-10, 211-12, 215-22
anarchism, 16, 105, 113, 114-15, 208
  and *Tender Buttons*, 119, 133
Anderson, Margaret, 144
Anderson, Sherwood, 143, 144, 147-50, 151, 220
Anglo-American modernism, 142-6, 147-50, 158
anti-Semitism, 233-4
Apollinaire, Guillaume, 91

Ardis, Ann, 20
Arendt, Hannah, 4, 11, 74
Armory Show (1913), 84, 89, 103, 104-12
  and reception, 112-17
art *see* visual art
Art of Being Ruled, The (Lewis), 168, 190, 192, 199-200
Arts and Decoration (journal), 89, 103, 107-9
Atlantic Monthly (magazine), 41-2
authoritarianism, 17, 18
authorship, 5-6
  and aberrant, 133-4
  and *The Autobiography of Alice B. Toklas*, 227, 230-6
  and Eliot, 181-2
  and *Geography and Plays*, 150-8
  and intelligence, 189-90
  and mass democracy, 19-21
  and modernism, 1-2, 9, 182-4
  and otherness, 76-7
  and Stein, 13-14, 168-70
  and *Tender Buttons*, 117-19, 124-32
  and *Useful Knowledge*, 212-13, 216-17, 222
Autobiography of Alice B. Toklas, The (Stein), 31, 227, 229-36
autonomy, 8
avant-garde, 7-8, 11, 29, 32n13, 36, 37, 86
  and Anglo-American, 144-5
  and Armory Show, 104-5
  and *The Autobiography of Alice B. Toklas*, 230-1

and Language poets, 14-15
and *Vanity Fair* (magazine), 143

Baker, Josephine, 220, 226n35
Baker, Ray Stannard
  Following the Color Line: An Account of Negro Citizenship in the American Democracy, 43-4, 52-5, 56, 57-8
Baltimore, 37-8, 46, 220
barbarism, 175
Barnes, Albert C., 233
Barnes, Djuna, 158
Beach, Sylvia, 144
Binding, Karl, *Authorisation for the Annihilation of Life Unworthy to be Lived*, 197
biography, 37-8
BLAST (magazine), 85
Blaue Reiter, Der (magazine), 85
Bluemner, Oscar, 'Audiator et Altera Pars: Some Plain Sense on the Modern Art Movement', 111-12
'Bon Marché Weather' (Stein), 98
Bonnard, Pierre, 100
Bookstaver, May, 61
Boston Globe, The (newspaper), 72, 75
Bourdieu, Pierre, 19
Bowers, Jane, 90, 92
Braque, Georges, 91
Brooklyn Daily Eagle (newspaper), 71, 72, 74-5
Broom (journal), 144
brotherhoods, 87-8
Brunkhorst, Hauke, 4
Burns, Edward, 144

Cambridge University, 164, 166-8
Camera Work (journal), 84, 85, 89-90, 107-8, 111, 114
capitalism, 105
Casanova, Pascale, *The World Republic of Letters*, 5-6, 7-8
Cather, Willa, 38, 42
Cezanne, Paul, 91, 100-1
Chadbourne, Emily, 220
Chaning-Pearce, M., *Chiron, or the Education of a Citizen of the World*, 208-9
character sketches, 41-9, 71, 73
'Cheating the Nature: A Literary Challenge to Opal Whiteley, Patience Worth and Gertrude Stein' ('Arthors'/*Vanity Fair*), 142-3
Chessman, Harriet Scott, *The Public is Invited to Dance*, 17

Chicago Record-Herald (newspaper), 72, 74, 77
childbirth, 66-7
citizenship, 10, 12
Claire Marie Press, 84
Clark, T. J., 122
class, 3, 69, 180, 208-9; *see also* working classes
collective behaviour *see* group culture
Composition as Explanation (Stein), 30, 143, 158, 164-70
consumerism, 2
Contact Collection of Contemporary Writers, 158
continuous present, 62, 167
Cortissoz, Royal, 112
cosmopolitanism, 10, 32n19, 156-7
Cox, Kenyon, 112
Crane, Stephen, 39
Criterion, The (journal), 159-63, 179, 192
Croker, Richard, 43
Crookshank, F. G., *The Mongol in Our Midst*, 194, 201-2, 203
Crowninshield, Frank, 142
cubism, 118, 119, 122, 126, 138n62, 140-1

dance, 152-3
Davies, Arthur B., 108-9
death, 63-5
Declaration of Independence, 108
DeKoven, Marianne, *A Different Language*, 17
democracy, 1-5, 8-9, 30
  and Agamben, 11-13
  and authorship, 19-21
  and *The Autobiography of Alice B. Toklas*, 227, 229, 230
  and Eliot, 179-80
  and futurism, 191
  and intelligence, 189-90, 199-200
  and Stein, 13-19, 24, 204-9
  and USA, 23, 25-6
  and *Useful Knowledge*, 209-18, 219-22
  and Wilson, 106, 107
Dial, The (magazine), 169, 180-1, 192
Diepeveen, Leonard, 122
  Mock Modernism, 183
disability, 193-7, 199-204
documentary, 41-2
Dodge, Mabel, 84, 89-90, 91, 100-4
  'Speculations, or Post-Impressionism in Prose', 110-11
Down's syndrome, 194, 201-2
Du Bois, W. E. B., 53, 63

Duffield, Pitts, 40–1
Dydo, Ulla, 16, 17, 147, 159

egalitarianism, 4, 14–15, 16, 21, 27, 68
Egoist (magazine), 85
Eliot, T. S., 9, 19, 169, 190
  and disability, 203–4
  and futurism, 192
  and print culture, 178–82
  and 'The Fifteenth of November', 158, 159–63
  The Waste Land, 147
English, Daylanne, 60, 66, 213
environment, 43–5, 47–9
ethnicity, 47–9
eugenics, 66–7, 191, 193–7, 201
evolution, 44–5, 52, 86–7, 107, 110–12
  and mental illness, 201
  and Rodker, 198
  and *Tender Buttons*, 117–18
  and *Three Lives*, 38, 58–9, 70, 72–4
Ex Libris (magazine), 145
exclusion, 8–13, 159–63, 233–5
exhibitions, 84, 86
experience, 129–31

Farragut, David Glasgow, 218–20
fascism, 12
fashion, 76–7
Fäy, Bernard, 17, 18
feminism, 17–18
Fernhurst (Stein), 36, 221
'Fifteenth of November, The' (Stein), 158
First World War, 22–3, 124–5, 153–4, 165, 218
Flanner, Janet, 91
Flaubert, Gustav, *Trois Contes*, 63
'Flirting at the Bon Marché' (Stein), 98
Flynt, Josiah, 42
'Food' (Stein), 129, 130
Ford, Ford Madox, 158
Forrest, Maud de, 220
Foucault, Michel, 11, 12, 31n5, 183
France, 23, 153; *see also* Paris
fraud, 126–7, 142–3
Free Verse, 23, 24
freedom, 68
Fry, Roger, 86, 89
futurism, 3, 122, 138n62, 169, 191–4; *see also* Rodker, John

Garland, Hamlin, 39
gender, 2
genealogy, 37–8
'Gentle Lena, The' (Stein), 64–6, 67

Geography and Plays (Stein), 30, 141, 143–4, 147–50
  and nationalism, 150–8
Gibb, Harry Phelan, 91
Glackens, William J., 109–10
Gladden, Washington, 44, 65
G.M.P. (Stein), 118, 119–22, 124
'Good Anna, The' (Stein), 47–9, 60, 63–4, 68–70
  and reproduction, 66, 67–8
Goodspeed-Chadwick, Julie, 16
Goody, Alex, 100
Grafton Galleries, 86, 89
Grafton Press, 37–8, 41, 78n4
Grant, Ulysses S., 22–3
Graves, Robert, 192
  A Survey of Modernist Poetry, 169, 170–3, 174–5, 176, 190
Gregg, Frederick James, 'The Attitude of the Americans', 109
group culture, 85, 94–9, 134n3, 144, 146
  and *G.M.P.*, 120–2
  and *Tender Buttons*, 118–19, 124

Hain, T. Jenkins, 'Beneath the "Bulldog's" Bilge', 51
Haldane, J. B. S., *Daedalus, or Science and the Future*, 193
Hanna, Mark, 43, 44–5, 47
Hapgood, Hutchins, 113–14
Harding, Jason, 178–9
Harding, Warren G., 154, 155
Harte, Brett, 72
Hartley, Marsden, 85, 91
Heap, Jane, 144
Hemingway, Ernest, 144, 147
hierarchies, 6, 16–17, 123, 196, 200
  and race, 50, 52–5, 57
Hitchcock, F. H., 41
Hoche, Alfred, *Authorisation for the Annihilation of Life Unworthy to be Lived*, 197
Hodder, Alfred, 42
Hogarth Essays, 30
Hogarth Press, 158
Holly, Flora M, 38, 41
Howells, William Dean, 39
human mind, 212–15; *see also* intellectual disability; intelligence; mental health

'If You Had Three Husbands' (Stein), 144
Impressionism, 101
inclusion, 8–13, 16, 232–3, 236

inheritance, 43–4, 47–9
institutionalism, 60–1, 62, 63–4
intellectual disability (and 'feeble-mindedness'), 194–7, 199–204
intelligence, 189–90, 193, 194–204, 208–9, 211
International Exhibition of Modern Art *see* Armory Show
internationalism, 10, 21–2, 25, 140
intimacy, 129–31
'Italians' (Stein), 1, 3

Jaffe, Aaron, *Modernism and the Culture of Celebrity*, 19
James, Henry, 72, 74
James, William, 40
Jennings, H. S., *Prometheus, or Biology and the Advancement of Man*, 194, 196–7
Jewett, Sarah Orne, 39
Jewishness, 233–4
Johns Hopkins School of Medicine, 38, 46, 62, 86, 125, 213
journalism *see* print culture
Jouve, Emeline, 150
Joyce, James, *Ulysses*, 147, 157–8, 174

Kansas City Star (newspaper), 71–2, 74, 77
Katz, Leon, 61
knowledge *see* Useful Knowledge
Kreymborg, Alfred, 126–7, 144–6
  American Caravan, 158

Laforgue, Jules, 46
language, 121, 122, 129–30
Language poets, 14–15
League of Nations, 20, 22, 24–8, 140–1
  and *Useful Knowledge*, 218, 221
Lee, Vernon, 211
  Proteus, or The Future of Intelligence, 208–9
Leick, Karen, 20
lesbianism, 61
Lewelyn, Ida, 220
Lewis, Pericles, 3, 148, 149
Lewis, Wyndham, 90, 168–9, 173–6, 177
  and disability, 199–201, 202
  and Eliot, 180–1
  and Russell, 192
liberalism, 9, 29, 87
Life (magazine), 20–1, 22–5, 115–16
literature, 5–6, 7, 28–9; *see also* authorship
'Literature of Fascism, The' (Eliot), 179

Little Review (journal), 144, 147
London, Jack, 39
Loy, Mina, 1–4, 11, 24, 190, 204–6
  and *Geography and Plays*, 147
  and *Useful Knowledge*, 211, 213

McCann, Sean, 49, 86–7
McClure's Magazine, 38–9, 41, 42–5, 51–2
McKinley, William, 44
magazines *see* print culture
Making of Americans, The (Stein), 30, 62, 87–8, 158
Manguin, Henri, 91
Marinetti, Filippo, 3
Marquis, Don, 118, 127, 128
  'Gertrude Stein on the War', 124–5
Marxism, 15
mass culture *see* popular culture
mass democracy *see* democracy
Matisse, Henri, 36, 75–6, 84, 113
  and *The Autobiography of Alice B. Toklas*, 231, 232
  and *G.M.P.*, 119–20, 122
  and portrait, 89, 92, 93–9
  and *Tender Buttons*, 122–4
'Melanctha' (Stein), 49, 50–1, 53, 55–8, 60–3
  and death, 64, 66
  and wandering, 69–70
Mencken, H. L., 127
mental health, 194–7, 199–204
migration, 10, 43–4, 46, 52
Miller, Andrew John
  Modernism and the Crisis of Sovereignty, 10
miscegenation, 50–1
Mitrano, G. F., 16
Mix, Deborah, 20
mockery, 182–3
modern art, 84–6; *see also* Armory Show
modernism, 1–5, 8–9, 84–5
  and Anglo-American, 142–6, 158
  and authorship, 11, 182–4
  and *The Autobiography of Alice B. Toklas*, 230–2
  and canonisation, 33n25
  and *Composition as Explanation*, 164
  and death of, 169–75
  and democracy, 204–6
  and *Geography and Plays*, 147–50
  and literary culture, 29–30
  and nationalism, 10
  and poetry, 206–8
  and popular culture, 19–20
  and primitivism, 176

modernism (cont.)
　and Stein, 13–14, 15–16
Monroe Doctrine, 25
Moody, William Vaughn, *A First View of English and American Literature*, 39–40, 71, 72
Morgan, J. Pierpont, 43
Moyn, Samuel, 8, 9–10
Munsterberg, Hugo, 58–9, 63
Mussolini, Benito, 3

Nadelman, Elie, 91
Nation, The (newspaper), 73–4, 75
Nation and Athenaeum, The (magazine), 147, 169, 178, 190, 192
national degeneracy, 195–6
nationalism, 3, 4, 5, 7–8
　and *Geography and Plays*, 150–8
　and rights, 10
　and Stein, 17, 18, 21–8
　and *Useful Knowledge*, 220–2
neo-Lamarckism, 44
New Criterion, The (journal), 168, 178–9
New Republic, The (magazine), 147, 148–9
New York Sun (newspaper), 71, 73
newspapers *see* print culture
Norris, Frank, 39

'Objects' (Stein), 129–30
openness, 16
otherness, 76–7, 177
Outlook (magazine), 105–6, 112
Oxford Magazine, 140
Oxford University, 164–8

Page, Thomas Nelson, 51
Paris, 36, 75–6
　and art world, 85, 90–1
　and Baker, 220
　and collective behaviour, 98–9
　and Peace Conference, 27, 140–1
　and rue de Fleurus, 227, 229–30, 235–6
parody, 142–3
participation, 16, 141, 189–90
　and Armory Show, 105–6, 107, 111–12
　and *The Autobiography of Alice B. Toklas*, 232–3
Payson and Clarke, 158, 209–10
Penguin Book of Contemporary Verse, 14
Perloff, Marjorie, *The Poetics of Indeterminacy: Rimbaud to Cage*, 15
Pershing, General, 23
Picasso, Pablo, 36, 84, 111, 113

　and *The Autobiography of Alice B. Toklas*, 232
　and G.M.P., 119–20, 122
　and portrait, 89, 90, 92, 93–9, 100, 101
　and *Portrait of Gertrude Stein*, 91–2
Pink, M. Alderton, *Procrustes: Or The Future of English Education*, 208
pioneers, 148–9, 150
Pittsburgh Daily Post (newspaper), 73
Pittsburgh Post-Gazette (newspaper), 75–7
place, 152
Plain Editions, 227, 228
plays *see Geography and Plays*
Poetry (magazine), 85
politics, 11, 24–6, 151, 153–7; *see also* democracy; nationalism; progressivism
popular culture, 19–20, 175–7, 178, 179, 230–1
portraits, 88–93
　and Dodge, 100–4
　and 'Matisse'/'Picasso', 93–9
　and *Useful Knowledge*, 218–20
Post-Impressionism, 89, 90, 100–1, 114
Potter, Rachel, 9, 74
Pound, Ezra, 90, 158, 169, 180–1
Powers That Prey, The (Flynt), 42
primitivism, 175–8
print culture, 29–30, 186n33
　and the academy, 166–8
　and Anglo-American, 144–5
　and Armory Show, 104–6, 107, 112–14
　and Eliot, 178–82
　and *Geography and Plays*, 147
　and *Tender Buttons*, 118–19, 124–9, 131–2
　and *Three Lives*, 71–8
　see also *Camera Work*; *Life* magazine; *McClure's Magazine*; *Vanity Fair*
progressivism, 29, 36–7, 38–9, 41–2
　and Anderson, 149–50
　and Armory Show, 104–12, 113–15, 115–17
　and problematising discourse, 59–70
　and race, 50–9
　and rejection, 140–1
　and social reform, 44
　and Stein, 86–7
　and *Tender Buttons*, 117–18
'Psychology of Nations, The' (Stein), 151–6

Q.E.D. (Stein), 36, 61

Quartermain, Peter, *Disjunctive Poetics*, 15
Quinn, John, 'Modern Art from a Layman's Point of View', 109

Rabaté, Jean-Michel, 172
race, 3, 4, 31n5, 177
  and Americanness, 234–5
  and Baker, 53–5
  and intellectual disability, 201–2
  and 'mulattos', 54–5, 57–8
  and 'negroes', 3, 4, 31n5, 177
  and reproduction, 67
  and *Three Lives*, 46, 50–3, 55–9, 60–3, 71–2
  and *Useful Knowledge*, 218, 220, 226n35
  see also ethnicity
Radcliffe College, 38, 39–40, 86, 125
radicalism, 106–7
Rainey, Lawrence, 92
realism, 36, 37, 38–41, 42
  and *Three Lives*, 46, 71–3
Renoir, Pierre-Auguste, 100
reportage, 41–2
reproduction, 66–8
Retallack, Joan, *Gertrude Stein: Selections*, 15, 16
revolution, 108–9, 114, 169
Rhythm (magazine), 85
Richardson, Dorothy, 158
Riding, Laura, 181–2, 206–8
  Contemporaries and Snobs, 173
  A Survey of Modernist Poetry, 169, 170–3, 174–5, 176, 190
rights, 4, 8–10, 12–13, 20, 36–7, 133–4
  and democracy, 30, 142, 150, 179–80, 212, 222
  and human, 28–9, 32n17, 74
  and intellectual disability, 194
  and nationality, 24, 185n20
  and race, 51, 53, 58, 62, 81n39
  and Wilson, 116
  and women, 78n1
Riis, Jacob, 42
Rivers, W. H. R., 203
Robeson, Paul, 226n35, 234–5
Rockefeller, John D., 43–4
Rodker, John, 192
  The Future of Futurism, 169, 175, 177, 190, 191, 197–200, 202–4
Rogue (magazine), 144
romance, 212
Roosevelt, Theodore, 39, 65, 105–7, 112, 115, 132
Rowland, Henry C., 'Oil and Water', 51

Ruddick, Lisa Cole, *Body, Text, Gnosis*, 17
Russell, Bertrand, 192, 201
  Icarus, or the Future of Science, 193
Russian Revolution, 25

'Saints in Seven' (Stein), 174
Sampson, Admiral William T., 43
Schiller, F. C. S., *Tantalus, or the Future of Man*, 193–4, 201
Schmidt, Karl, 11
Schocket, Eric, 99
Schraner, Elise, 191–2
Schurz, Carl, 51
self-education, 209–11
settlement houses, 6
sexuality, 2; *see also* lesbianism
Sitwell, Edith, 143, 147
slavery, 51
social Darwinism, 29, 36, 44
social history, 37–8
socialism, 106, 115, 133
Spahr, Juliana, *Everybody's Autonomy*, 15, 17
Spencer, Herbert, 44
State of Exception (Agamben), 11–12
statelessness, 156
Stein, Gertrude
  and aberrance, 133–4, 141–2
  and American identity, 7–8
  and Armory Show, 107
  and authorship, 5–6, 10–11
  and 'democratic' writing, 13–19, 204–9
  and Dodge essay, 110–11
  and Dodge portrait, 100–4
  and Eliot, 178, 179, 180–2
  and futurism, 192–3
  and *G.M.P.*, 119–22
  and Hapgood, 113
  and image, 76–7
  and intelligence, 189–90, 197–204
  and Kreymborg, 144–6
  and 'Matisse'/'Picasso' portraits, 93–9
  and mockery, 182–4
  and modernism, 1–4, 170–5
  and nationalism, 21–8
  and New Art, 84–6
  and popular culture, 19–20
  and portraits, 88–93
  and primitivism, 175–8
  and publication, 158–9, 228
  'The Fifteenth of November', 159–63
  'Two Cubist Poems. The Peace Conference', 140–1
  and *Vanity Fair* (magazine), 142–3

Stein, Gertrude (*cont.*)
  and women, 6–7
  see also *Autobiography of Alice B. Toklas, The*; *Composition as Explanation*; *Geography and Plays*; *Making of Americans, The*; *Tender Buttons*; *Three Lives*; *Useful Knowledge*
sterilisation, 194, 197
Stieglitz, Alfred, 85, 89–90, 111
Stonebridge, Lyndsey, 9, 28–9, 74, 156
suffrage, 2, 154–5, 179, 194
  and African Americans, 51, 52
supplication, 159–60
'Suzie Asado' (Stein), 151

Taft, William, 105
Tanner, Allen, 220
Tarbell, Ida, 39, 43–4
Taylor, Frederick Winslow, 66
Tender Buttons (Stein), 77, 84, 86
  and authorship, 117–19, 124–32, 133
  and Matisse, 122–4
  and Wilson, Edmund, 157
Thompson, Aidan, 16–17
Three Lives (Stein), 20, 29, 36–41
  and American press, 71–8
  and character sketch, 41–2, 45–9
  and Lewis, 176
  and progressive discourse, 59–70
  and race, 50–3, 55–9
Three Stories and Ten Poems (Hemingway), 144
Time and Western Man (Lewis), 168–9, 173–5, 190, 200–1, 202
To-day and To-morrow (pamphlet series), 191–4, 196–7, 201, 208–9, 222n3
Toklas, Alice B., 91, 129, 151, 219; see also *The Autobiography of Alice B. Toklas*
totalitarianism, 11–12
Transatlantic Review, The (magazine), 30, 147, 158, 190
Tredgold, A. F., *Mental Deficiency: Amentia*, 194–6, 201
Tribune (Paris) (newspaper), 147
Troubadour (Kreymborg), 144–6
Twain, Mark, 39, 72

Uncle Sam, 25–6
United States of America (USA), 6–8, 15–16
  and *Geography and Plays*, 155–6
  and identity, 21, 147–50
  and nationalism, 22–3
  and print culture, 186n33

  and *Three Lives*, 41
  see also Americanness; Roosevelt, Theodore; Wilson, Woodrow
Useful Knowledge (Stein), 21, 30–1, 158, 189, 209–22

'Vacation in Brittany' (Stein), 144
value judgement, 163
Van Vechten, Carl, 91, 209–10, 220, 226n35, 235
Vanity Fair (magazine), 142–3, 147, 157–8
Villa Curonia (Italy), 101–3
visual art, 68–70, 77–8; see also Armory Show; cubism; Matisse, Henri; modern art; Picasso, Pablo; portraits
Vollard, Ambroise, 91, 100–1

Wagner-Martin, Linda, 61, 62
Walker, Marion, 234
wandering, 49, 50–1, 56–7, 61–2, 64, 68–70
war see American Civil War; First World War
Washington, Booker T., 53, 63
Washington, George, 22–3
Washington Herald (newspaper), 73
'Wear' (Stein), 144
White, William Allen, 43, 44–5
white supremacy, 53, 54, 55
Whiteley, Opal, 184n4
whiteness, 53
Will, Barbara, 21
  Gertrude Stein, Modernism and the Problem of 'Genius', 15–16, 217
  Unlikely Collaboration, 17, 18
Wilson, Edmund, 143, 147, 157–8
Wilson, Woodrow, 11, 105, 106
  and 'A League', 20, 22, 23–4, 26–8
  and campaign, 108, 109, 110
  and cartoons, 25–6
  and *Geography and Plays*, 153–5
  and internationalism, 140
  and *Life* magazine, 115–16
  and *Useful Knowledge*, 218, 220–1
  women, 6–7, 46; see also suffrage; *Three Lives*
Woolf, Leonard, 30
Woolf, Virginia, 30
  Jacob's Room, 147
working classes, 2, 6–7, 67
  and *Three Lives*, 41, 46, 50, 56, 71, 73
World of Graft, The (Flynt), 42
Worth, Patience, 184n4